READING THEIR WORLD

Reading Their World
The Young Adult Novel in the Classroom

edited by

Virginia R. Monseau & Gary M. Salvner

BOYNTON/COOK PUBLISHERS
Heinemann
Portsmouth, NH

Boynton/Cook Publishers, Inc.
A Subsidiary of
Heinemann Educational Books, Inc.
361 Hanover Street, Portsmouth, NH 03801
Offices and agents throughout the world

Every effort has been made to contact the copyright holders and students for permission
to reprint borrowed material. We regret any oversights that may have occurred and
would be happy to rectify them in future printings of this work.

Reading their world: the young adult novel in the classroom/edited by Virginia R.
  Monseau, Gary M. Salvner.
      p.   cm.
  Includes bibliographical references.
  ISBN 0–86709–306–4
  1. Young adult fiction, American—Study and teaching (Secondary)
2. Young adult fiction, English—Study and teaching (Secondary)
3. Young adult fiction—History and criticism—Theory, etc.
4. Young adults—Books and reading.   5. Young in literature.
I. Monseau, Virginia R., 1941–   . II. Salvner, Gary M.
PS42.R4 1992
813.009′9283—dc20

Cover design by Jenny Jensen Greenleaf
Printed in the United States of America.
92 93 94 95 96 9 8 7 6 5 4 3 2 1

TO PAUL AND KATHY

Contents

Acknowledgments

We are grateful to the Youngstown State University Research Council for its support of this project and to the many students, teachers, and colleagues who have offered encouragement and valuable suggestions along the way. We also thank our research assistant, Bonnie Molnar, for her diligent work and conscientious attention to detail. We are especially grateful to our editor, Peter Stillman, for his belief in what we've done here, for his patience in nurturing us along, and for his wonderful sense of humor that saw us through some difficult moments. Thanks, finally, to our contributors, whose hard work made this collection possible and whose enthusiasm made it a joy.

Acknowledgment

Introduction

This book was born of our desire to provide students, teachers, and all interested readers with a collection of essays that address issues of selection, pedagogy, and worth of the young adult novel. Such a book is needed, we feel, not only because the genre is receiving increasing attention among both adolescents and publishers, but also because young adult novels have come of age and proven themselves to be literature of quality.

While early novels for young readers tended to be excessively moralistic, rigidly formulaic, or both, today's books for and about young people, taken together, display the same elements of all masterfully crafted works of fiction: complex main characters who seek to resolve conflicts of tremendous consequence to themselves and the world; vividly drawn minor characters who not only create texture in the works they inhabit, but also advance the action of those stories and serve as meaningful foils and allies for the protagonists; vivid settings, both real and imaginary; plots that hold the reader to the story through deft pacing, skillful use of suspense, and the use of flashbacks and other manipulations of time sequence; and, most recently, experimentation with various points of view from which the stories are told. Above all, as Ted Hipple notes in his essay in this book, young adult novels have come of age through their treatment of themes that matter not just to teens struggling with adolescence, but to all of us—the quest for justice; the savagery of war and hatred; and the struggles for love, acceptance, and understanding, to name a few. Young adult novels have come of age because they have demonstrated the same skillful craftmanship employed in all good literature and because they have translated to the world of the young adult the same conflicts and issues with which all humans struggle.

Unfortunately, despite the quality of many young adult books, their acceptance in classrooms has remained limited, due partly to misconceptions about the genre and partly to uncertainty about how such works fit into the prescribed curriculum. How, for example, can young adult novels be incorporated into an historical survey course? What might be their role in a thematic approach to literature study? How can such novels be used to teach the literary elements? To answer these questions, teachers must come to know student readers better, as our title reminds us, by "reading their world," for only through entering the world of young adult readers will we know how to encourage and direct their reading, and only through reading those works that captivate and move young adults will we be fully able to understand and appreciate them as readers. A primary purpose of this book, then, is to enter the world of young adult readers through a literary form they know well, the modern young adult novel.

Another purpose of this book is to encourage the reading of young adult novels as a way of extending our own experiences with literature. Reading their world, after all, is also a means of reading our own, for we inhabit the same places, encounter similar struggles, and respond with similar emotions. As adult readers, we re-encounter in young adult novels the baffling and oftentimes painful experiences of adolescence, and we become better readers as a result.

Our concern for the experiences of both adolescent and adult readers has led us to the work of Louise Rosenblatt, who has helped many readers to understand better the nature of the literary transaction. Rosenblatt uses a musical metaphor for the act of reading literature: "The reader performs the poem or novel, as the violinist performs the sonata. But the instrument on which the reader plays, and from which he evokes the work, is — himself" (279). This metaphor reminds us that readers create the "music" of texts as they perform them and that the harmonies of reading come from placing the experience of a book alongside the experience of the reader. To adolescents, the advantage of young adult novels is that these books harmonize well with the experiences they have had in their young lives. As a result, instead of merely learning *about* the literature they read in school, as so often happens when they analyze literary classics, students become involved *in* the literature as a result of the connections they make between their experience and the text.

This book, then, invites us as readers and teachers of literature to take a closer look at the reading worlds of both our students and ourselves and at what we are doing in our classrooms when we read and study literature. Learning theory tells us that we best acquire new knowledge by relating it to what we already know. Do we give our students this opportunity in the literature class, or do we consistently present them with literary worlds to which they have no connection described in language that they find difficult to understand? Because young adult novels are written in straightforward language that reflects the adolescent world, they can become the means through which young adult readers gain new knowledge of themselves and others. But the best novels don't stop there. Through skillful writing and a keen awareness of the human condition, the authors of these works leave us with universal questions to ponder about our very existence.

To facilitate reading and to provide a logical structure, we have divided the book into three sections. In Part I, Reading the Young Adult Novel, Ted Hipple discusses the universality of young adult books, exploring the thematic significance of various young adult novels. In examining the attitudes of readers toward the young adult novel, Donald Gallo demonstrates how preconceived notions about the genre affect our acceptance of young adult books as literature. Barbara Samuels gives teachers some valuable ideas for using young adult novels as transitions to more difficult works, and Linda Shadiow traces the evolution of the young adult book from its earliest days as a cautionary tract to its present form as substantive literature. In Part II, Writing the Young Adult Novel, Sue Ellen Bridgers, Richard Peck, and Sandy Asher, contemporary authors of young adult books, discuss young people and their literature, focusing on their own processes of writing and speculating on the needs and interests of young adult readers. Part III, Teaching the Young Adult Novel, takes a look at various issues surrounding the genre and suggests innovative, provocative ways of incorporating this literature into the curriculum. Virginia Monseau illustrates ways in which the literature classroom can become a community of readers, encouraging student engagement and response, while Gary Salvner discusses the use of young adult novels in the traditionally structured literature curriculum. The possibilities of reading young adult novels across the curriculum are explored by Jeanne Gerlach, who provides theoretical background as well as practical suggestions. Lois Stover and Eileen Tway explore the world of cross-cultural young adult novels, providing sound reasons for their inclusion in the English curriculum, and Patricia Kelly discusses the issue of gender in young adult books, focusing specifically on same-gender and cross-gender relationships. In the final essay James Davis examines the censorship issue as it relates to young adult novels, providing an historical perspective while at the same time suggesting strategies for dealing with censorship problems.

As a final note we call attention to the fact that some of the quoted material in this volume, published earlier in this century, contains what now appears to be sexist language. To avoid awkwardness and to preserve the integrity of this reference material, we have not attempted to alter the quotes in any way. We trust that readers will understand the significance of leaving the language intact.

We hope this book will demonstrate that reading the adolescent's world can result in an enriching and enlightening literary journey, whether we trod the path for the first time or retrace footprints made long ago.

Work Cited

Rosenblatt, Louise M. *Literature As Exploration*, 3rd ed. New York: Modern
Language Association, 1988.

Part I
Reading the Young Adult Novel

1

The Universality of the Young Adult Novel

Ted Hipple

Literature captivates its readers in various ways. With many novels it is the story we remember. Our need to know what will happen next in the events Dickens weaves together in his *A Tale of Two Cities* keeps us turning over the pages long after we should have been turning off the bedlamp. In other works characters loom significant and become as known to us as family and friends. Few readers of Twain's *Adventures of Huckleberry Finn* will forget central figures like Huck or Jim or even lesser ones like Pap or the duke and the king. Setting, too, can be an important element in our enjoyment of literature. Egdon Heath so clearly plays a role in Hardy's *Return of the Native* that it might well be listed in the *dramatis personae* of any staged version of that magnificent novel.

The foregoing paragraph could just as easily have contained adolescent novels as illustrations of its points. Thomas Baird's *Where Time Ends*, a young adult novel that has not received the attention it deserves, presents the possible end of the world, the result of a nuclear war and its aftermath; readers who get beyond just the opening twenty or thirty pages will very soon finish this compelling story. Authors of adolescent novels also shape characters whom we love or hate or pity but absolutely never forget. In Robert Cormier's *The Chocolate War* both Archie and Brother Leon lodge themselves in our memories, even though we squirm a bit in terror at the recollection of their seemingly innate evil. And what of the setting in Sue Ellen Bridgers's *All Together Now*, the small North Carolina town that rises up as a single entity to protect the retarded Dwayne and prevent his being sent to a mental institution?

Yet possibly what most makes literature LITERATURE, what moves it from words on a page that we read to ideas to which we return again and again, is theme, the underlying philosophy embodied in the work, the view of the human condition it offers. Even in classic novels like those just mentioned, the themes are as forceful as are their stories or their characters or their settings. Dickens painted vivid portraits of class struggles on both sides of the English Channel between those with money and those without it. The repeated explorations into good and evil, with Huck Finn usually astraddle them, give us pause for our own thoughts and make us rise out of our seats in triumphant joy when Huck refuses to turn Jim in. Though set in the most appropriate of places, the harsh and unforgiving Egdon Heath, Hardy's novel is really about humankind's minimal chances against a malevolent fate.

So also with young adult literature: it must be read with attention not simply to its story lines or its characters or its setting but also and very importantly to its themes. Those less familiar with young adult literature tend sometimes to believe that its thematic treatments are slight, superficial, "teenage" if you will. They are not. Like the best of literature written for adults, good novels written for adolescents possess themes that merit and reward examination and commentary. This chapter will explore some of the more common themes found in adolescent novels.

Alienation

"They murdered him." Cormier's *The Chocolate War* begins with those three words. Though the murder described is not quite literal — it takes place during football practice — that sentence foreshadows the rest of the novel. "They" — Archie and the malevolent fraternity he manages, Brother Leon, fate maybe — do conspire to murder Jerry Renault or at least the spirits of this anti-hero of an outstanding novel about alienation and its complement, loneliness. The cards seem a bit stacked against Jerry: his mother is dead, his father is indifferent not only to Jerry but to most of life; he has no siblings; his one close friend Goober succumbs easily to the power of the Vigils. Jerry is isolated. At first he obeys the Vigils's command for initiation into their group — he will not sell the school chocolates — but then he goes off on his own, refusing to sell them even after being ordered to do so by Archie. Jerry asks the question Eliot's Prufrock asks: "Do I dare disturb the universe?" He does dare, and he suffers for that presumption.

Like many adolescents, Jerry suffers alone, pressured by peers, unable to control events, buffeted by life. In him many adolescent readers see themselves, more pawns than kings or queens or even knights. Yet Jerry resists; he fights. And in doing so he adds to the alienation, the separation, the loneliness. He is, throughout, on his own and the message is clear: Life is tough.

Whether or not *The Catcher in the Rye* is an adolescent novel may depend on one's definitions, as J. D. Salinger clearly wrote it for an adult audience. Yet it has been and is being read each year by thousands of young people and is consistently found among the required readings in both high school and college literature classes. One of the reasons for its staying power—it was published in 1951—is its compelling, portrait of an alienated adolescent. Holden Caulfield's troubles are many, including the very serious physical illness which removes him from New York City to the California sanitarium from which he tells his story of that "madman stuff that happened to me around last Christmas," but chief among them and the cause of the others is his inability to relate to anyone else, save possibly his younger sister Phoebe. He reveres innocence—imagined former girlfriend Jane who keeps her kings in the back row when they play checkers, the nuns he meets during his sojourn in Manhattan—but finds it too seldom. More common is his revulsion about the hypocrisy he sees everywhere about him: the cool Stradlater at school, his theater date Sally Hayes who always seems to be looking over his shoulder for someone more important, the three tourists from Seattle who yearn to see a movie star. Holden's intolerance for these people extends to an intolerance for society as a whole and he withdraws, socially and physically. Like Jerry, he has been defeated by the universe.

Friendship

For many adolescents, however, the loneliness of a Jerry Renault seems remote; they have a good friend, maybe several. Perhaps more than most authors, Paul Zindel explores friendship as a theme, particularly in *The Pigman* and, ten years later, *The Pigman's Legacy*, and also in such intervening novels as *Pardon Me, You're Stepping on My Eyeball*, *The Undertaker's Gone Bananas*, and the more recent *Harry and Hortense at Hormone High*. Setting him apart from many of his fellow writers, Zindel crosses sex lines in his friendships—John and Lorraine in *The Pigman* books, "Marsh" Mellow and Edna Singlebox in *Pardon Me*, Bobby and Lauri in *The Undertaker*, Harry and Hortense. Friendship signifies in a Zindel novel just as it does in teenage life and adult life. One has someone to talk to, to share with, to grow with. At a time when most adolescents are moving apart from family, especially parents, friends assume even more importance in their lives and, thus being able to read about friendships, even fictional ones, becomes telling.

Zindel's boy-girl couples do not have sex. Neither do Owen Griffith and Natalie Field, the protagonists of Ursula LeGuin's *Very Far Away from Anywhere Else*. Bright, shy, introspective, they become wonderful companions for each other and develop a friendship that will, in all likelihood, mature into love (unlike the relationships frequently found in the novels of Judy Blume and Norma Klein in which love, at least sex, precedes friendship). Owen describes his feelings one December day when he and Natalie are sitting on a deserted beach:

> And it was cold and it was the high point of my life. I'd had high points before. Once at night walking in the park in the rain in autumn. Once out in the desert under the stars, when I turned into the earth turning on its axis. Sometimes thinking, just thinking things through. But always alone. By myself. This time I was not alone. I was on the high mountain with a friend. There is nothing, there is *nothing* that beats that. If it never happens again in my life, still I can say I was there once. (41)

Yet friendship, like alienation, is many-faceted. *Among Friends* by Caroline Cooney explores this topic with a different slant, that of the friendship which has gone awry. Three girls — Jennie, Emily, Hilary — have been fast friends seemingly forever; they call themselves the Awesome Threesome. But in this novel made up of their diary entries, the friendship begins to disintegrate, the result, not of bad behavior, but of good: Jennie is too successful, too attractive, too intelligent. Because her friends can't match her, they begin to dislike her. The friendship dissolves. And it hurts.

Still another exploration of friendship is that found in Bridgers's *All Together Now*. It is 1951 and Casey, a twelve-year-old, comes to small-town North Carolina to spend a summer with her grandparents. Almost her first acquaintance is Dwayne, a retarded adult thirty-three years of age, who, thinking Casey is a boy, invites her to play baseball with him. Casey goes along with the deception and soon she and Dwayne are good friends, fast friends, sufficiently so that when Dwayne finally learns the truth about Casey's gender, they remain friends. The two of them even discuss friendship, with Dwayne advising Casey, "You be nice to folks and they be nice to you right back. That's one thing for sure" (52).

In this same novel Bridgers examines friendship among adults, an unusual but needed study in adolescent literature that is intended for teenagers who will, after all, very soon become adults. Casey's grandmother Jane and her lifelong neighbor, Pansy, "had been friends for so long, as long as either of them could remember, but there had never before this been any apprehension between them, no fear that what they said to each other could do irreparable damage to their affection, no inhibitions that kept them from speaking the truth" (71). Adolescents who read of friendships as strong as this one are, whether they know it or not, absorbing values about companionship and "otherness" that will inform their own ways of living, thus providing no meager justification for the use of young adult fiction with young adults.

Just these few examples of the way friendship is differently treated in different adolescent novels offer a suitable paradigm to explain the universality of the themes found in this kind of literature and its appeal for not only adolescent readers but adult readers as well. What happens to teenagers happens to us all: the need, say, for friends is not limited to six-year-olds or sixteen-year-olds or sixty-year-olds; it is everyone's need. Hence, treatment of this important life concern, when well done as it is in these and numerous other adolescent novels, supports the contention that adolescent literature is thematically linked to all substantial literature, no matter the intended age of its readers. It is perhaps a critical overstatement to link Cormier with Conrad, Blume with Balzac, but their differences are more of degree than of kind; all of them take as their domain the study of the human condition.

The study of still other themes may reinforce the point.

Family

Tolstoy opened *Anna Karenina* with a sentence that has since become famous: "All happy families are alike; every unhappy family is unhappy in its own way." Unhappy families frequently make up the cast of characters in adolescent novels. For example, Lois Duncan's *Don't Look Behind You* features that happy family that is like all of the other happy families in suburban Washington and then, unlike those others, it becomes completely unhappy. They are totally uprooted, their former identities abolished, new and unfamiliar names and roles provided them, all the result of the father's having to flee Washington as part of a witness-protection program. The forced change tests all four of the Corrigans, even as they become the Webers to escape the threats of a hired killer they know only as the Vamp.

Life falls apart, too, for the members of the family Susan Beth Pfeffer creates in *The Year Without Michael*, a book whose title tells the story. Michael has disappeared and no one knows where he is, why he is gone, what has happened to him, early on *when* he will show up, later on *if* he will show up. Previously tentative but still stable relationships among the members of Michael's family begin to crumble under this new pressure — the family becomes unhappy.

A variation on the theme occurs in novels like S. E. Hinton's *The Outsiders* and Harry Mazer's *When the Phone Rang*. In each novel the unhappiness occurs after the accidental death of loving and caring parents, leaving the three adolescent siblings in each book wondering what will come next for them. In both novels they attempt to stay together.

Death

Adolescents die in real life. They die in young adult fiction. In fact, from a thematic point of view, death is one of the more common elements found in adolescent literature (just as it is in literature intended for adult audiences), mainly, of course, because of the powerful drama always associated with death. Katherine Paterson's remarkable *Bridge to Terabithia* makes ten-year-old Jess confront death for the first time, but not the more remote death of a seldom-seen and old grandparent or the death of a friend of his parents. Rather, it is Leslie, his ten-year-old buddy with whom he had created the island kingdom of Terabithia. Ironically it is while she is trying to swing across to their island that Leslie falls into the raging river and is drowned. Disbelieving, disconsolate, Jess has to mature too soon, one thinks, yet death has that effect on the young.

Or they prove unable to handle it and, suffused with guilt, become mentally unstable. In Judith Guest's *Ordinary People* Conrad's older brother Buck is killed when they are boating together and come up against a storm. Conrad holds himself responsible not simply (or legitimately) for Buck's death but also for surviving himself and attempts suicide. His recovery, aided by a wonderfully drawn psychologist, parallels the disintegration of the family unit, particularly the problems faced by Conrad's mother Beth. Thus, like all good novels, whether adult or adolescent, and like all of life, *Ordinary People* interweaves themes, offering thoughtful commentary not only on death but on family life, on self-judgment, on love.

Suicide, a successful attempt this time, also is central in Fran Arrick's *Tunnel Vision*. The novel opens with simple sentences about complex events: "Anthony died. He died in his own house and by his own hand." From that point the novel tracks the lives of people involved in one way or another with Anthony—siblings, parents, aunt and uncle, girlfriend, swim teammates—many of whom blame themselves for Anthony's unexpected suicide. Just as life fails to offer easy answers, so also does Arrick not provide any kind of final closure. To be sure, *Tunnel Vision* is a novel written for young adults, but equally sure is its mature treatment of a major societal problem, teenage suicide, the second leading cause (after accidents) of teenage death.

Other societal problems also appear in young adult novels. While sometimes focused on topics of particular interest to teens, these novels also deal with universal societal issues.

Mental Illness

The most devastating result of mental illness among teenagers is, of course, suicide, but not all sufferers commit suicide; somehow they struggle on. In *Lisa Bright and Dark* the title character is better aware of her schizophrenia than her parents, who think she is faking it, or her friends, who regard her as weird. But a few of the latter finally begin to sense that something is seriously wrong and provide her the help she needs to try to make a new beginning. Wisely, author John Neufeld doesn't end the novel with optimistic pronouncements.

Another protagonist who is mentally ill, though readers are unsure about that, is found in Cormier's troubling *I Am the Cheese*. Young Adam is on a bicycle trip, or so we readers are allowed to infer. In fact, we learn that he is imprisoned not only in a home for the mentally unstable but in his own mind, the results of his seeing the murder of his parents, who were in a protected witness program, like the Corrigans in *Don't Look Behind You*.

But mental illness in young adult literature is not simply a problem of the young. Commonly, it is the adolescent's reaction to the mental illness of an adult that becomes a central theme in novels. Few authors have explored this theme more adroitly than Sue Ellen Bridgers, who makes such illness a major element in three different novels. (Significantly, Bridger's father was himself mentally ill while she was in junior and senior high school and she invests in her adolescent characters many of the guilty feelings she experienced — was she in any way the cause of her father's illness? — and the fears she had — will the illness of the father be repeated in the life of the child?) In *All Together Now* Dwayne is a retarded adult, thirty-three, who passes his days the way a twelve-year-old would — baseball, movies, just "hanging out." Twelve-year-old Casey becomes his greatest friend, and it is she who galvanizes community reaction to keep Dwayne from being committed to a "home." More autobiographical in some ways among Bridgers's novels is *Notes for Another Life*, in which father Tom is mentally ill and teenage son Kevin is filled with anger at Tom's inability to be the father he wants, and with doubts and fears about his own sanity. In *Permanent Connections* Bridgers explores agoraphobia, an illness she has hinted at in characterizations in her earlier novels. But here it is a central problem in the novel: Coralee Davis, the protagonist middle-aged spinster aunt, will not leave her house. It takes the wise prodding of a sensitive neighbor, Ginny Collier, to help her overcome her fears and to move, first to the porch, then to the backyard, and then to the frightening world "out there." Coralee's (and Ginny's) triumph merits an accompaniment of "Ode to Joy," but, beyond story, the significance lies in the novelistic exploration of this common and dreaded disease.

Sex

Few young adult novels examine sex quite so graphically or so commercially as Judy Blume's *Forever*. It opens with "Sybil Davison has a genius I.Q. and has been laid by at least six different guys" and becomes even more specific thereafter. Kathy, a high school senior, a virgin, though not terribly hung up on remaining one, meets Michael, also a senior, not a virgin, and terribly hung up on Kathy's not remaining one much longer. In very explicit scenes, even to the point of naming Michael's penis Ralph, Blume presents first sex for Kathy in a way that gives one set of answers to the many questions all teens have about sex. Though "forever" isn't quite forever in their developing love, Kathy has no regrets about her sexual experiences with Michael and appears to regard them as one further stage in her maturation, a view Blume seems to share.

Not all readers take this tolerant perspective. While Blume's book is one of the most widely sold novels written for young adults, it is also one of the most widely censored, with most proponents of its abolition from school and public libraries arguing that the sexual content is one problem, the seeming amorality another and more serious one. Yet it cannot be denied that for many teenagers Blume's book is their *Joy of Sex*.

Turning on its head the traditional boy-as-aggressor image of teen-aged sex, *It's OK If You Don't Love Me* by Norma Klein features Jody and Lyle, the former much more experienced and much more eager to make sex a regular part of their lives. Norma Klein usually includes sex as a central activity in the lives of her adolescent characters. As with Blume's books, though less successfully, Klein's typically assume a matter-of-fact attitude about sex among teenagers, one many readers no doubt find refreshing as well as instructive.

A much older novel (in the relatively short span of time young adult literature has been around), Ann Head's *Mr. and Mrs. Bo Jo Jones* seems antiquated to many of today's teens, yet read by them still. High schoolers Bo Jo and girl friend July have sex, just once, but she gets pregnant, they get married, and the novel chronicles the difficulties they face. Head barely avoids overt didacticism, but her message is clear nonetheless: Teenage marriages have little to recommend them.

July Jones becomes pregnant; Blume's Kathy is directed to get birth control information by a savvy grandmother; Klein's characters are generally sexually active yet seldom get pregnant. But sometimes they do and among their choices then is abortion. In *Beginner's Love* Leda has such an abortion, one presented as legally and socially acceptable in her New York City set and medically safe. Over a decade earlier than this 1983 book by Norma Klein, Zindel had portrayed all the ugly features of back-alley abortions in *My Darling, My Hamburger*. Thus, in this as in other instances, does young adult literature reflect the changing of the times.

Not all the sex in adolescent fiction is heterosexual. Sandra Scoppettone has written two novels that treat teenage homosexuality.

Trying Hard to Hear You, though told from the point of view of a heterosexual young woman, has as one of its central themes—and problems—the homosexual relationship of two young men whose secret becomes known, with tragic consequences. *Happy Endings Are All Alike* features Jared and Peggy, high school girls who are lovers. Though secret (only Jared's mother knows), their relationship is jeopardized when Jared is brutally raped by a school acquaintance who learns about her and Peggy and threatens Jared with a you-tell-on-me-and-I'll-tell-on-you ultimatum.

Jack by A. M. Homes offers still another perspective on the theme of homosexuality. Jack's parents divorce when he is eleven, but it is not until he is fifteen that his father confesses about his gay life. Outraged and shattered by this revelation, Jack cannot keep it to himself and soon is victimized by schoolmates who call him "faggot's son" or even "faggot" himself, a term that Jack had thought about in connection with his father.

Both Scoppettone and Homes present balanced books about homosexuality, just as Blume and Norma Klein do in their treatments of heterosexuality. Judgments are avoided, issues are thoughtfully explored, and both teens and adults act, albeit emotionally, with some ultimate intelligence. Again, these books provide examples of how seriously serious themes are treated in adolescent literature. The long held view that books written for teenagers rarely display affection beyond hand-holding—or at least they ought not to—clearly is naive, as unsophisticated about the literature of teenagers as it is about the lives of teenagers.

Drugs and Alcohol

Scoppettone again, this time not on sex but on alcohol. As in her books about teen homosexuality, her characters are not wrong-side-of-the-tracks sleazebags but ordinary kids who, in the instance of *The Late Great Me*, drink. In Chapter One, after establishing herself as a relatively normal high school junior, with a brother at Harvard, a mother and father who are themselves successful even if they may be on her back overmuch, the narrator ends with these lines: "I am, I have discovered, many things. I am a young woman, an artist, both considerate and inconsiderable, generous and selfish, funny and sulky, rigid and open, arrogant and humble, and absolutely, definitely, without any doubt a drunk. My name is Geri Peters and I'm an alcoholic and I think you should know about it" (5). Most readers take up Geri's challenge to "know about it" and, in the course of their education, learn a good bit about this increasing teenage scourge.

The sometimes deserved criticism that adolescent novels sugarcoat life's problems and solve them too easily, a point of view more readily exemplified a decade ago than today, certainly does not apply to *Go Ask Alice*. The anonymous diary of a hooked-on-drugs teenager, this compelling account of her victories and defeats in the adolescent drug culture perhaps has done more — one really does not know — to deter other young people from a similar fate than all the "just say no" commercials ever recorded. Intense, devastating, *Go Ask Alice* pulls no punches in its message that drugs destroy.

The foregoing paragraphs barely skim the thematic surfaces of young adult literature; space does not permit a fuller treatment of these themes presented or of other themes found in fiction intended for teenaged audiences: crime (see the novels of Lois Duncan or *Up Country* by Alden R. Carter); ethical dilemmas (Robert Newton Peck's *Justice Lion*, another novel too often overlooked, places a boy squarely at odds with the father he had heretofore idolized); school life (*Harry and Hortense at Hormone High* by Paul Zindel implies in its title the less-than-positive picture of school life typically found in the novels by that popular author, himself a former teacher for ten years); AIDS (see *Night Kites* by M. E. Kerr or Alice Hoffman's *At Risk*, in which the victim is eleven-year-old Amanda, who five years earlier had an operation and had been given a transfusion of contaminated blood); obesity (Robert Lipsyte has produced three books about overweight Bobby Marks: *One Fat Summer*, *Summer Rules*, and *The Summerboy*); sibling rivalry (in Lynn Hall's *Half the Battle* the reader's emotions are as torn as the relationship between the two brothers, one of them blind); divorce (novelistic treatments as different as the optimistic *It's Not the End of the World* by Blume, the thoughtful *Notes for Another Life* by Bridgers, and the humorous *Divorce Express* by Paula Danziger).

Racial intolerance plays a part in Bruce Brooks's *The Moves Make the Man*, religious intolerance in Arrick's *Chernowitz*. Cancer kills people in Carter's *Sheila's Dying*. Walter Dean Myers's historical *Fallen Angels* portrays teenagers fighting the Vietnam war and William Sleator's futuristic *House of Stairs* pits teens against a malevolent social psychologist. *Things Are Seldom What They Seem* by Sandy Asher provides a picture of sexual abuse by a teacher; *Abby, My Love* by Hadley Irwin offers a similar portrait, this time by an incestuous father. Handicapped teenagers are found in Robin Brancato's *Winning* and Chris Crutcher's *The Crazy Horse Electric Game* and Emily Hanlon's *It's Too Late for Sorry*.

And so it goes, on and on. The generalization that adolescent literature, in some form or another, in some way or another, covers all of adolescent life and, for that matter, all of adult life, where the same themes are universal, can be defended, as these many examples make abundantly clear. The themes treated in novels written for young people cover the physical, social, and emotional waterfront so completely that many such novels are appropriately variations on themes, different treatments from different perspectives, writing "with a slant," as Emily Dickinson put it.

Which, of course, brings us directly to another element of adolescent fiction that adds to its staying power and its universal appeal (and not always, by the way, just among teenaged readers; adolescent novels get their fair share of adult readership): its literary quality. No matter what the subject treated — divorce or mental illness or teenaged sex — a bad book is a bad book and will garner few readers.

The books themselves offer, of course, the best argument about their quality, but other exemplars may be adduced. Writers as far different as Fran Arrick and Paul Zindel, and between them Brancato and Bridgers and Brooks and literally hundreds of others, get reviewed regularly in the pages of journals devoted to the study of seriously attempted and successfully written literature, the *New York Times Book Review*, for one example, *Booklist*, for another. And a whole host of journals focusing more specifically on adolescent literature has sprung up, most particularly *The ALAN Review*, *The School Library Journal*, and *VOYA, the Voice of Youth Advocates*. These journals not only review new books for adolescents, but offer sound and scholarly critical analyses of the field and its significant authors. Adolescent literature courses now are found at virtually every college and university and are among the fastest growing in the curriculum. Countless term papers and even many doctoral dissertations have been written on adolescent literature.

Twayne Publishers has for years published single volume critical biographies of the major canonical literary figures, writers like Shakespeare and Joyce and Twain and Faulkner. In the late 1980s it added a new series imprint, "Twayne's United States Authors Series, Young Adult Authors," and it has now published studies on, among others, S. E. Hinton, Richard Peck, M. E. Kerr, and Sue Ellen Bridgers. More volumes are forthcoming.

ALAN, the Assembly on Literature for Adolescents of the National Council of Teachers of English, has grown in its seventeen-year existence from a handful of founders to almost 2500 members. Its convention each November tops out at the maximum number of registrants allowed — 300 — within weeks of the opening of the registration period, but other folks crowd their way in to hear authors of young adult literature speak about their own writing and scholars speak about those authors. A field of lesser worth would not have this drawing power.

Thus, the broad appeal of adolescent literature lies in part in its treatment of universal themes and in part in its high quality. Its writers write well. They tell good stories, inhabit them with memorable characters, place them in well-described settings, and do it all with prose that causes readers to linger now and again for a second reading, a moment of appreciation for the well-turned phrase or the artistic metaphor. Three examples from three different authors may make the point and end the discussion:

(a) Sue Ellen Bridgers lets Rob, the protagonist of *Permanent Connections*, provide his own autobiography in his thinking about an English assignment he has neglected:

> Right now he should get up and write something. He would write about how it feels when you wake up in the night because your folks are arguing about you, about how lousy it is never to be left alone, about what a pain in the butt your twelve-year-old perfect sister is, about how you're already messed up. Already, at seventeen, boxed in with no way out. Not enough guts to scramble, never enough bucks to float. Sinking, always sinking. Holding tight and falling away at the same time. (6)

(b) M. E. Kerr opens *Gentlehands*, a novel that explores both class and racial intolerances, with words that get directly into one of the key themes of the novel—status differences:

> I wonder what the summer would have been like if I'd never met Skye Pennington. They always seem to have names like that, don't they? Rich, beautiful girls are never named Elsie Pip or Mary Smith. They have those special names and they say them in their particular tones and accents, and my mother was right, I was in over my head or out of my depth, or however she put it. My father said, "She's not in our class, Buddy." This conversation took place the first night I took her out. (1)

(c) Their own hearts torn asunder with the doctor's report, her parents tenderly and lovingly break the news to eleven-year-old Amanda that she has AIDS in Alice Hoffman's *At Risk*:

> She ran up to her room and locked herself in, and they let her. They let her sit in the dark and cry, they let her listen to one cassette tape after another, and when she came back downstairs at a little after nine that night, they nodded when she said her eyes might look funny because she was tired. They sat around the kitchen table, eating chocolate ice cream. But they didn't look at each other; they didn't dare speak above a whisper. They've become sleepwalkers, wandering through their own nightmares, each avoiding the others for fear that a word, a conversation, a kiss will make them realize they aren't dreaming. (57)

Yes, literature written for young adults is fine literature, about themes that are universal, with quality that is stunning. Such literature merits—and rewards—attention.

Works Cited

Arrick, Fran. 1981. *Chernowitz!*. New York: Bradbury.

———. 1980. *Tunnel Vision*. New York: Dell.

Asher, Sandy. 1984. *Things Are Seldom What They Seem*. New York: Delacorte.

Baird, Thomas. 1988. *Where Time Ends*. New York: Harper & Row.

Blume, Judy. 1976. *Forever*. New York: Pocket Books.

———. 1972. *It's Not the End of the World*. New York: Bradbury.

Brancato, Robin. 1977. *Winning*. New York: Knopf.

Bridgers, Sue Ellen. 1979. *All Together Now*. New York: Knopf.

———. 1981. *Notes for Another Life*. New York: Knopf.

———. 1986. *Permanent Connections*. New York: Harper & Row.

Brooks, Bruce. 1984. *The Moves Make the Man*. New York: Harper & Row.

Carter, Alden R. 1986. *Sheila's Dying*. New York: Putnam.

———. 1989. *Up Country*. New York: Putnam.

Cooney, Caroline. 1987. *Among Friends*. New York: Bantam.

Cormier, Robert. 1974. *The Chocolate War*. New York: Pantheon.

———. 1977. *I Am the Cheese*. New York: Dell.

Crutcher, Chris. 1986. *Crazy Horse Electric Game*. New York: Greenwillow.

———. 1983. *Running Loose*. New York: Greenwillow.

Danziger, Paula. 1982. *Divorce Express*. New York: Delacorte.

Dickens, Charles. 1906. *A Tale of Two Cities*. London: Dent.

Duncan, Lois. 1989. *Don't Look Behind You*. New York: Delacorte.

Go Ask Alice. 1976. New York: Avon.

Guest, Judith. 1976. *Ordinary People*. New York: Viking.

Hall, Lynn. 1982. *Half the Battle*. New York: Macmillan.

Hanlon, Emily. 1978. *It's Too Late for Sorry*. New York: Bradbury.

Hardy, Thomas. 1912. *Return of the Native*. New York: Harper & Row.

Head, Ann. 1967. *Mr. and Mrs. Bo Jo Jones*. New York: New American Library.

Hinton, S. E. 1967. *The Outsiders*. New York: Viking.

Hoffman, Alice. 1988. *At Risk*. New York: Putnam.

Homes, A. M. 1989. *Jack*. New York: Macmillan.

Irwin, Hadley. 1987. *Abby, My Love*. New York: New American Library.

Kerr, M. E. 1978. *Gentlehands*. New York: Harper & Row.

———. 1986. *Night Kites*. New York: Harper & Row.

Klein, Norma. 1983. *Beginner's Love*. New York: Hillside Books.

———. 1977. *It's OK If You Don't Love Me*. New York: Dial.

LeGuin, Ursula. 1982. *Very Far Away from Anywhere Else*. New York: Bantam.

Lipsyte, Robert. 1977. *One Fat Summer.* New York: Harper & Row.

———. 1981. *Summer Rules.* New York: Harper & Row.

———. 1982. *The Summerboy.* New York: Harper & Row.

Mazer, Harry. 1985. *When the Phone Rang.* New York: Scholastic.

Myers, Walter Dean. 1988. *Fallen Angels.* New York: Scholastic.

Neufeld, John. 1970. *Lisa Bright and Dark.* New York: New American Library.

Paterson, Katherine. 1977. *Bridge to Terabithia.* New York: Crowell.

Peck, Robert Newton. 1981. *Justice Lion.* Boston: Little, Brown.

Pfeffer, Susan Beth. 1988. *The Year Without Michael.* New York: Bantam.

Salinger, J. D. 1951. *The Catcher in the Rye.* Boston: Little, Brown.

Scoppettone, Sandra. 1979. *Happy Endings Are All Alike.* New York: Laurel Leaf.

———. 1984. *The Late Great Me.* New York: Bantam.

———. 1974. *Trying Hard to Hear You.* New York: Harper & Row.

Sleator, William. 1975. *House of Stairs.* New York: Avon.

Tolstoy, Leo. 1970. *Anna Karenina.* New York: Norton.

Twain, Mark. 1948. *The Adventures of Huckleberry Finn.* New York: Holt, Rinehart, and Wilson.

Zindel, Paul. 1984. *Harry and Hortense at Hormone High.* New York: Harper & Row.

———. 1969. *My Darling, My Hamburger.* New York: Harper & Row.

———. 1976. *Pardon Me, You're Stepping on My Eyeball.* New York: Harper & Row.

———. 1968. *The Pigman.* New York: Harper & Row.

———. 1980. *The Pigman's Legacy.* New York: Harper & Row.

———. 1978. *The Undertaker's Gone Bananas.* New York: Harper & Row.

2

Listening to Readers: Attitudes Toward the Young Adult Novel

Donald R. Gallo

English teachers are novel lovers. That *double-entendre* boldly proclaimed on bumper stickers and lapel buttons might just be the cause of one of English teaching's most serious problems.

English teachers love literature. That's why most of us became teachers of English. We enjoyed reading at an early age. During our teenage years we read voraciously. While some of our classmates were reading true romances and comic books, we devoured and appreciated great works of literature: *Little Women, The Adventures of Huckleberry Finn, Great Expectations, Les Miserables, Wuthering Heights, Tess of the D'Urbervilles*, plays by Shakespeare, and novels by Dostoyevsky, Camus, and Faulkner.

We want students in our classes to react in the same way. Thus we are delighted when one of our sophomore students tells us she read *Anna Karenina* during her summer vacation, and we commend the eleventh grade boy who has taken our suggestion to read Malamud for his term paper. On the other hand we become frustrated and disappointed when other students don't evince the same kinds of responses. We sigh dejectedly when one student after another asks permission to read the latest Stephen King or Danielle Steel novel for outside reading; we scowl at girls reading the most recent edition of Sweet Valley High during study hall.

It's satisfying to remember that we loved and valued literature so much — and still do. But we also need to look critically at how our experiences affect the way most of us teach literature in classes filled with students who do not — or who *can* not — respond to literature in a similar manner.

Because many of our students don't have the same tastes and attitudes (not to mention experiences, world views, and genetic predispositions) as we had and have, if we hope to develop *any* interest in reading in the majority of our students — who are not at all like us — we ought to use different pieces of literature than we read at their age. Consider this topic from the perspective of a student in our lowest ability group, or from the perspective of one of the least enthusiastic readers in our heterogeneous classes. What books would that student recommend for required reading if he or she were to become an English teacher five or ten years from now? Would that student view literature and teach it the same way as do those of us who devoured books with ease when we were teenagers? Although there is no way to determine the answer to that question, it seems logical that such a student would look at literature quite differently because he or she has experienced it from a different perspective. Such an individual could not think: *These are the books I loved as a teenager and, therefore, these are the books I will in turn teach my students to love in the same way.* He or she would not be likely to conclude: *This is the way literature was taught to me; therefore, I will teach literature the same way to my students so that they will appreciate it the way I did.* The opposite is more likely to hold true.

In spite of the growth of young adult literature and the expanded use of paperbacks in junior and senior high school classrooms during the past twenty years, three observations have been unquestionably confirmed in a recent and extensive study of literature teaching conducted by the Center for the Learning and Teaching of Literature at the State University of New York at Albany — *A Study of Book-Length Works Taught in High School English Courses.* Arthur Applebee reports that 1) more than ninety percent of English classrooms employ anthologies, emphasizing genre in the lower grades and chronology in the upper grades; 2) familiarity is the second most important characteristic of the literature taught in junior and senior high schools — i.e., traditional classics dominate the literature curriculum; and 3) most English programs in our nation make little distinction between literary works taught to college-bound students and those taught to non-academic students (Applebee 1989a).

To examine the effects of traditional literature on students and to compare those with the effects of young adult novels, we need first to listen to what teenagers have to say about their reading preferences and their responses to literature. Then it will be valuable to examine what teachers and other adults say about literature for teenagers.

Students' Responses

As part of a 1982 study of reading interests of nearly 3400 students in grades four through twelve in over 50 schools in 37 towns and cities throughout Connecticut, students were asked if they liked the novels and other books they were assigned to read. In junior high schools, 40 percent of the boys and 35 percent of the girls indicated that they **seldom** or **never** liked the required selections. In senior high schools, 41 percent of the boys and 23 percent of the girls said **seldom** or **never**. In comparison, only one student in every five **usually** or **always** liked the assigned books (Gallo 7–8). There is little reason to believe those percentages are markedly different in most communities today when the Applebee study (1989a) shows relative stagnation in literature curricula across the nation.

Bob Carlsen and Anne Sherrill, in their insightful book *Voices of Readers: How We Come to Love Books*, illustrate the diverse responses that individuals have had to books during their secondary school years. One adult respondent recalls:

> During my high school days, I read most of the classroom assignments, but was bored by the masterpieces, or perhaps I failed to understand them. They seemed to be written in another language and seemed not to entertain, but confuse. (132)

Another college student recalls a much more positive experience:

> In the ninth grade I was exposed to the classics by my English teacher. I read *Jane Eyre* and became so involved in it that several mornings I read until four a.m. It was so cold in my room that winter that I used to read with wool mittens on. (132)

But about that same book another respondent states:

> I hated almost all of the books we studied in English classes. ... I hated Charlotte Bronte the most. I was to read *Jane Eyre* for a seventh grade book report, but I couldn't finish it and have never been able to force myself to try it again. (131)

Among reasons for not enjoying assigned literature, Carlsen and Sherrill's respondents note the difficulty in comprehending ponderous texts, having to dissect and over analyze the books, "rehashing the same material for days," the lack of "fun and sense of wonder," having to search for the "meaning" without acknowledgment of the reader's feelings, and being forced to read sophisticated texts when the students lacked the experience and maturity to deal with them (129–136).

Many contemporary students whom I have surveyed dislike traditional classics because the books lack the kind of action kids have become accustomed to in novels as well as in films and on television; have "antiquated" styles; contain too many unfamiliar words; are "too dry, historical, or old fashioned." Classics, proclaims Keisa, an above-average student in an inner-city high school, "are well written but *dull*."

For many students the themes and conflicts of classical novels have no apparent connection with the lives of today's students. "The books have nothing to do with me," says one resentful tenth grade boy. "Reading literature is keeping in touch with the dead," pronounces a tenth grade girl.

Furthermore, most students feel the way another tenth grader states it: "Our teacher doesn't *want* you to enjoy literature; she wants you to read it for the details and the themes."

Carlsen and Sherrill conclude from their study that "teachers profess that, by presenting the classics, they are really increasing reading enthusiasm for and an appreciation of the great works of literature. It is quite disturbing to find that the protocols indicate exactly the opposite situation for many of the young" (136).

What most students want — whether they are in advanced classes or not — is involvement with the literary text. "I want to read something with a pulse!" one exasperated high school boy told me. "I like young adult novels because they catch your attention very quick," asserts a middle school boy. In a recent study in Texas, a University of Houston researcher has noted that reading for avid readers — as opposed to students who read little — is an emotional activity; they want to interact with the text (Beers). "I like to read books about people my age . . . 'cause you can relate to it," declares Cindy, a suburban Connecticut eighth grader.

When comparing self-selected independent reading with teacher-selected required reading, students in the 1982 Connecticut survey indicated similar responses to reading: with self-selected books, "I usually put myself in the place of the person I am reading about." "I learn something from my choices." "The books I read on my own you never want to put them down" (Gallo 8).

In examining the characteristics of favorite books selected by junior high school readers in the Southwest during the 1981 Children's Choices survey, Betty Carter and Karen Harris confirm that, along with a lively style, one of the most important literary elements in a book for teenagers is characterization. Kids are most attracted to books about characters who are like themselves in some way, especially in having to deal with personal problems and solve moral dilemmas (43–44).

That shouldn't be at all surprising when we consider what teenagers' most important concern is at this point in life: Themselves! Who am I? is a teenager's most consistent (if unspoken) question. In young adult novels teenagers are the main characters, and teenage concerns are their focus. Teenagers, however, are conspicuously absent in almost all classics taught in junior and senior high schools. In fact, in *Silas Marner*, which continues to be in the top forty most widely taught novels in the country, Eppie enters the story at age two in Part I and then reappears at age eighteen in Part II, her teenage years having been completely ignored.

When kids, especially those in junior high/middle schools, read a book they like, they see the characters as friends. It's easy for them to see Ponyboy Curtis in *The Outsiders* or Jackie McGee in *The Girl in the Box* as a personal friend because the main characters in those stories (as in most young adult novels) address the reader directly and intimately through their personal narration. It's not so easy for most fourteen year olds to see Hester Prynne or Willy Loman or Hamlet as personal friends.

From the perspective of a few years, one of the students in my university class in young adult literature recalls her earlier response to books:

> When I was in junior high school . . . I couldn't relate to most of the books that I had to read in school. *The Scarlet Letter*, for example, confused me and bored me. I didn't understand why Hester Prynne, the protagonist, stayed in a town where she was treated worse than a criminal simply because she committed adultery.
>
> Instead, I read about other teenagers who had problems that I could identify with. I turned to books about drugs and street life, such as *Go Ask Alice, Kathleen, Please Come Home,* and *Run, Shelly, Run* to help me come to terms with my own experiences as a teenager and to solidify my understanding of myself. I compared my thoughts and feelings about a given situation to those of characters in the books that I read to see if I was normal. . . . Reading helped me come to terms with my problems and to create my sense of self.

A senior English major looks back and remembers that her first contact with a novel that involved her emotionally occurred when her best friend handed her a book in seventh grade:

> As I began to read, I found myself enthralled by its protagonist. I knew her; her thoughts were so much like the ones that were rambling through my thirteen-year-old mind. I devoured the book in a few hours and quickly ran to the local library to read others. Its title is easily recognized by any adolescent girl in the United States today. It has, like make-up and designer jeans, become an intricate part of growing up. It is the famous *Are You There God? It's Me, Margaret*.
>
> It was not long before I had read all of Judy Blume's novels — over and over again. Soon, I had graduated to Paula Danziger and, as I grew older, Norma Klein became my close companion.

Today, it is not difficult to understand why such books were so important to me as a teenager. They depicted adolescents like me facing different situations, experiencing puzzling feelings and overcoming challenging obstacles. ... I found refuge from the pain of growing up with these girls who, unlike my parents, understood my turmoil.

A third student, recalling her search for the right role to play in life, says:

As a teenager, I was able to be myself when I was reading, while the rest of the time I was fitting in. Because a lot of the novels I read dealt with teenagers with similar problems, I felt comfortable.

Possibly the most important difference between the traditional classics and contemporary young adult novels is that YA novels help students to feel normal, comfortable, understood. But do most English teachers recognize that?

Educators' Responses

In a damning but not very well publicized study of members of the Massachusetts Council of Teachers of English conducted in the late 1970s, Patricia Aubin reported the despicably poor attitude that most teachers had toward the young adult novel. Not only were most of the teachers unaware of the range or the quality of books being produced for teenage readers, but many of the one hundred English teachers sampled also did not "have a clear image of what a Young Adult Novel is; nor [were] they aware of the reading tastes of their students" (3). A large part of the problem was that many of those teachers said they didn't read young adult novels. Half of them had never taken a course in adolescent literature and more than half of those were not interested in ever doing so. In addition, most of the teachers didn't read professional journals or attend conferences where books for teenagers were discussed. Worse, a majority of the teachers viewed young adult novels as "a basically inferior form of literature," describing it as "simplistic" and "immature" (5). If they used it at all, it was with remedial or less-able readers.

Diane Ravitch and Chester Finn exhibit that same attitude in their widely publicized 1987 book *What Do Our 17-Year-Olds Know?* when they bemoan the changes in the traditional literature curriculum which they hold responsible for American students' lack of literary knowledge. "At the precollege level, the substitutes for works by the likes of George Eliot, Nathaniel Hawthorne, and Ralph Waldo Emerson were a new generation of realistic melodrama known as 'young adult fiction' . . . ," they claim. "All too often, the new reading material was such that it could not be called literature by *anyone's* standards" (11).

At a workshop that I presented in a large Connecticut urban high school last year recommending wider use of young adult novels, one member of the English department declared: "We shouldn't be spending school funds to buy those kinds of books. If kids want to read that *stuff*," she snarled, "let them go buy it in the stores."

Too many teachers unfairly equate young adult novels only with Sweet Valley High, teenage romances, shallow sports biographies, mass-produced mysteries, and sensational thrillers such as those written by V. C. Andrews. The sophisticated novels of Sue Ellen Bridgers, Bruce Brooks, Alden Carter, Brock Cole, Aidan Chambers, Alice Childress, Robert Cormier, Chris Crutcher, Virginia Hamilton, M. E. Kerr, Kathryn Lasky, Norma Fox Mazer, Walter Dean Myers, Katherine Paterson, Gary Paulsen, Richard Peck, Susan Beth Pfeffer, Ouida Sebestyen, Cynthia Voigt, and others are unfamiliar to those teachers. Some teachers, in fact, have maligned young adult literature while they teach novels they don't even realize are classified in that genre.

For example, the 1988–89 Connecticut Teacher of the Year—a lively and enthusiastic English teacher in a suburban high school—disparaged young adult novels in a published interview by asserting that she prefers to teach "quality literature" that "has meaning and is discussable." She said: "Everybody talks about teaching critical thinking. There isn't much to think about in *The Cat Ate My Gymsuit*" (Queenan 8). Instead, she teaches *Antigone* and *Oedipus* because they "challenge" students. "I like to challenge students with quality literature that continues to speak to people over the years and touches them . . . " (7).

Although I and many young readers would disagree that there isn't much to discuss or think about in Paula Danziger's popular novel, I do agree that *The Cat Ate My Gymsuit* is not a novel worthy of thoughtful reading and critical discussion *in a high school*. It is much more appropriately suited to the sixth grade, where middle school readers, especially girls, have found great pleasure and personal insight in it. What this talented and exemplary English teacher has done is limit her view of what a young adult novel is, mistakenly thinking like many others that the young adult genre consists primarily of lightweight humorous novels. This same teacher a few weeks later, at a state conference of English teachers, publicly admitted to using Robert Cormier's *After the First Death* with one of her high school classes and finding it a worthwhile novel to teach.

Some sophisticated high school students, especially those in wealthy Connecticut suburbs, assess young adult literature the same way. When asked if they now read any young adult novels, such students often say something like: "Oh, no. I did when I was in sixth and seventh grades. I read Judy Blume and S. E. Hinton and the *Chronicles of Narnia* and almost everything that Lois Duncan wrote. But I grew out of that stuff." Have you, I ask them, ever read *The Chocolate War*? "Oh, yeah. We read that last year. It was really good." It seems that if it's called young adult literature, it's for younger kids; if a book's themes or conflict are more sophisticated, then it isn't seen as young adult.

This attitude suggests a concept widely accepted among members of the English teaching profession as well as among the general public: *If a work of literature is to be "studied," it must be difficult to begin with.* The logic behind that concept goes this way:

1. The works we teachers studied in secondary school as well as college had *substance*. They were often difficult to understand; we relied on English teachers to help us interpret them correctly.

2. Conversely, if a text is easy to read and understand, and if students can read it on their own without a teacher's help, it is of little substance and can't be worth teaching.

3. The most substantive books we've read are the classics; they have been respected and have lasted this long because they have substance.

4. Therefore, if our students are going to be taught properly, we must use the books that have been part of the English literature curriculum for as far back as any of us can remember.

This concept — or one much like it — is to a large extent behind the calls for excellence in education as well as for "cultural literacy" along with the proposal for a national literature curriculum we've heard about since the mid-1980s.

One problem with this approach is that by equating longevity with quality, we deny quality in contemporary works, especially in literary selections that lack sophisticated vocabulary, convoluted sentence structures, and complex plots. Complexity does not necessarily equal greatness, nor does simplicity equal simple-mindedness. Another flaw is the assumption that all students can best learn to interpret and appreciate literature by reading difficult material. If there are too many unfamiliar words, if the sentence structures are too complex to follow easily, if the concepts are too obscure . . . many students will not comprehend enough of the text to even begin to appreciate it, no less enjoy it.

The emphasis on traditional classics also ignores, and usually even scorns, newer and less well-known literary works. Furthermore, it disregards the intellectual and emotional development of teenagers while also underestimating the role that interest plays in developing literary appreciation and, ultimately, positive lifetime reading habits.

Many English teachers, librarians, and parents in my graduate course in young adult literature share similar misconceptions at the beginning of the course each semester. A middle-aged male teacher writes: "I really did not know what to expect from books for young adults. If pushed, I would have guessed that they were the easier classics or watered down versions of the great works." A female teacher states: "I always considered Young Adult novels to be poorly written fluff about better-than-life non-existent teenagers (you know, class presidents, straight-A students, cheerleaders, star athletes, etc)." A mother of five children admits: "To my mind, they were only a step above those comic books based on the classics that were so popular some years back ... poor writing, stories with little meaning or value."

But once these adults read and discuss a variety of good books in the genre, most of them have a different response. For example, a middle school reading teacher states: "I never, never would have expected there to be such a variety and wealth of books available. The more I read, the more I want to read! Nor did I ever imagine the diversity and complexity of situations the characters would be involved in." A graduate student, who has himself written novels (all as yet, alas, unpublished), writes:

> [One] thing that has surprised me is how good some of these books are in and of themselves, regardless of who they are intended for and what their subjects are and how old the main character may be. *Sheila's Dying* by Alden R. Carter and *A Day No Pigs Would Die* by Robert Newton Peck are both moving, serious works of literature.

A middle school teacher found insights for herself as well as a better perspective on her students, as she explains:

> I knew that many of my students were really enjoying books by authors like Blume, Clearly, L'Engle, O'Dell, etc., but I expected all these young adult books to be beneath my own reading repertoire as I supposed they were all "juvenile" and immature fluff! Wrong, wrong, wrong.

For many adult readers the characters and conflicts in young adult novels can have as strong an emotional impact as they have for teenagers. A high school librarian describes her first experience with a young adult novel after reading *The Outsiders* by S. E. Hinton:

> I was quite surprised to find myself so deeply involved with these characters. I supposed I would find them foreign or repulsive. Instead, I cared for them, even cried over them. I never expected to find a plot or characters I would react to, or identify with, so strongly. I had anticipated being shocked by graphic subjects, or being bored by a trivial treatment of those issues. Yet I found normal people grappling with concepts and issues everyone deals with in some form. While the youth of the characters, and maybe the author, came through in dialogue, choice of activities, etc., the themes they dealt with (loyalty, insecurity, self-image, the need to be loved, etc.) are universal.

Some adult readers are surprised, even confounded, by the complexity of some young adult novels. After reading Robert Cormier's *I Am the Cheese*, an experienced English teacher wrote in her response journal: "It bothered me to be so confused by a piece of young adult literature."

New to the joys of reading young adult books, many teachers discover insights for themselves as well. A former Peace Corps worker and graduate student in library media writes:

> One of the secrets of getting the most out of literature is being able to step into the story. The YA literature I have read . . . had made this an easy task. I was Adam in *I Am the Cheese*, Robert in *A Day No Pigs Would Die*, Jerry in *The Chocolate War*, Lorraine in *The Pigman*, and Jody in *The Year Without Michael*. I believe through these fictional characters, I have been enabled to become a better me — better than I could have been had I never read the story.

By giving us insights into ourselves as well as into the worlds of teenagers, these novels can help us better understand and interact with the teenagers we deal with in the real world every day. Written for teenagers, these novels can help us teachers, librarians, and parents "see through kids' eyes."

Because teenagers appreciate and need books that speak *to* them instead of *at* them, that does not mean we can't use classics in our classrooms. But it does mean we shouldn't use *only* classics. If we at least start our courses with selections that interest students from the beginning, we will be acknowledging that we care about what students think and feel. Moreover, if we try to see the curriculum through our students' eyes and provide a variety of literary experiences, we will increase the odds that our students will find things they like and can learn from. And by increasing the pleasure associated with literature, we will increase the likelihood that students will want to read more. Furthermore, because increased interest usually results in increased dialogue about books in general as well as about the content of the specific literary works we examine in depth, our class time will be livelier and more rewarding for us as well as for our students.

Most importantly, as we have seen, young adult novels are valuable tools for helping teenagers to understand themselves and to see their place in a world that is far different from the one in which many of us English teachers grew up. Although the books might not be the same ones that got us hooked on reading when we were teenagers, our students, by reading books that *they* care about, can become novel lovers too.

Notes

I want to thank the following undergraduate and graduate students for permission to quote from their papers and journals throughout this chapter: Ava Biffer, Christine Boulanger, Nancy Burce, Susan Gates, Dawn Hansen, Barbara Haydasz, Linda Podgwaite, Alice Rodrigues, Paul Rosenberg, Rita Santostefano, and Thomas Siemiatowski. Thanks are also due Louann Reid for her insightful editorial suggestions.

Works Cited

Applebee, Arthur N. 1989a. "Current Approaches in American Schools." Report presented at the annual convention of the National Council of Teachers of English, Baltimore, MD, November 19.

Applebee, Arthur N. 1989b. *A Study of Book-Length Works Taught in High School English Courses*. Albany: State University of New York.

Aubin, Patricia A. 1980. "The Young Adult Novel in the English Class — Do Teachers Use It?" *Connecticut English Journal* 12.1: 1—6.

Beers, Kylene. 1990. "Books and Basics: What Students Have to Say about Reading." Report presented at the spring conference of the National Council of Teachers of English, Colorado Springs, CO, March 8.

Carlsen, G. Robert, and Anne Sherrill. 1988. *Voices of Readers: How We Come to Love Books*. Urbana, IL: National Council of Teachers of English.

Carter, Betty, and Karen Harris. 1982. "What Junior High Students Like in Books." *Journal of Reading* 26.1: 42—46.

Gallo, Donald R. 1984. "Reactions to Required Reading: Some Implications from a Study of Connecticut Students." *Connecticut English Journal* 15.2: 7—11.

Queenan, Margaret. 1989. "Wait Till You Meet Carol Virostek!" *Connecticut English Newsletter* 23.1: 1, 7—8.

Ravitch, Diane, and Chester E. Finn, Jr. 1987. *What Do Our 17-Year-Olds Know?* New York: Harper & Row.

3

The Young Adult Novel as Transitional Literature

Barbara G. Samuels

George's mother telephoned in despair one June. "George just finished eighth grade," she said, "but he hasn't read a single book this year. How can I get him to read this summer?"

When questioned, George admitted that he had not finished a single novel. "We read *Great Expectations* in school this semester. It was so boring. I hated it. So after the first few chapters, I just read the *Cliff's Notes*."

Joanne enjoyed reading in elementary school, loved *Charlotte's Web*, *Ramona Quimby*, the series books, Judy Blume, Lois Lowry, and Betsy Byars. Suddenly in middle school she stopped going to the library. Reading assignments from school didn't seem to relate to her concerns.

Jonathan always read late into the night. His mother had become accustomed to checking on him to make sure he had finally turned out the light and gone to sleep. He read all the Hardy boys books, then started reading biographies and war stories. Lately his parents noticed that he rarely had his nose in a book.

For all three of these students, adolescence signaled a gradual movement away from reading for pleasure. What happened to these budding readers? What can be done to help them?

In their study of years of reading autobiographies to find out how people come to love literature, Robert Carlsen and Anne Sherrill report a variety of reasons teens turn away from reading. Beginning in secondary school, students complain that assigned reading takes too much of their time so that they no longer have time to select books they enjoy reading for pleasure. In many schools in the United States, literary education takes an historical approach presented in a literature anthology and based upon the "classics." For some people, this introduction to the classics opens a world of language and literature. Others, however, are neither intellectually nor psychologically ready to appreciate the sophisticated ideas and complex language of *The Scarlet Letter* or *A Tale of Two Cities*. Like George, they are overwhelmed by the novels assigned before they are ready for them. If not helped, many of these people join the large number of non-readers in this country.

Looking back on their secondary school years, adults complain about the particular selections they were forced to read. One adult respondent to Carlsen and Sherrill's study reported, "During my high school days, I read most of the classroom assignments, but was bored by the masterpieces, or perhaps I failed to understand them. They seemed to be written in another language and seemed not to entertain, but confuse" (132). Another said, "Every English teacher handed out a long list of classics that every college bound student should read. From then on, my reading appetite was inhibited, because I felt guilty reading anything else and didn't have enough background or support from the teacher to enjoy the classics" (100). Those "classics" that were appealing and are remembered fondly tend to be the ones that mirror adolescent reading interests, like *Huckleberry Finn*. Carlsen and Sherrill conclude that it seems clear that tastes have to mature before classics can be appreciated.

While many of the adult novels read by secondary school students as part of the curriculum introduce students to adolescent protagonists, the central focus of these novels is often on issues beyond the developmental tasks of adolescence. For example, according to Henry Nash Smith, the three major themes of *The Adventures of Huckleberry Finn* — one of the most frequently studied novels — are "the flight toward freedom," the "social satire of the towns along the river," and "the developing characterization of Huck" (114). Huck's characterization ties the other threads of the novel together and accentuates the book's "coming of age" theme. However, the other interwoven themes make the novel much more complex and sophisticated and therefore more difficult for some teen readers.

The adolescent novel provides a perfect vehicle to help the adolescent cross the bridge between literature for children and adult classics. Written about the developmental concerns of teenagers and addressing the problems they worry about, young adult novels address their psychological needs. Muller compiled the characteristics of adolescent novels and concluded that they "mirror adolescent interests accurately," dealing with all aspects of contemporary life (291). In 1979, Small also presented characteristics of the young adult novel and concluded that they have a "clear theme related to adolescent concerns and problems" (72). In a study of five adolescent novels, Linda Bleich concludes that young adult novels address the entire range of developmental tasks. She asked teachers to question their goals in reading instruction and to be more cognizant of adolescent needs and interests in their choice of classroom reading.

Generally shorter than adult novels, less complex in structure, but often well written and tightly constructed, young adult novels also serve as models to lead students to a better understanding of the novel form. Study of these novels can enable adolescents to understand the craft of fiction in such a way that they are better able to read and comprehend the message and the literary mode of the classics. Robert Small (1977) suggests that students can experience success studying an adolescent novel for aspects of the art of the novel as preparation for reading more adult novels in the future.

> If you were, for example, trying to teach a child how a jet or an automobile engine works, it surely would be better not to use the engines of a 747 or the most advanced racing cars. Their size, complexity, and refinement would make them poor starting places for the beginner. You would, instead, probably want to start with a simple jet engine, a combustion engine with a single cylinder. In other words, you would use a working model so that the number of parts and the size would help, rather than interfere, with making its workings perfectly clear. The working model of the mature piece of literature is the junior adolescent novel. (57–58).

Experience with a number of young adult novels helps teens acquire the tools they need to better approach the complexities of more adult novels. Nugent argues that "learning difficult concepts (point of view, symbolism, or internal monologue) while reading difficult and often unfamiliar content prematurely places too many demands upon students" (35). Adolescent novels can be used to help secondary school students discover such literary conventions as character development, style, symbolism, or plot structure as well as to introduce students to some of the themes, settings, and ideas developed in more complex adult novels. Rather than struggle with abstract concepts of freedom and social satire in *The Adventures of Huckleberry Finn*, for example, students who encounter similar themes in the simpler novel *Sounder* or the more complex adolescent novel *The Chocolate War* are better prepared to discuss and understand Twain's genius.

For teaching students about characterization, novels by Chris Crutcher and Kathryn Lasky are appealing to teens while offering opportunities to study how strong, round characters are developed. Nortie, Lion, Walker, and Jeff, the four friends in Crutcher's *Stotan!*, are all developed as distinct and memorable young men. Told in first person in a journal format by Walker, the novel introduces each of these characters with both a description from Walker's point of view as well as dialogue and action. When Nortie's father's behavior at home becomes more than he can bear, Nortie, whose older brother had committed suicide rather than continue to be abused by his father, comes to live with Walker. Lion, the artist of the group, who "brings a certain zany grace to things," resides alone in a small apartment that becomes the home of all four during Stotan Week. And Jeff, creative problem solver, "Alfred Hitchcock when it comes to creating suspense," sucks out his abscessed tooth and spits on those who offend him. Crutcher introduces each of these boys by presenting some situation or quality that identifies him as an individual.

In one particularly memorable vignette typical of adolescence, Lion describes the time just prior to the Football Frolics dance, during which he hopes to gather up the courage to ask the enchanting Melissa Lefebvre to dance.

> I was visited upon by the first of a forest of pimples yet to come. This wasn't an advance man, an insignificant pimple scout sent ahead to determine whether this peach-fuzz frontier could support a whole pimple nation. This was Sitting Bull. The pimple was red and sore and angry and given to harmonic tremors. Friends asked if I were growing another head. Enemies said it must be my date to the dance. This was a big zit. (72)

To solve his problem, Walker had recommended the Coke bottle treatment. Following Walker's suggestion, Lion had boiled a Coke bottle, wrapped it in a freezing rag, and slipped

> the piping hot mouth of the bottle over the monstrous zit — the idea being that as the air inside cooled and contracted, it would suck the boiling core of the Vesuvian blemish *whappo!* right into the bottle, rendering it dormant and harmless. (72)

Unfortunately, Walker's remedy didn't work and Lion instead ended up with an ugly ring around the pimple, "forming a perfect three dimensional bull's-eye right in the middle of my head" (73). Stories like this one about the four friends help the reader to know them not only as unique characters who come together to swim competitively, but also as young men who support and defend each other through some difficult times.

Throughout the novel, Walker reflects on his friends' conversations and actions. When Nortie denies Elaine's hope that their dying friend Jeff might be reincarnated in another form, Walker thinks, "Nortie was right. All the cosmic, philosophical explanations of life and death don't amount to a medium sized pile of dog dung when your friend is dying" (149). The boys are called upon to make important decisions in their senior year of high school, the year of Stotan Week, when they are tested physically and emotionally to the limits of their endurance and they learn what it is to win it or come "awful close." Drawn to *Stotan!* by its treatment of adolescent concerns like friendships, relationships with members of the opposite sex, high school sports, and peer loyalties, young adult readers who study the novel learn about authors' techniques for creating unique and compelling characters who grow through adversity and pain.

Beyond the Divide, Kathryn Lasky's historical fiction story about the Gold Rush days, introduces Meribah, a strong-willed female protagonist, who is forced to make some important value decisions. Meribah's father has been shunned by their Amish community in Pennsylvania because he attended the funeral of a man who was not considered strictly Amish by the community. Meribah hates the tension in her household and thinks her mother and the rest of the community are wrong, unfair in refusing to talk to her father. When her dad joins a covered wagon train going west, she decides to leave home and join him. In telling Meribah's story, Lasky details the difficult and dangerous life of the pioneers. Along the way, Meribah's best friend Serena Billings is raped by the Timms brothers, and the wagon train community shuns the victim of the rape in much the same way as the Amish community had shunned Meribah's father. Mr. Wickham, who before the rape incident was courting Serena, now seems offended by her presence in the group. Other members of the wagon train ignore her. Once again, Meribah has to make a decision, and she tries to sort out her feelings as she asks her father:

> Well, tell me this then: What is happening now? Why does Mr. Billings drink all the milk for Serena and her mother? Why are the Whitings forgiving *me* for walking with *her?* Why is Serena "her" and "she" and Mr. Wickham still "Mr. Wickham"? Why are the Timms never mentioned and Serena, the victim, is judged? Why? Why? Why? (132)

The parallels between the two incidents of shunning are striking. Once again, Meribah realizes how hypocritical and self righteous the group behavior is. And again, she makes the moral decision to support her friend, as she had earlier supported her father. Through such decisions, we come to know and admire this unusual young woman. A study of character development in *Beyond the Divide* enables the reader to appreciate an author's ability to create an interesting and strong character. At the same time, students who analyze Meribah's growth in the novel learn how to analyze a character's development from childhood to maturity (Samuels et al. 1987). In addition, the chronological plot line and adolescent point of view in the novel make it particularly appealing to readers who are not yet ready for the multiple plot lines, abstract themes, internal dialogues, and the general complexity of an adult historical fiction novel like *The Red Badge of Courage* or *The Scarlet Letter*.

Adolescent readers also have difficulty understanding the ways in which authors structure the plots of their novels. In a speech to the ALAN Workshop participants in Baltimore in 1989, Cynthia Voigt suggested analyzing novels by mapping the events in each chapter. In this way, the reader often can gain insight into the author's intention in the novel. As one example, she emphasized looking at the first and last lines of a novel, saying that significant patterns may emerge. Mapping her Newbery Award winning novel *Dicey's Song*, we are immediately struck by the fact that the book begins "And they lived happily ever after" and ends with the line "So Gram began her story." The circularity implied by the reverse of beginning and ending lines suggests a cumulative tale or a ballad. It also suggests the continuity between generations, the "reaching out" and the "holding on" that Gram tells Dicey she must do and that Gram is doing herself by forging a relationship with the children. We also understand the idea that a beginning with Gram is really an ending of their life on the road told in *Homecoming*, but the ending of the book is really a beginning of their future with Gram as their guardian. A further analysis of the chapters in the novel reveals that Voigt builds the story from Dicey's initial need to rest from the responsibilities thrust upon her by the abandonment of their mother to Dicey's realization that her mother is dead and she needs to accept responsibility, along with Gram, for her brothers and sister and for her own reaching out to others and to adulthood. The final chapters show Dicey, whose name implies risk taking, beginning to take the chance of reaching out and developing friendships with Mina and Jeff. Life isn't as simple as a song, even the songs Jeff sings about being a stranger in a new place, but *Dicey's Song* adds additional verses in this continuation of her story:

> The pictures her memory made had songs in them, clearer than the noise of the train. All the songs seemed to be blending together, into music as complicated as some of Maybeth's piano pieces. But Dicey could pick them out, each one, each separate melody. (201)

Each person's song is individual, but for Dicey, to whom all the characters turn for strength, the songs are blended into a complicated melody.

By studying the patterns of conflict, rising action, climax, and falling action in a novel in which the order of the chapters reflects the message the author intends to convey, students begin to understand the craft of the novel. They can also reflect upon the ways in which character development interacts with the plot development in a novel, usually making it difficult to separate one from the other. In this way, young adult novels serve as simpler models than more sophisticated adult novels.

Adult classics often use objects as symbols to reinforce or enhance a point the author is trying to convey. The rosebush at the door to the prison in *The Scarlet Letter*, for example, is a symbol as Hawthorne states, "of some sweet moral blossom," that may "relieve the darkening close of a tale of human frailty and sorrow" (46). Experienced readers may make the connection between little Pearl and the rosebush, but less practiced teen readers often miss this kind of relationship implied in a symbol. Whereas a more complex adult novel might imply the connection between a symbol and a character, the novelist for young adults tends to make such symbols explicit and obvious, helping the adolescent who is learning to read the novel as an art form.

Just as students learn about the significance of plot structure by studying the ordering of the chapters of an adolescent novel, they can also easily see the symbolism in these novels that involve them and reflect their developmental needs. In addition to the role of music in the novel, other symbols in *Dicey's Song* add interest to the plot and are presented in such an obvious and explicit way as to make their meaning clear to the less sophisticated reader. At the beginning of the book, Dicey's sailboat is at rest, being sanded, the rough edges being smoothed, the gaps being filled in. Dicey looks forward to the time when she can launch the boat and it will sail freely. In the same way, Dicey herself is at rest in this book about the Tillerman family. She too is getting her rough edges smoothed as she learns how to reach out to those different from herself like Mina, Millie, and Maybeth. By the end of the book, both the boat and Dicey are almost ready to set sail,

> As if Dicey were a sailboat and the sails were furled up now, the mainsail wrapped up around the boom, and she was sitting at anchor. It felt good to come to rest, the way it felt walking up to their house on a cold evening, seeing the yellow light at the kitchen window and knowing you would be warm inside while the darkness drew in around the house. But a boat at anchor wasn't like a boat at sea. ... Furled sails were just waiting to be raised, when the sailor chose to head out again. (202)

Voigt's explicit statement of the connection between Dicey and her boat makes the symbol clear to the less sophisticated reader who otherwise might miss the connection. Teaching a difficult concept like symbolism with the simpler form and familiar content of a young adult novel can help students to grasp the concept before attacking the more difficult form of the adult or classic novel.

Just as inexperienced readers can discover through young adult novels how authors use symbolism, they can also learn to appreciate the significance of an author's choice of setting. In some books, the setting is not an integral part of the structure and message. In others, readers need to reflect upon the writer's decision to set a novel in a particular place. *The Chocolate War* is an excellent example of the role setting plays in a novel. Although peer pressure occurs in every adolescent milieu, placing this story at Jesuit Trinity High School adds an ironic twist and power to the struggle between good and evil that is making the book a classic in the field of adolescent literature.

In addition to studying setting, other benefits are derived from using *The Chocolate War* in the classroom. From the first line, "They murdered him." (7) to the final scene in which Jerry Renault is again being murdered on the football field, where the shadows of the goal posts look like "a network of crosses, empty crucifixes" (17), the reader is hooked by this powerful tale of one boy's decision not to go along with the crowd. The novel's treatment of the subject of peer pressure in a high school is intensely relevant to all teenagers. *The Chocolate War*'s stark realism, its fast-moving action, and its theme of retaining individualism in the face of overwhelming institutional evil have made it among the most-taught adolescent novels in the secondary school curriculum (Samuels 1982).

Using young adult novels to teach literary conventions is one way to provide a transition to adult novels and the classics. Another strategy teachers have been using more and more frequently is pairing young adult novels with the more sophisticated adult books they are required to teach. To help students ease into reading required classics or to deepen students' understanding of adult titles, a comparative study using adolescent novels along with required titles can be useful. Donelson and Nilsen say,

> One reason that such pairing is successful is that as educational attitudes have moved away from the free thinking of the late '60s and early '70s into the 'back to basics' movement of the late '70s and on into the 'push for excellence' philosophy of the '80s and '90s, teachers feel more anxious that young readers make observable progress. The pairing of books helps both students and their teachers feel this sense of progression. (357)

The idea of pairing books is to introduce students to a theme, situation, or setting they find appealing and manageable, rather than giving them books they find overwhelming. Then, having mastered the concepts and having had a positive reading experience, students can be introduced to the more complex format and ideas of the adult book. The pairing system can involve matching books or authors. Within a single class, students might even be reading a variety of books in a thematic unit as preparation for the whole class reading of a single adult classic.

Among the first of the classics read in middle or junior high school is *Great Expectations*. Yet adolescents find Dickens difficult, struggling with the setting, with the unusual characters Dickens creates, and with his challenging sentence structures. In an article in *Focus: Books for the Junior High Years*, Virginia Monseau builds a case for introducing students to Dickens' England with the books of Leon Garfield. Garfield's characters, his settings in eighteenth-century England, and the general style and spirit of his novels are very reminiscent of Dickens. Featuring rich figurative language, exciting plots that weave into complicated coincidences, and characters who are mistreated by society, Garfield's novels prepare students to approach the classic Dickens novels with some background. In spite of the similarities, Garfield's adolescent novels are shorter than Dickens' novels, with plots full of action, written in a more contemporary style, making them effective companions for *Great Expectations* or *Oliver Twist*.

The main character in *The Sound of Coaches*, for example, an orphan born one stormy night on a stage coach to a mysterious young woman who dies during childbirth, is in some ways like Pip in *Great Expectations*. Both are orphaned as infants, and both leave home at a young age in search of a wealthy savior. Their growth as characters is dependent on the trials and tribulations they experience as they journey toward self-realization. Similarly, twelve-year-old Smith, the hero of Garfield's *Smith*, like Dickens' characters in *Oliver Twist*, makes his living picking pockets in the streets of London. Like Oliver, who is eventually adopted by the wealthy Mr. Brownlow, Smith is befriended and helped by the blind magistrate. According to Monseau, so similar is Garfield's style to Dickens' that he completed Dickens' unfinished novel, the *Mystery of Edwin Drood*, in 1980. She adds:

> Knowledgeable teachers can make good use of Garfield's books, since they are such wonderful connectors to Dickens' works. So often we are disappointed by our students' indifference to or dislike of Dickens' books. Those of us who read and enjoy Charles Dickens would hate to see young readers turn away from his works permanently simply because they are not intellectually or experientially ready for these books when they encounter them in high school. We as teachers can try to keep this from happening by using books by authors like Leon Garfield to ease our students into more difficult works and to help them appreciate and enjoy more complex books later on. (33)

A teacher might introduce students to a variety of Leon Garfield novels in a unit on the author in preparation for reading one of Dickens' works as a class. Comparing and contrasting Garfield's books to Dickens' work will then help students to deepen their understanding of both authors.

Students preparing to read Stephen Crane's *The Red Badge of Courage* might better understand the feelings about the war and the theme of guilt and shame if they first read some adolescent war novels. *Across Five Aprils*, *Rifles for Watie*, *The Sacred Moon Tree*, *Thunder on the Tennessee*, *The Tamarack Tree*, and *Which Way Freedom*, all Civil War stories written for adolescents, help to provide background about the war itself and the emotions of those who were fighting as well as those left at home. But pairing *The Red Badge of Courage* with a book like Harry Mazer's *The Last Mission*, a World War II story, also helps students to think critically about the similarities and differences in the situations of two young men who go off to war thinking that the life of a soldier is glorious and exciting. Since secondary school students today generally have more background to help them understand World War II than they have for the Civil War, reading *The Last Mission* first may help them find *The Red Badge of Courage* more accessible. Like Henry Fleming, the protagonist of *The Red Badge of Courage*, who dreams about being a hero in battle, Jack Raab dreams of personally killing Hitler. He wants to fight so desperately that he steals his older brother's birth certificate to enlist when he is only fifteen years old. When he gets to fly missions over Germany, he realizes that the bombs that his plane drops kill women and children whose only crime is being German. War was not what he had dreamed it would be. He begins to fight an internal war as well. Whereas Henry Fleming feels guilty about his retreat under fire, Jack Raab feels guilty because of the lies that got him into the war. Whereas Jack assuages his guilt by telling people his story, Henry's guilt is coupled with shame which is not resolved at the end of the novel. It is through discussions of what is the same and what is different in these boys' wartime experiences that students begin to better understand the feelings expressed in the adult novel.

Other novels with an antiwar theme can also be paired. To achieve a better understanding of the issues in Erich Maria Remarque's *All Quiet on the Western Front*, the young adult novel *No Hero for the Kaiser* by Rudolf Frank could serve as an excellent transition. Both novels are about young men who served with the German army during World War I. Both novels were originally published in Germany between World War I and World War II as anti-war messages. In *No Hero for the Kaiser* fourteen-year-old Jan Kubitzky is "adopted" as a mascot by the German soldiers who attacked his village in 1914. Paul Baumer in *All Quiet on the Western Front* patriotically volunteers to fight. Like the characters in *The Red Badge of Courage* and *The Last Mission*, these two young men learn the evils of war.

In his novel for adolescents, Frank assumes that young readers need explanations of some of the military issues and terminology. He talks about the uniform soldiers wear and explains that although the word *uniform* means equal, in the military differences in uniforms give clues as to rank and power (118). Students who read his book first, then, are given the background to comprehend the difficulties associated with rank and power that become a major issue in *All Quiet on the Western Front*.

The two young men ponder some of the same issues related to war as well. In Frank's book, Jan thinks about his father fighting for the Russians, remembers earlier times they had spent together, and wonders why the earth means so little to the soldiers. "Why could they not tend the field together as before? . . . a real field does not kill . . . a field is where things grow. He had caught the military in a lie. The soldiers were sent into a field of deceit" (46). The adult novel, more vicious in its anti-war imagery, its philosophical discussions, and in the fact that the hero dies in the end, also presents a view of the earth. Paul explains, "To no man does the earth mean so much as to the soldier. When he presses himself down upon her . . . from the fear of death . . . then she is his only friend . . . his mother. She shelters him and gives him a new lease on ten seconds of life, receives him again and often forever" (30–31).

Young adults in the United States today probably most clearly associate antiwar messages with the Vietnam War. Richie Perry's story in Walter Dean Myers' *Fallen Angels* pairs very effectively with all of the war stories mentioned. Like Henry Fleming, Jack Raab, and Paul Baumer, Richie volunteers for Vietnam. Although he really would prefer to be in college learning to write like James Baldwin, the reality of his Harlem poverty causes him to join the Army. Life in Vietnam leads him to reevaluate his life. At first he is impatient with all the waiting around before he actually meets the enemy. As Stephen Crane in *The Red Badge of Courage* says, "The youth had been taught that a man becomes another thing in battle. He saw his salvation in such a change. Hence this waiting was an ordeal for him" (73). Like the characters in the other novels, facing death serves as an initiation rite which helps Richie Perry find his manhood.

> I had come into the army at seventeen, and I remembered who I was, and who I had been as a kid. The war hadn't meant anything to me then, maybe because I had never gone through anything like it before. All I had thought about combat was that I would never die, that our side would win, and that we would all go home somehow satisfied. And now all the dying around me, and all the killing, was making me look at myself again, hoping to find something more than the kid I was. Maybe I could sift through the kid's stuff, the basketball, the Harlem streets, and find the man I would be. I hoped I did it before I got killed. (187)

Diana Mitchell, a teacher at Sexton High School in Lansing, Michigan, described the enthusiasm with which her students discussed the similarities and differences between *The Red Badge of Courage* and *Fallen Angels*. Students talked about the difference in the first person narrative of Myers and the third person introspective narrative of Crane. They enjoyed comparing the two main characters and their internal and external conflicts, finding many parallels in the two books. Students considered the question of how each of these young men would be able to reenter the civilian world and noted that the Vietnam War was an unpopular war while the Civil War soldiers were heroes when they returned to their homes. Mitchell said that her students developed a deeper understanding of both books because of the comparisons and contrasts.

Examining and comparing the role of war in the lives of several young men, historical figures from the Civil War, World War I, World War II, and Vietnam can help today's young adults develop a deeper understanding of Crane's magnificent novel. Whereas teenagers frequently select books with an emphasis on plot and action, Crane's focus is on his hero's internal struggle, on the psychological effects of war. The adolescent reader who may have difficulty following the plot of Henry's internal struggle and the descriptions in the novel, may be helped by prior reading and discussion about the Civil War and about other soldiers' responses to wartime situations. Allowing students to read other war stories along with *The Red Badge of Courage* and to discuss the similarities and differences will heighten appreciation of Crane's craft.

A group of young adult novels may also help the contemporary teen to comprehend *The Scarlet Letter*. One of the novels most frequently taught in American high schools, *The Scarlet Letter* is also one of the most difficult for contemporary adolescents to understand. An article in *The ALAN Review* (Samuels et al. 1987) suggests that when *The Scarlet Letter* is taught after study of a few adolescent novels, it may become more accessible.

> Teens struggle with it for many reasons apart from issues of sentence structure and vocabulary. It is difficult to understand the background of the Puritan mind as well as conflict Hawthorne explores. Many of the novel's themes are hard for young readers to comprehend: suffering purifies; there are moral consequences to a sexual relationship; guilt becomes overpowering and physical in form; and vengeance can rule one's life. In terms of style, the symbolism and use of setting as an emotional participant in the action also make the book a struggle. (44)

Thinking about these issues of theme, setting, and symbolism and addressing them in other novels first may make study of *The Scarlet*

Letter more rewarding for some young readers. The Newbery Award winning novel, *The Witch of Blackbird Pond*, or *Tituba of Salem Village*, two stories of young women newly arrived in Puritan New England, can help students to begin to understand the milieu of Puritanism. An exploration of these young adult novels, followed by reading and study of Arthur Miller's play, *The Crucible*, might establish the setting of Hawthorne's novel.

Another issue related to setting in *The Scarlet Letter* is the way in which the setting is an integral part of the plot, reflecting moods, emotions, and serving in a symbolic relationship with Pearl. Pearl is like the rose which grows next to the ugly, weather-stained door of the jail. Like the rose, she too represents beauty and purity in the midst of evil and darkness. Pearl dances in the sunlight while Hester walks in the shade. At another point in the novel an "A" is burned in the sky by a meteor as a signal to those on earth. This use of setting as symbol can better be understood by adolescents who have discussed the symbolism of the mulberry tree growing outside the house in *Dicey's Song* or the symbolic role of Anne Burden's peaceful valley in Robert O'Brien's science fiction novel *Z for Zachariah*.

Several young adult novels provide opportunities for students to discuss the theme of guilt and its ramifications before attempting to consider the issue in *The Scarlet Letter*. Paul Zindel's *The Pigman* is told in first person by John and Lorraine as a tribute to the Pigman in an effort to deal with the overwhelming guilt that they feel about the deceit they used in meeting him and in letting him down. It works particularly well for class discussion because at one point in the story Mr. Pignati plays a game with John and Lorraine in which they list levels of guilt in the imaginary death of a woman. Right after this discussion, the Pigman himself has a heart attack while roller skating with John and Lorraine. The game prepares the reader for the struggle the two teens have about their role in Mr. Pignati's death. John Knowles' *A Separate Peace*, another novel frequently taught in high school, might also be used with *The Scarlet Letter* to examine the theme of guilt.

Contemporary teens have difficulty relating to the Puritan stigma on an unmarried woman who gives birth to a child. Adolescent novels about teen pregnancies might provide some material for spirited discussion of these issues. Reading such books as Jeanette Eyerly's *Someone to Love Me*, John Neufeld's *Sharelle*, Ann Head's *Mr. and Mrs. Bo Jo Jones*, or others about the subject may help adolescents understand how experience as a lonely young mother can make women more wise and compassionate and how suffering can provide insight. Since the young adult novel promotes society's value system, all of these young women learn from their unwanted pregnancies. A comparison with *The Scarlet Letter* helps to make Hawthorne's book more relevant to students today. In other words, reading *The Scarlet Letter* within the context of a number of other books that relate to the setting, theme, and subject matter may help provide a cognitive basis for understanding.

In a rationale for a curriculum change, Houston teacher Mary Santerre suggested a sequence of books for study of the human struggle between good and evil leading from the adolescent novels *Killing Mr. Griffin* and *The Chocolate War* and then to the adult novel *Lord of the Flies*. *Killing Mr. Griffin* is Lois Duncan's chilling adolescent novel about a group of high school students who kidnap their English teacher in retaliation for what they consider his humiliating treatment of them in the classroom. Unfortunately, their plan backfires when Mr. Griffin dies of a heart attack during the abduction. Charismatic Mark, a boy able to manipulate those around him, is the originator of the plan. David thinks, "But somehow with Mark things always seemed so sensible. When Mark looked at you with those odd gray eyes of his . . ." (99). Evil Mark continues to provoke lawlessness as the students bury Mr. Griffin and tell lies to hide his death. The deceit continues until Susan's sense of outrage and Mrs. Griffin's interference bring reason to the situation and overcome Mark's psychopathic domination of the group.

Evil in *The Chocolate War* is embodied in adolescents Archie Costello and Emile Janza as well as in an adult religious figure, Brother Leon, the acting Headmaster of Trinity School. Jerry Renault's refusal to go along with the pressure to sell chocolates represents a lone voice against power. Ironically Cormier has the evil Brother Leon make the connection between the situation at Trinity School and the ultimate evil of Hitler. It takes the courage of someone like Jerry Renault to stand up against characters like Mark in *Killing Mr. Griffin* and Brother Leon in *The Chocolate War*.

Left alone on an island, a group of boys in *Lord of the Flies* struggle in a war for physical and psychological domination. The voice of reason in *Lord of the Flies* comes in the form of Piggy, like Jerry a Christ figure, who is savagely killed by Jack. Ironically, Piggy's death is a sacrifice for Ralph, who is able to hide from the murderers. Secondly, the fire that Ralph had fought for is what finally alerts the rescue party that saves him. As in *Killing Mr. Griffin* and *The Chocolate War*, *Lord of the Flies* suggests that the aggressor is both physically able and psychologically manipulative. Golding's novel seriously questions whether human beings are innately evil. Reading and discussing the two adolescent novels prior to a discussion of *Lord of the Flies* will help students to build on and expand their understanding of all three of the novels. More advanced students might go on to study good and evil in Melville's *Billy Budd* or *Moby Dick*.

As teachers consider novels frequently taught in the secondary school curriculum, they should consider the advantage of teaching pairs or groups of books together. Robert LeBlanc says:

> These book teams have several advantages over teaching significant literature in isolation. The reader is hooked on the theme by reading the easily manageable adolescent novel first. The more difficult book has the advantage of being based on a familiar theme and is associated with the positive experience of reading the young adult novels. (35)

Among other pairs, LeBlanc suggests grouping *Roll of Thunder, Hear My Cry* with *To Kill a Mockingbird*. Both stories are narrated by young girls, take place at approximately the same time in American history, and explore similar themes. Both girls are initially ignorant of prejudice and naive. Both grow towards maturity and understanding. Both learn from their parents. Both novels have episodic plots. *Roll of Thunder, Hear My Cry* has a simple first person narration by Cassie. The action is fast-paced and direct, keeping the student reader involved and interested. The richness of detail about Southern life during the Depression provides many issues for students to think about. Young adults will find it valuable to consider the dual themes of prejudice and self-respect with regard to Cassie and some of the other characters in the novel.

However, *To Kill a Mockingbird*, while relatively simple in structure and language for an adult novel, is more multifaceted than *Roll of Thunder*. The interconnected stories of Boo Radley and Tom Robinson slowly come together in the narration. Harper Lee allows the reader to see more deeply into Scout's thoughts and feelings than Mildred Taylor allows the reader to see into Cassie's. The narration is more complex also. Although Scout is telling the story at age nine and thinking back on the past three years, the reader also sometimes hears the adult voice of Scout filling in the background to the novel. Lee's story introduces more than one event in each chapter, and the theme is paralleled with a few different situations of prejudice. In addition to prejudice towards blacks, the novel explores the idea of tolerance toward Boo Radley and anyone who is different. Scout learns that everyone has something to offer:

> Mockingbirds don't do one thing but make music for us to enjoy. They don't eat up people's gardens, don't nest in corn-cribs, they don't do one thing but sing their hearts out for us. That's why it's a sin to kill a mockingbird. (94)

Many other fine young adult novels can be paired with adult novels and classics to help students develop a deeper understanding of the ideas in the books. Samuels, Ingham, and Lowery-Moore suggest that *The Grapes of Wrath* might be better understood after studying *Home Before Dark* (Sue Ellen Bridgers), *Homecoming* (Cynthia Voigt), or *Words by Heart* (Ouida Sebestyen). Since all three of these novels explore issues of home and place, they are interesting to compare thematically with *The Grapes of Wrath*. Author Patricia Lee Gauch suggests in an article in *Top of the News* that *Roll of Thunder, Hear My Cry* be paired with *I Know Why the Caged Bird Sings* by Maya Angelou. "This isn't babying kids into reading decent prose. It's yoking 'good stuff' with 'good stuff' to take advantage of the length and teen-centered subject of the younger book" (125). Reading other books about the Holocaust like *The Devil's Arithmetic*, *Upon the Head of a Goat*, and *Upstairs Room* in preparation for or along with *Diary of a Young Girl* by Anne Frank deepens students' understanding of Anne Frank's powerful story. Susan Nugent recommends studying literary style in Barbara Wersba's *Run Softly, Go Fast* and Maia Wojcie-chowska's *Don't Play Dead Before You Have To* before reading the more complex *The Catcher in the Rye* (36). *The Secret Diary of Adrian Mole, Aged 13¾* is also an excellent introduction to the adolescent narrative voice in preparation for reading *The Catcher in the Rye*. Silas Marner's love for little Eppie brings him back into wholesome, normal living much as Mr. Tom's relationship with an eight-year-old abused child in *Goodnight, Mr. Tom* helps him to regain the love and human feeling he has within him.

Hazel Rochman, in *Tales of Love and Terror*, an ALA publication about booktalking, suggests a variety of ways books may be grouped thematically for booktalks. The appendix is particularly helpful in providing lists of book titles that are linked together by some common theme or idea. Rochman notes that in every classroom there are students who are reading at a variety of levels. She uses a theme to provide unity to a series of twelve to fifteen booktalks aimed at luring readers into a wide variety of books. Connecting to *Wuthering Heights*, for example, she says she has booktalked "books about love, ghosts, rage, family conflict, mystery, self-betrayal, outsiders, a desolate setting, terror, and survival" (37). The same variety of connections might be made in classroom activities in which individual students pair *Wuthering Heights* with any one of a number of books that by comparison and contrast help to build students' understanding and critical thinking.

The reading logs of secondary school students reveal interesting patterns. For recreational reading a single student might read such diverse books as Beverly Cleary's biography *A Girl from Yamhill*, adolescent novels like *Home Before Dark* and *Seven Days to a Brand New Me*, an adult bestseller like *The Prince of Tides*, and a nineteenth-century classic like *Tess of the D'Urbervilles* within a semester. Students who are themselves bridging the years between childhood and adulthood shift in their reading interests among books for children, books for adolescents, and books for adults. The single link among these books may be that one of the main characters is a young person who is moving towards some kind of maturity and self-understanding.

Pairing adolescent novels with more sophisticated books for class-room study and using young adult novels to teach about literary conventions are certainly ways in which specific adolescent novels serve as transitions to contemporary adult books and the classics. We have learned from looking at Carlsen and Sherrill's research on the development of readers that all readers move through a variety of stages of reading before they learn to love reading adult literature. Shifting from picture books to short novels and series books to adolescent novels and then to popular fiction is a common practice for young people who eventually become adult readers of fiction. Robert Leblanc suggests, "The jump from Nancy Drew and the Hardy Boys to *Moby Dick* and *Crime and Punishment* leaves out adolescent literature which can serve as a bridge between these two very different kinds of reading experiences" (35). Adult readers generally report a time in their lives when they read extensively the books that are transitional.

What research and observation suggest is that in addition to assigning specific books which will lead our students to understanding the tools of literary analysis and pairing books for a depth of understanding of concepts beyond their experience, perhaps the way in which adolescent novels best serve as transitions to adult literature is by providing young people with books they enjoy. Students should be allowed the opportunity to select books they want to read in addition to being assigned books they have to read. Extensive reading of any kind may be the key to developing readers. Making reading a pleasurable experience by making adolescent novels available to students may be the best vehicle teachers have to help adolescents cross the bridge from childhood books to adult classics.

Works Cited

Angelou, Maya. 1971. *I Know Why the Caged Bird Sings*. New York: Bantam.

Bleich, Linda L. 1980. "A Study of the Psychological and Social Characteristics of Adolescence in Adolescent Literature 1945–1975." Unpublished dissertation, Indiana University.

Bridgers, Sue Ellen. 1985. *Home Before Dark*. New York: Bantam.

Bronte, Emily. 1983. *Wuthering Heights*. New York: Bantam Classics.

Brooks, Bruce. 1986. *The Moves Make the Man*. New York: Harper Trophy.

Carlsen, G. Robert, and Anne Sherrill. 1988. *Voices of Readers: How We Come to Love Books*. Urbana: NCTE.

Cleary, Beverly. 1989. *A Girl from Yamhill*. New York: Dell.

Conford, Ellen. 1982. *Seven Days to a Brand New Me*. New York: Scholastic.

Conroy, Pat. 1987. *The Prince of Tides*. New York: Bantam.

Cormier, Robert. 1983. *The Chocolate War*. New York: Dell.

Crane, Stephen. 1972. *The Red Badge of Courage*. New York: Scholastic.

Crutcher, Chris. 1988. *Stotan!* New York: Dell.

Dickens, Charles. 1989. *A Tale of Two Cities*. New York: Bantam Classics.

———. 1982. *Great Expectations*. New York: Bantam Classics.

———. 1964. *Oliver Twist*. New York: Bantam Classics.

Donelson, Kenneth L., and Alleen P. Nilsen. 1989. *Literature for Today's Young Adults*. 3rd edition. Glenview, Illinois: Scott, Foresman and Company.

Duncan, Lois. 1979. *Killing Mr. Griffin*. New York: Dell.

Eyerly, Jeanette. 1987. *Someone to Love Me*. New York: Lippincott.

Fitzgerald, F. Scott. 1981. *The Great Gatsby*. New York: Scribner.

Fox, Paula. 1985. *One Eyed Cat*. New York: Dell.

Frank, Anne. 1952. *The Diary of a Young Girl*. New York: Doubleday.

Frank, Rudolf. 1986. *No Hero for the Kaiser*. New York: Lothrop, Lee, and Shepard.

Garfield, Leon. 1987. *Smith*. New York: Dell.

———. 1974. *The Sound of Coaches*. New York: Viking.

———. 1969. *Black Jack*. New York: Pantheon.

Gauch, Patricia Lee. 1984. "'Good Stuff' in Adolescent Fiction," *Top of the News*. 50 Winter: 125–129.

Golding, William. 1955. *Lord of the Flies*. New York: Putnam.

Hansen, Joyce. 1986. *Which Way Freedom*. New York: Walker.

Hawthorne, Nathaniel. 1981. *The Scarlet Letter*. New York: Bantam.

Head, Ann. 1968. *Mr. and Mrs. Bo Jo Jones*. New York: New American Library.

Hunt, Irene. 1986. *Across Five Aprils*. New York: Berkley.

Keith, Harold. 1987. *Rifles for Watie*. New York: Harper.

Knowles, John. 1984. *A Separate Peace*. New York: Bantam.

Lasky, Katherine. 1986. *Beyond the Divide*. New York: Dell.

LeBlanc, Robert. 1980. "An English Teacher's Fantasy," *English Journal*, 69 October: 35–36.

Lee, Harper. 1961. *To Kill a Mockingbird*. New York: Harper.

Magorian, Michelle. 1986. *Good Night, Mr. Tom*. New York: Harper.

Mazer, Harry. 1981. *The Last Mission*. New York: Dell.

Miller, Arthur. 1976. *The Crucible*. New York: Penguin.

Mitchell, Diana. 1990. Personal communication, March.

Monseau, Virginia. 1989. "From Leon Garfield to Charles Dickens: A Step Toward 'Excellence' in the Literature Class." Focus: *Books for the Junior High Years*. Southeastern Ohio Council of Teachers of English, XV, 2, Spring: 30–34.

Muller, Al P. 1973. "The Currently Popular Adolescent Novel as Transitional Literature," Unpublished dissertation. Florida State University.

Myers, Walter Dean. 1988. *Fallen Angels*. New York: Scholastic.

Neufeld, John. 1984. *Sharelle*. New York: New American Library.

Nugent, Susan M. 1984. "Adolescent Literature: A Transition into a Future of Reading." *English Journal*, November: 35–36.

O'Brien, Robert. 1987. *Z for Zachariah*. New York: Macmillan.

Remarque, Erich M. 1967. *All Quiet on the Western Front*. Greenwich: Fawcett.

Reiss, Johanna. 1973. *The Upstairs Room*. New York: Bantam.

Rochman, Hazel. 1987. *Tales of Love and Terror: Booktalking the Classics, Old and New*. Chicago: American Library Association.

Salinger, J. D. 1984. *The Catcher in the Rye*. New York: Bantam.

Samuels, Barbara G. 1982. "A National Survey to Determine the Status of the Young Adult Novel in the Secondary School English Classroom, Grades 7–12." Unpublished dissertation, University of Houston.

Samuels, Barbara G., Rosemary O. Ingham, and Hollis Lowery-Moore. 1987. "Bridging the Basics: The Young Adult Novel in a Back-to-Basics Society." *The ALAN Review*. 14, 2. Winter: 42–44.

Santerre, Mary. 1990. Unpublished curriculum document, Houston Baptist School.

Sebestyen, Ouida. 1983. *Words by Heart*. New York: Bantam.

Siegal, Aranka. 1983. *Upon the Head of a Goat*. New York: New American Library.

Small, Robert C. 1977. "The Junior Novel and the Art of Literature." *English Journal*. 66, 7, October: 55–59.

———. 1979. "The Young Adult Novel in the Composition Program." *English Journal*. 68, 6, September: 71–73.

Smith, Henry Nash. 1962. *Mark Twain: The Development of a Writer*. Cambridge: Belknap Press of Harvard.

Speare, Elizabeth George. 1978. *The Witch of Blackbird Pond*. New York: Dell.

Steinbeck, John. 1976. *The Grapes of Wrath*. New York: Penguin.

Taylor, Mildred. 1984. *Roll of Thunder, Hear My Cry*. New York: Bantam.

Townsend, Sue. 1984. *The Secret Diary of Adrian Mole, Aged 13¾*. New York: Avon.

Voigt, Cynthia. 1982. *Dicey's Song*. New York: Macmillan.

———. 1981. *Homecoming*. New York: Macmillan.

Wersba, Barbara. 1979. *Run Softly, Go Fast*. New York: Greenwillow.

White, E. B. 1952. *Charlotte's Web*. New York: Harper.

Wisler, G. Clifton. 1983. *Thunder on the Tennessee*. New York: Lodestar.

Yolen, Jane. 1988. *The Devil's Arithmetic*. New York: Penguin.

Zindel, Paul. 1983. *The Pigman*. New York: Bantam.

4

The Development of the Young Adult Novel: A Progression of Lessons and Lives

Linda K. Shadiow

1881

Popular novels have doubtless done more to arouse curiosity in the young, and to excite and foster passion and immorality, than the obscene literature for the suppression of which such active measures have recently been taken ... Novel-reading has led to thousands of lives of dissoluteness.

(J. H. Kellog)

1982

The reading of works of fiction is one of the most pernicious habits to which a young person can become devoted. ... The novel-devotee is as much a slave as the opium-eater or the inebriate. The reading of fictitious literature destroys the taste for sober, wholesome reading, and imparts an unhealthy stimulus to the mind. ...

(Hall 1982)

Who and what are adolescents? What are they or should they be reading? Today we take the cliches and jokes about "the teenage crisis years" as much for granted as we do the labels of childhood like "the terrible two's," but the truth is that the label "adolescence" is a relatively recent invention. When G. Stanley Hall published the two-volume work *Adolescence: Its Psychology and Its Relations to Physiology, Anthropology, Sociology, Sex, Crime, Religion, and Education* in 1905, he paved the way for a systematic consideration of the period between childhood and adulthood. This "invention" both coalesced previous observations of the characteristics of young people and provided a theory for additional study. Hall's adolescence was a stage of development "corresponding to the historical period of savagery, vagrancy, and nomadic life" with young people who were "savages, too unrestrained, too filled with the spirit of adventure and the 'wanderlust,' to adapt easily to the adult roles laid out for them" (Nasaw 88).

The fictional representation of the lessons and lives in books read by and written for young readers is one key to understanding the historical legacy of this genre. The lessons and lives from past books characterize the evolution of what an "adolescent" or "young adult" is thought to be. At the same time, the degree of unedited reality within the books illustrates the evolution of literature for this age group and assists our contemporary understanding of the judgments applied to both the books and to the consequences of reading them. By getting to know a few characters from books representative of historical strands in young adult literature and by peering into the authors' representations of the lessons and lives in these books, we can let this multifaceted history speak for itself.

In William Pene DuBois' children's book, *Lion*, there is a "chief designer" who has turned over the administrative responsibilities in the world's animal factory to Artist Foreman. In the past, Artist Foreman has been an animal originator himself. Now, in his supervisory position, he rarely exercises his own creative abilities but instead oversees the work of the other artists as they add new animals to the kingdom of the world. One particular day, however, Artist Foreman comes up with a wonderful name for an animal: "Lion." Because he is out of practice in creating his own drawings he walks through the room to see what all the artists are working on. As he surveys their current projects, he becomes inspired to design an animal to go with the new name. He sits down at his desk to draft this "lion," and a compilation of all the designs he has just seen emerges—a long-haired, rainbow-colored, four-footed animal that only remotely resembles what eventually becomes his "final draft."

Because the terms "adolescence," and "adolescent novel" or "young adult novel" are relatively recent labels, the earliest forms of this genre take on qualities much like those of Artist Foreman's first draft of the lion—a patchwork of the characteristics of books and their literary purposes drawn from other places and compiled out of a desire to shape something in the way one wants it to be shaped before it takes on a life of its own. The spheres of influence and action in books for young readers emerge as organizers for categories that contributed to the eventual shaping of young adult literature. While these spheres or settings are identifiable in contemporary titles, they are also keys to the genre's vigorous past: the church, the home, the "outer" world, the workplace, the "inner" world.

The Church—
"Literature of the Sunday School Union"

In the early part of the 1800s, churches played an important role in the education of children. In seeking to school young people on the virtues of religion and the rewards of being guided by religious principles, the churches developed materials to be read to and by young people. Because a large number of young teenagers were already in the work force, the education of this group was of particular concern to the churches. The American Sunday School Union was a non-denominational group (first founded in Philadelphia in 1817) that eventually produced and distributed numerous books to teach basic skills and at the same time to "inculcate essential truths" (Shaffer 21).

In an unpublished paper, Ken Donelson cites Hubert Lee's 1849 book, *The Prize Garden* as a typical book produced for the Sunday School Union. The story describes the competition between two boys, Walter Sherwood and George Lincoln, as they try to keep their gardens "in neatest order" through the summer so that they can win the prize—a Bible—from their beloved teacher, Mr. Russell. Walter believes his widowed mother would like to have the prize, but because he has so many other duties and responsibilities he doubts he can win, and he is right. He foregoes his chance at the prize when he neglects his garden in favor of fulfilling his duties as a humble, dutiful son and young scholar.

George, however, wants to win badly enough that he neglects some of his responsibilities (including completing his schoolwork and playing with his younger sister) and he inappropriately works in his garden on a Sunday. When his sister, Kitty, asks him to play with her, he replies: "Oh, no, Kitty—not to-day. I cannot. I must work in the garden all afternoon. I have much to do there." And a few lines later after she persists: "I must work in my garden to-day. You know I am working for the prize, and I must not lose a minute."

Kitty then makes a judgment that foreshadows how George will feel after he wins the prize (which he eventually does): "Oh, George, you used to love me better than the flowers ... and now you love the flowers better than me. I am so sorry." Although he is judged to have the prize garden and wins the Bible, the possession brings more rebukes than rewards. Even in the solitude of a concluding moment his eyes fall on a telling passage in his new book: "What shall it profit a man, if he gain the whole world and lose his own soul?" Then, in order to reiterate the point, the reader is provided with this note in the book's concluding pages:

> Dear children who read this book, — there is a prize offered to each one of you, which you cannot labour too earnestly, or strive too diligently to obtain. It is a crown of glory — a place in the eternal and glorious kingdom of your Father in heaven! Oh! it is a great and wonderful prize to be offered to poor sinful creatures, and great and wonderful is God's goodness in offering it. Then make every thing in life bend to gain it. Watch and pray for it — in faith and patience — and never cease while life lasts, whether in sickness or in health, in joy or in sorrow, in prosperity or in poverty, to press toward the mark for the prize of the high calling of God in Christ Jesus our Lord.

Some critics at the time characterized these books as "parodies" and "moral monstrosities" with children who were "impossible little prigs" and parents who were "so inflexibly serious that they never opened their lips without preaching." But the books filled the gap believed to be created by popular fiction with its corrupt principles that according to one nineteenth century critic "destroy the love of sober investigation, and blast the hope of mental improvement." The didactic tracts of the Sunday School Union were replaced by other works with similar strong moral tones in the late 1800s, but the lessons and lives of characters like Walter Sherwood and George Lincoln continue to have echoes in some titles intended for contemporary young adult readers.

The Home — "Domestic Novels"

In the middle 1800s a school of writing called "domestic novels" emerged. While intended to be read by adults, these books became very popular with young adults. The domestic novels had something in common with the novels of the Sunday School Union in that they sought to tell stories and to educate simultaneously (and none too subtly). Among the prominent characteristics of the domestic novels was the elevation and celebration of the power of good women to salvage humanity especially when combined with the power of righteous living promoted by conservatism and religion. Readers of these books came to expect a variety of devices: stock characters (the orphan girl, the mysterious man), plot formulas (the reform of a "bad" man by the influence of a "good" woman), gothic elements (hidden doors, disappearing letters), and imbedded allusions ("When the echo of her retreating footsteps died away, St. Elmo threw his cigar out of the window, and walked up and down the quaint and elegant rooms, whose costly *bizarrerie* would more appropriately have adorned a villa of Parthenope or Lucanian Sybaris, than a country-house in *soi-disant* 'republican' America" [79]).

According to Donelson's 1989 description, the heroines of these novels had a set of common characteristics no matter who the writer. The heroines were "self-sacrificing and self-denying beyond belief, interested in the primacy of the family unit and a happy marriage as the goal of all decent women. They abhorred sin generally, particularly divorce, drink, tobacco, and adultery" (468). *St. Elmo*, the most popular book of this type, was written by Augusta Jane Evans Wilson and published in 1867. The popularity of the book was such that towns, cigars, boats, trains, and hotels were all named after St. Elmo Murray, the errant-but-soon-to-be-reformed character for whom the novel is named.

In *St. Elmo*, Mrs. Murray rescues young Edna Earl after her father is killed in a train wreck and her grandfather (the sole remaining relative) dies. This wealthy, aristocratic sponsor plans to raise the young orphan as her own daughter and takes her into the Murray home. St. Elmo Murray leaves soon after his new stepsister arrives; since he has a wicked reputation (for both violence and seduction), the reader applauds his departure but anticipates the plot and looks forward to the complications that will be caused by his ultimate return. The local pastor takes responsibility for Edna's education, and when St. Elmo does return four years later, he finds that she has blossomed into an educated and desirable young woman. The pastor has, in St. Elmo's absence, schooled Edna in Arabic, Chaldee, Greek, Hebrew, Latin, and Sanskrit. St. Elmo attempts to make friends with Edna after a betraying blush has signaled her affirmative answer to a question he poses about her fear of him: "Edna Earl, you are at least honest and truthful, and those are rare traits at the present day. I thank you for preserving and returning my Dante." Poor Edna cannot hide her uneasy feelings about this mysterious man.

> She closed the door, ran lightly across the rotunda, and regaining her own room, felt inexpressibly relieved that the ordeal was over—that in the future there remained no necessity for her to address one whose very tones made her shudder, and the touch of whose hand filled her with vague dread and loathing (78–79).

The perceived future of "no necessity" indeed foreshadows exactly the opposite. Eventually he returns again with reasons why she should reconsider her judgment. It is only after she has become a successful novelist and he has become a Christian and then a minister that she agrees to marry him. Upon each of her rejections is built another layer of his redemption. Multiple editions of this book gave it a widespread prominence and the more homes it was in, the more young readers had access to it.

The Outer World — "Dime Novels"

The melodrama of the domestic novels, their adventure, intrigue, and suspense, became even more widely available (and more widely condemned) with the advent of the dime novels in the mid-1800s which moved the stories to wider and more adventurous settings. Inexpensive books with tales of sensational escapades introduced readers to the worlds outside their homes. The popularity and dangers of doing so met with outcries from critics, legislators, and even song writers (memorialized in the American musical, *Music Man's* "We got trouble, right here in River City" where in addition to playing pool the city's youngsters are caught reading dime novels behind the corn crib).

In 1858 two Beadle brothers (Erastus and Irwin) and Robert Adams opened an office in New York City and published some inexpensive non-fiction, including a *Dime Song-Book* and later a *Dime Cook-Book*. In 1860 they advertised a dime-novel series: "Books for the Million! A Dollar book for a dime!! 128 pages complete only Ten Cents!!!" The firm published thirteen titles during the first year, and Beadle & Adams Publishers were on their way to success in providing readers with views of worlds outside of the ones they inhabited. When the publishers discovered that young boys were among the most avid readers of the novels, the price was held down, a half-dime library appeared, and the novels were distributed to troops on both sides of the Civil War ("the soldier's solace and comfort in camp and campaign"). Titles like *Seth Jones; or, the Captives of the Frontier*, *The Prairie Pilot; or, The Phantom of the Sky*, and *Daring Davy, The Young Bear Killer; or the Trail of the Border Wolf* invited readers to explore what critics were to call "pernicious", "corruptive," and "obscene" reading material.

John Vose's 1878 dime novel, published by Beadle & Adams, was an account of a series of pranks by college students: *B'Hoys of Yale; or The Scrapes of a Hard Set of Collegians*. This tale chronicles the adventures of a secret fraternity from its formation in the back room of a local greasy spoon to the graduation of its most illustrious members. Twenty-six Yale students (one for each state in the union) swear each other to secrecy, adopt the name "The Philistine Society" and draw up a constitution complete with by-laws, rules, and regulations. Under the banner of *reform*, Joggles (who drinks too much) and Derby (who smokes too much) and Tim (who gambles too much) lead the others through a maze of antics more memorable than any course of study. In the wake of their reform efforts, they let a horse loose on the campus

mall, reconstruct a professor's buggy in his office, stage a fake philosophical lecture, remove the clapper from the campus wake-up bell,
and take down the creaking signs on all the local business establishments.
Because of their need for publicity, they also publish (and secretly
post) an underground newspaper which satirizes their own colleagues
and characterizes community folk (including the two town gossips,
both "on the wrong side of thirty").

The melodramatic style, the undeveloped characters, the lack of
motivation for some twists of plot and the predictable nature of others
did not intrude on the ability these books had to engage their readers.
Fees for writing this kind of fiction were large enough to attract some
notable writers including Louisa May Alcott, who wrote some under a
pseudonym. In stories like *Pauline's Passion and Punishment* (1863),
The Mysterious Key, and What It Opened (1867), *Behind a Mask; or,
A Woman's Power* (1866), Alcott did what her character, Jo March,
did in the story of *Little Women*; she wrote "necessity stories."

In a contemporary collection of Alcott's blood-and-thunder tales,
editor Madeleine Stern borrows part of her title from one of Alcott's
own, *Behind a Mask: The Unknown Thrillers of Louisa May Alcott*
(1975), and quotes from a conversation Alcott once had with a friend:

> I think my natural ambition is for the lurid style. I indulge in gorgeous
> fancies and wish I dared describe them upon my pages and set them
> before the public. ... How should I dare to interfere with the proper
> grayness of old Concord? The dear old town has never known a
> startling hue since the redcoats were there.

As she contributed stories to the *Ten Cent Novelette* series and
later to a protective *No Name Series*, she exhibited the pompous style
of the genre and explored its "ghostly-gruesome" themes. In 1867 one
of the publishers of her stories suggested she write a "girls' book." In
her diary Alcott recounts the conversation and writes, "Said I'd try."
The result was *Little Women*, the first part of which appeared in 1868,
the second part in 1869.

While most critics decried the wide availability of dime novels (to
the point that legislation was discussed branding the sale of such to
young people as contributing to the delinquency of minors), some
recognized that going "back to the basics" was not an acceptable
option. Writing on the "Dime Novel Nuisance" in an 1890 issue on the
Journal of Pedagogy, William McCormick tried to bring a voice of
reason to the discussions of literary choice for young readers:

> Yet I have no hesitancy in stating my belief that as many false ideas
> of life have emanated from the selves of the Sunday School library as
> from the cheap bookstalls. Many a rough and ready street-boy has
> had his mind trained by the perusal of a so-called dime novel, and by
> it been lured to a life of crime. But that same impetuous boy will, ten

to one, be repelled and disgusted by the cant phrases and pious talk
of the average Sunday School book. (210)

After a discussion of the characteristics of "book-loving lads" he has
known and the difficulties of assisting them in making the "transition
from trash to the best literature," McCormick concludes:

> If the ever growing curse of corrupt fiction is to be exterminated, it is
> in the replacement of trash by wholesome books, that shall steer as
> clear of the Scylla of namby-pambyism as of the Charybdis of vice.
> (211)

By the beginning of the 1900s, dime-novels had been replaced in
popularity by a variety of other books — the replacement was led most
prominently by the series books and Horatio Alger stories which
garnered increasing readership. In many ways, the search for the
literary life raft that would enable young readers to avoid the Scylla
and Charybdis that McCormick wrote about was carried on by authors
who were awakening to the fact that young readers were making
choices different from the choices being made for them by others —
that the imposition of lessons and lives in the fiction *planned* for the
reading of young people might not be the source of lesson-learning and
life-building that such authors had hoped.

The Workplace — "Series Books"

From the mid-1800s on, another strand was developing in books for
young readers. In detailed accounts of the history of adolescent literature, the books are placed in more discreet categories with labels
describing their plots: Horatio Alger stories, bad boy literature, and
adventure stories. While the settings for the books were varied, a
number of them revolved around topics related to work — not having a
job, trying to get a job, getting a bad job (but being good at it), and
getting a good job. Stories with details about one's "work" whether at
home, in school or in the military, were one part of this literature
which attracted readers with characters who were a bit more believable,
in settings which were a bit more realistic, but in plots that were no
less sensational or sentimental.

Horatio Alger, a Harvard-educated Unitarian minister, submitted
a story about Ragged Dick, a poor New York street boy, for serialization
in a juvenile magazine edited by Oliver Optic. The story was published
as a book the next year, 1867. All of Alger's heroes (heroes like *Phil
the Fiddler; or, the Story of the Street Musician* and Luke in *Struggling
Upward; or, Luke Larkin's Luck*) moved upward, outward, or forward
due in large part to their honesty, hard work, and abilities to resist
temptation.

This was a time of formulaic writing accompanied by the conviction that if the formula worked once, it would work again. So, plot patterns were repeated by one author and adopted by others. And characters were introduced in one book with adventures that carried them into several others. Sarah Chauncey Woolsey (pen name Susan Coolidge), for instance, introduced fourteen-year-old Katy (the oldest of a mother-less family of seven children, a headstrong protagonist with a desire to become surrogate mother to her siblings) in *What Katy Did* (1872). Although Katy overcomes physical adversity in the first book and tames her headstrong nature enough so she is observed by others to be "gentle, womanly, polite and tactful," readers have the opportunity to see what happens to Katy next in four books published between 1873 and 1891. Similarly, through the story-telling of Martha Farquharson, readers could follow the life of Elsie Dinsmore as she is introduced (*Elsie Dinsmore* 1867), grows up (*Elsie's Girlhood* 1872), faces life without a spouse (*Widowhood* 1880), and gets old (*Christmas with Grandma Elsie* 1888).

The story of Derrick Sterling was published during the middle of this period and combines some of the characteristics of the Horatio Alger rags-to-riches formula along with the melodrama present in adventure series (as well as a sprinkling of "bad boys"). In *Derrick Sterling: A Story of the Mines* (Munroe 1888), the young hero is followed through an adventure reminiscent of earlier melodramas. The plot moves quickly and a barrage of verbs and adjectives sounds throughout the text. Even a quick re-telling of the story can barely escape the trance induced by such a style. Derrick Sterling (fatherless, determined, intelligent, staunch, and manly-looking) is called home from private school to work eleven-hour shifts in the coal mines where he can earn thirty-five cents a day to support his little sister, Helen, and his mother, Mom. He befriends Paul Evert (delicate, deformed, wistful, even-tempered, pitiful) and saves his life in the first ten pages. As a result, the mine boss takes Derrick into his confidence and asks him to spy on other miners, and during the next two hundred pages Derrick is promoted, beaten up, trapped, and promoted again. In the midst of all this he cries, prays, shivers, stumbles, thinks, wins, loses, fights, yells, plans, defies, protects, and saves three people. And he meets the boss's niece, Nellie. Near the end of the book, and after many twists and turns of plot, Derrick discovers he and his mother are heirs to some valuable property, which he plans to sell, and, vows to use the money wisely. The book concludes with text supposedly written five years later; Derrick (now refined, handsome, and sun-tanned) will soon graduate from college first in his class with special honors in math, and he is respected far and wide for his wit and wisdom. Derrick Sterling, as with characters before him like Walter Sherwood and

St. Elmo Murray, led a life full of incidents and adventures plotted as if on a graph to demonstrate what young readers could become if they followed the directions of others.

No overview of this period is complete without references to books that are still read today as "classics" and not just as curiosities. In books like these some of the rules of predictability were broken in the presentation of the characters, and some of the lessons emerged from their lives rather than from an imposition of external ideals. The adventures of Jo March and her sisters (in Alcott's *Little Women*, 1868), of Twain's *Tom Sawyer* (1876) and *Huckleberry Finn* (1884), of Pyle's *The Merry Adventures of Robin Hood* (1883) and of Stevenson's Long John Silver in *Treasure Island* (1883), and David Balfour in *Kidnapped* (1886) gave readers more substance in character and more congruity in plot. The unexcelled popularity of books in the series produced by the Stratemayer syndicate in the early 1900s was built on a combination of the richly textured books produced from the mid to late 1880s and the increased demand for books that had more of an "inside" rather than "outside" view of the experiences of young adults.

The Stratemeyer Syndicate Novels were pushed to unimagined limits (of both success and popularity) with the market-analysis acumen and the entrepreneurial spirit of Edward Stratemeyer. As a writer of fiction himself who had ghost-written some Horatio Alger books on the benefits and rewards of a life of hard work, Stratemeyer was responsible for combining the concept of plot formulas in a succession of books and multiple sequels. He was a prolific writer and apparently relished the task of expanding the situations in which his characters found themselves. The Rover Boys, for instance, went from military school (in 1899) to an ocean voyage and an adventure in Africa—and then, almost eleven years and eleven volumes later readers found them at college (and this was after they had been, among other places, out West, on the Great Lakes, in the mountains, on the river, and so on and so on).

Eventually the popularity of the multiple series he had created resulted in a demand for new titles that he could not meet himself. The Stratemeyer Literary Syndicate evolved around 1906 when he enlisted the assistance of aspiring writers. Authors were sent plot outlines, they spent up to six weeks filling in the details suggested in the blueprint, and they submitted the manuscripts. The resulting series then, although each title within it carried the name of the same author, was the work of many different writers. The discovery that books about Nancy Drew, The Hardy Boys, Tom Swift, The Bobbsey Twins, and The Dana Girls were not in fact written by clearly identifiable authors is akin for some readers to learning that there isn't a Santa Claus. It is an interesting footnote that in the 1980s *The New Bobbsey Twins* series became available at bookstores, complete with the Bobbsey twins shopping at the mall, eating fast foods, and playing punk rock. The books produced by the Stratemeyer Syndicate did make more widely available books with increasingly realistic characters who did more than play the value-laden parts of a larger morality drama.

The Inner World

Prior to the early 1900s most books for young readers presented worlds *given* to readers by others: "Here is your world as I believe it should be, so learn from it" and "Here is your world the way it can never be, but enjoy it." From this foundation emerged increasing numbers of books where characters described "my" world, but this "my" was still to a large extent determined by an outside rather than inside view. In the mid-1900s, however, another shift took place. With the appearance of a very personal "me" within the books, characters did start to explore the church, the home, and other worlds from an internal rather than external perspective. Mabel Robinson's *Bright Island* (1937) illustrates the transition that books for young readers were going through during the early part of the 1900s.

Thankful Curtis (her mother named her for the Rest-and-Be-Thankful Cemetery after she learned that her seventh child was her first daughter) is growing up on an island off the coast of Maine where some family members are trying to teach her what a young woman should become; this could be the beginning of a Sunday School tract or a domestic novel. But because she has developed a special relationship with her grandfather, he leaves her some valuable property when he dies; this could be part of a Horatio Alger story. Thankful is enrolled in a private school in Maine and her challenges there include confronting the complexities of life in a world with electric lights, running water, and adventuresome classmates; this could be the outline for a dime novel.

Instead of repeating previous patterns of characterization and exposition, however, this novel presents a character who leads herself into her own future. While he was alive, Thankful's grandfather saw something in her that was unnoticed by others as they tried to squeeze her into the trappings of femininity. Unbeknownst to her (and earning the eventual consternation of surprised relatives), Grandfather bequeaths Thankful not only Bright Island, but also money and plans for her attendance at a private school. When her mother tries to explain this and the fact that her father and brothers all went unmentioned in the will, she says, "It's a man's world, Thankful, and they like to lead us. You would never be a good follower. Your Gramp knew it."

As Thankful deals with school (the results of her placement tests surprise everyone and she is invited to enroll as a senior), with boys (three different young men are introduced as potential suitors), and with her own future (she has some of Jo March's characteristics for strength and self-sufficiency), the reader sees that neither the character of Thankful Curtis nor her creator, Mabel Robinson, are, in fact, good followers.

The book differs from Sunday School novels and domestic novels because there is little inculcation of predetermined values. It differs from dime novels in that little is overstated; the story is bare and the details are restrained. It differs from the Stratemeyer books because the emphasis is on psychological rather than physical action. And it foreshadows books where the reactions and inner emotions of a character are more than one-dimensional, where relationships between characters have depth and influence and therefore a more believable impact, and where the lessons and lives represented on the page are left untouched by a heavy editorial hand.

The bulk of the books published for juvenile readers between 1900 and 1960 are today generally characterized as being sentimental, moralistic portraits of the experiences of adolescents. In spite of exceptions, like *Bright Island*, that gave readers a view of what was on the horizon, most books purported to present "real" lessons and "real" lives. The distance between acceptable and unacceptable topics negated their claims, however. Books were about school, but not about drugs or alcohol; about home, but not about divorce or less-than-ideal parents; about dating, but not about sex; and about jobs, but not about exploitation. A few book titles illustrate how the writers defined the territory, but the texts are evidence that many parameters remained unexplored: *Sue Barton, Student Nurse* (Boylston), *Donna Parker on Her Own* (Martin), *Prom Trouble* (Budlong), *Double Date* (DuJardin), *Campus Melody* (Emery). In addition to the books in the Stratemeyer series, titles like these prompted critics in the following decades to compare them to the problem realism books that were to emerge. In the opening paragraph of a one-page article, "New Novels for Juniors," in a 1974 issue of *Newsweek* Jean Seligmann reflected:

> Once upon a time, most books written for young people — aside from out-and-out adventure stories — were populated by cheerful white teen-agers whose biggest worries were how to get a date for the senior prom or whether the home team would win the Saturday-night game. Not any more. A pandemic of realism has invaded young people's fiction. ... In books with titles like "Dinky Hocker Shoots Smack!," "Diary of a Frantic Kid Sister," My Dad Lives in a Downtown Motel," and "Mom, the Wolf-Man, and Me," today's youthful heroes and heroines are smoking dope, swallowing diet pills, suffering

mental breakdowns, worrying about homosexuality and masturbation, watching their parents squabble and split up, being battered by racial discrimination, confronting serious illness and even death. In short, they are doing things that real kids do. (83)

The titles most frequently cited as groundbreakers in this movement to a more dramatic realism, a realism characterized by G. Robert Carlsen as one "showing adolescent life, not from the adult's point of view as he looks back, but rather from the adolescent's viewpoint as he moves through his experiences" (42) include: *Seventeenth Summer* (Daly 1942), *The Outsiders* (Hinton 1967), *Mr. and Mrs. Bo Jo Jones* (Head 1968), *The Pigman* (Zindel 1968), *Go Ask Alice* (Anonymous 1971), and *The Chocolate War* (Cormier 1974). Rosa Guy's character, Ruby, from a 1976 book of the same name, is one who illustrates the change.

Eighteen-year-old Ruby Cathy is a teenager from the West Indies who, along with her sister, brother, and father, lives in an apartment in Harlem. Ruby's life is peopled by others who have built up defense mechanisms to protect themselves from what they each view as the harshness of life. Ruby's father moves in shadows and threats: "You want to jump? Jump! Go ahead, jump! I'll put your tail back on that ledge and if you ain't jump I split your tail. ... You want to kill yourself? I'll give you something to kill yourself about" (178). Her younger sister, Phyllisia, escapes "all things by producing a book." Her teacher, Miss Gottlieb, hides behind cynicism and anger: "These parents who send their morons to school expect *us* to do something with them. They know where those morons will end up" (33). Classmates hide behind teenage lasciviousness and coarseness; the tutor in an apartment upstairs hides behind intelligence and shyness; the housekeeper hides behind dreams of romance. Ruby observes all the masks and then she tries, unsuccessfully, to see if any will work for her. Instead, she finds friendships "as fluid as water, fragile as those modern buildings ... quickly erected and as easily destroyed" (3). In a manner different from almost all of the characters in the book, Ruby is open and vulnerable. In making the transition from adolescence to adulthood, she has not yet discovered the masks that might make it easier to survive.

And then she meets Daphne Dupre, a girl who is the result of a carefully planned and rehearsed script. Daphne is "one hundred per" and, in her own words, "cool, calm, collected, poised, sophisticated, cultured, and refined, and intelligent." As the book explores the relationship between Ruby and Daphne — their friendship and the friendship's end — the relationships Ruby has with all of the other characters come into play. Without sensationalism or sentimentality, the book provides both voice and insight to a "lived-through" process, a nearly unedited reality of what being a teenager is like for *one* teenager.

When looking at the history of young adult literature, answering questions beyond the obvious ones, like "what are the important books?" is one of the ways to understand the relationship between the past and the present. Questions like "Who *is* the writer?" "For what purposes was the book written?" "Who does the writer think the reader is?" can be answered in descriptions of literary periods and categories, but the most accurate responses are seen in examining the lessons and lives portrayed in the books themselves. Superimposed and highly edited *representations* of the lives, thoughts, problems, and worlds of young people result from one set of beliefs and assumptions about the nature of adolescents and the role of books; internally generated and tightly edited *presentations* result from another. Young adult literature today is built upon and reflects a dynamic past that encompasses books (and techniques and assumptions) representing both ends of this continuum. The changes have not always occurred in chronological order or discreet categories, and the books are a part of the larger social contexts of the times. Whether the books promote, report, or challenge the context, they become part of the conversation about what it means to live and grow up in an external world that is often as confusing as one's internal world.

Works Cited

Alcott, Louisa May. 1868. *Little Women*. Lee and Shepard.

Carlsen, G. Robert. 1971. *Books and the Teen-Age Reader*. New York: Harper & Row.

Coolidge, Susan. 1911. *What Katy Did*. Boston: Little, Brown, and Company.

Donelson, Kenneth L., January 1980. "Some Notes on Two Early Forms of Children's and Adolescent Literature: The American Sunday School Union and the American Temperance Society." Department of English, Arizona State University, Tempe. Photocopy.

Donelson, Kenneth L., and Alleen Pace Nilsen. 1989. *Literature for Today's Young Adults*, 3rd ed. Glenview, IL: Scott, Forseman & Co.

DuBois, William Pene. 1956. *Lion*. New York: Viking.

Farquharson, Martha. 1867. *Elsie Dinsmore*. NY: Dodd, Mead and Company.

———. 1872. *Elsie's Girlhood*. NY: Dodd, Mead and Company.

———. 1880. *Elsie's Widowhood*. NY: Dodd, Mead and Company.

———. 1888. *Christmas with Grandma Elsie*. NY: Dodd, Mead and Company.

Guy, Rosa. 1976. *Ruby*. New York: Bantam.

Hall, George F. 1982. *Plain Points on Personal Purity or Startling Sins of the Sterner Sex: A Book for Men Only.* Chicago: Columbian.

Hall, G. Stanley, 1905. *Adolescence; Its Psychology and Its Relations to Physiology, Anthropology, Sociology, Sex, Crime, Religion and Education.* 2 vols. New York: D. Appleton & Co.

Kellog, J. H. 1881. *Plain Facts for Old and Young.* Burlington, Iowa: Segner & Condit.

Lee, Hubert. 1849. *The Prize Garden.* Philadelphia: American Sunday School Union.

McCormick, William. 1890. "The Dime Novel Nuisance." *Journal of Pedagogy* 3: 209–11.

Munroe, Kirk. 1902. *Derrick Sterling: A Story of the Mines.* 1888. Reprint. New York: Harper & Row.

Nasaw, David. 1979. *Schooled to Order: A Social History of Schooling in the United States.* Oxford: Oxford University Press.

Pyle, Howard. 1883. *The Merry Adventures of Robin Hood.*

Robinson, Mabel. 1937. *Bright Island.* New York: Random House.

Seligman, Jean A. 1974. "New Novels for Juniors." *Newsweek*, March 4, 1974: 83.

Shaffer, Ellen. 1966. "The Children's Book of the American Sunday School Union, *American Book Collector* 17 (October): 21.

Stern, Madeleine, ed. 1975. *Behind a Mask: The Unknown Thrillers of Louisa May Alcott.* New York: William Morrow & Co.

Stevenson, Robert Louis. 1886. *Kidnapped.*

———. 1883. *Treasure Island.*

Twain, Mark. 1884. *The Adventures of Huckleberry Finn.*

Twain, Mark. 1876. *The Adventures of Tom Sawyer.*

Wilson, Augusta Jane Evans. 1867. St. Elmo. New York: Carleton.

Vose, John. 1878. *B'Hoys of Yale; or, The Scrapes of a Hard Set of Collegians.* New York: Beadle & Adams Publishers.

Part II
Writing The Young
Adult Novel

5

Creating a Bond Between Writer and Reader

Sue Ellen Bridgers

I came to write books of interest to young people quite inadvertently, having spent part of 1974 and 1975 writing a story about a migrant girl living in the south who wanted a place to call her own. It was a story set in a southern farming community, and the landscape and the home place were as important to me as the characters were, perhaps more so. Once the manuscript was finished, I thought *Home Before Dark* was a good story but I had no idea who might want to read it. It didn't seem to fit anywhere.

An editor at *Redbook Magazine* suggested I send the manuscript to Pat Ross at Alfred A. Knopf, where the readership issue eventually became the publisher's decision. I didn't know there was such a thing as a young adult novel until Ross asked me how I felt about *Home Before Dark* being designated as such.

I was so delighted to be published by Knopf, to have an editor who understood my intention and celebrated my attempt, to have readers of any age, that I certainly wasn't compelled to question their judgment. Although the book was marketed as a young adult novel, the mail I received about *Home Before Dark* (a condensed form also appeared in *Redbook* and *Reader's Digest* Condensed Books) indicated a broad readership. Letters came from elderly readers, nostalgic for the rural life the story evoked, as well as from young people who were curious about Stella's family and intrigued by her determination to have the life she'd envisioned.

When I began thinking about my second book, I knew I wanted to keep the rural southern setting, but I hoped to find a more lighthearted story to tell. A person out of my husband's past, a retarded man who was loved and protected by his community, provided the impetus, but I immediately felt the need for a companion for Dwayne Pickens, someone whose mind would be more accessible to me than his could be. At first I envisioned another man, then a boy in his late teens, and eventually a young girl who could pretend to be a boy. This deception on Casey's part added a dimension to their friendship that I knew would hold my interest. So by process of selectivity, I found myself with a protagonist even younger than Stella Willis, a flat-chested twelve-year-old tomboy who met the needs of the story I wanted to tell.

During the struggle to find my story, I wasn't thinking about the reader at all. In fact, although I now feel some pressure to write for the teenage audience, I still try to write to please myself, to write the story I want to read. This is especially true during the first stage of the process while I am getting to know my characters. The reader I imagine, if I imagine one at all, is hidden behind the book.

The fact remains that since all my books have young people in them, teenagers have turned out to be my sustaining audience — and what a wonderful audience to have! They read with enthusiasm. They are impatient and forthright. When they like a book, they pass it around. When they love one, they hold the memory of it close. They let it affect them.

Young people energize me. I like the intensity with which many of them live. Their lives seem more exciting, more on the edge than those of adults. But many middle class young people seem sad to me, too. If they are aware of world events, they have reason to be concerned, and I am appreciative of the positive outlets many have found to let their voices be heard about social and political issues such as the students in Colorado who succeeded in having tuna banned in their school cafeteria. Surely they will use that experience to tackle other environmental issues in the future.

But frequently teenagers' worries are turned inward, and they grapple with their problems alone. Too many of them don't seem to have appropriate skills or information to cope successfully. Then there are the kids in jail, on drugs, truant; there are children having children or suffering abuse many of us didn't know existed a few years ago. Kids who go to school hungry and sleep in abandoned automobiles, vacant buildings, boxes. Then there are the students who seem to be sleepwalking through school, their major interest their after-school jobs which provide car payments and gas. Their most urgent cause is getting an "open campus" lunch policy. Even those students intrigue me. What is going on behind their sleepy eyes? What motivates the teenage athlete? What kind of home life does the perfect student have? How will the decisions they make today affect their adult lives? What are they thinking, feeling, longing for?

In fiction I can ask: Who are you? And over a period of months, the answers come. Once I described this process as one of having an empty room inside myself that gradually fills, the clutter of a life haphazardly pushed into corners and against the walls. A life collects itself within my own life—a separate identity I am always questioning. What do you think? How do you feel? What will you do next?

But how does this process begin? Usually it starts with a visual experience. I see a person in my mind's eye. In the case of *Sara Will*, I saw this woman coming down the road in the twilight. She had work gloves tucked in her belt and carried a rake over her shoulder. I knew what her name was. I went to my typewriter and wrote exactly what I had seen. Then I started questioning her. Where are you going? Where have you been? What was your life like before this moment? What Sara Will told me was intriguing—I discovered she had a closed-up life and very limited experience. I learned she was frequently frustrated and sharp-tongued; what others may have considered composure was actually rigidity. Sara Will rarely took a deep breath. Her determination and forcefulness was a cover-up for an emptiness she didn't know how to fill. Not an especially pleasant person, this middle-aged Sara of firm lip and flashing eyes! So why did I spend three years with her? The main reason is that I am a lot like Sara. My exterior life may not be—it is, in fact, very different from hers—and yet we had similar interior lives—fear of failure, a protective rigidity in our thinking, an unwillingness to change. A friend called while reading *Sara Will* to report tearfully that she was just like Sara. "Oh," I said to comfort her, "we all are."

By the time I had this visual experience of Sara Will coming down the road, I had learned to be accepting of these experiences. The first one, however, was somewhat startling in its immediacy. It occurred while I was traveling toward my hometown with my family. Suddenly I saw this girl there in the car with us, and I knew she wanted the home we were going to. But why did she want it, and how would she go about getting it? She didn't have a name; she didn't have a past. She was just present with her scruffy family. We made quite a crowd in the car, even though my family seemed unaware of the extra passengers. All weekend at my mother's, I thought about these people. In fact, they were on my mind for several months, and I wrote fifty pages about them before putting the manuscript away as a failed short story. After a couple of years of what must have been much subconscious ruminating, I began working on Stella's story again. By then she had a new name, a history, and identifiable people in her life. Suddenly and inexplicably, I had a great deal of faith in her.

My first recognition of the characters in *Notes for Another Life* also occurred in an automobile; perhaps it is the movement of the car, the sense of not being completely grounded anywhere that causes these experiences. At any rate, these characters were singing, and I didn't have my radio on! On the edge of a pocket calendar I wrote, "They would start out singing" and listed the songs I heard. When I reached my destination, I quickly wrote down what these people looked like and what their names were.

Now that I understand my process, those early experiences with a new character before the story begins to take shape are the most exciting time for me as a writer. In my enthusiasm for these people I am about to know, I don't think about which genre they will fit into. I am too busy just getting to know them because it is through their past and present that I discern their future — the story I will tell. More often than not, the character that interests me most is a young person.

The two most obvious reasons for my interest in young people are that I was once one myself and that I have children to keep me knowledgeable about what young people are up to. Both these reasons are valid ones, although while my children were teenagers I never used them or their situations for subject matter. It seemed too much an infringement on their privacy. But another reason may have been that I was too involved in their ups and downs to see literary merit in their stories. Whatever the reason, it was not until *Permanent Connections* that I used my children in any way, and by then they were grown. There is a brief argument between the mother and daughter in that book which is similar to an argument I had with one of my daughters. When I asked permission to use it, she couldn't recall the incident, although I remember thinking at the time that what she was saying was bookworthy. I also asked my son who had played high school football to write a conversation about an up-coming game, which I was able to use, except for necessary expurgations.

My memories of my own teenage years are probably the true catalyst for discovering these young characters. I remember my teenage years much better than I do more recent times, but I find it isn't the events I need to remember so much as the feel of things. The gamut of teenage emotions I experienced is somehow always at my disposal. Envision a character, give him or her an internal life and a problem, and I'm on a journey full of all the emotional turmoil I knew thirty years ago.

I have always written about people and places I love. I can't imagine spending three years living with characters who bore me. I avoid the sinister in my fiction just as I do in my real life. When bad things happen to my characters, I want to take the time to understand the circumstances and to find whatever good might be in the event.

In *Home Before Dark*, Mae's death, although painful to write, turned out to be the impetus for the family's liberation from a life of hopelessness and poverty. Dwayne's brother's attempt to have him institutionalized in *All Together Now* gave his community a chance to act and gave Casey a growth experience that would help shape her life. In *Notes for Another Life*, the father's emotional illness and the difficult relationship between mother and children gave the young characters the conflict required for a successful story. *Permanent Connections* gave me a chance to write about the mountains of western North Carolina where I now live and to deal with issues affecting young people here.

The basis for fiction is always conflict, and the most prevalent form conflict takes in my work is the character who wants something worthwhile but difficult to achieve. The ensuing struggle provides the plot. Stella Willis wants a place to call her own. Casey wants to feel close to her extended family, to have Dwayne for a friend, and ultimately, to protect him. Kevin and Wren, the teenage siblings in *Notes for Another Life*, want a functional family—their father well, their mother with them. Rob and Ellery in *Permanent Connections* want to feel connected. None of these goals is perfectly achieved—easy goals make for lightweight fiction—but there is always growth and personal achievement. There is always the beginning of acceptance of themselves as they are.

I wish I could say I have some finely honed method of plotting the action. It would relieve my mind considerably to have an outline for reference, index cards in order, a plan. While I don't have a plot, I don't exactly fly by the seat of my pants either. The year in which I think about my characters, without writing more than the opening few pages and notes on bits of paper, provides me with time to know them fairly well. I start writing when I sense the characters are ready to tell their story. This process is not as hit-and-miss as you might think. By having a comfortable setting and a basic conflict which has been provided by the main character, I begin with a situation that is bound to develop into action. Occasionally a young reader complains that my characters think too much. I never worry that they are thinking too much, but I do worry that there's not enough action.

"Nothing is happening," I moan to my family when I stumble out of my study at the end of an unproductive morning. Eventually my husband reads the uneventful pages and jots down a list of all that happens, giving me temporary solace. It is good that I worry about the action. Ever conscious of the necessity of movement in the work, I keep it moving as best I can.

I don't know of any writer who claims to have been born with a style—certainly I wasn't. I remember well my struggle to find one. In my youth, this process involved several months of trying to write like a favorite author and then moving on to another writer whose style had attracted me. Periodically I tried to write like Charlotte Brontë, Ernest

Hemingway, Thomas Wolfe, John Steinbeck, Boris Pasternak, Jane Austen, Eudora Welty, and a host of others. They were wonderful teachers but frustrating, too. Their material was so different from mine.

I envy the young writer of today who can find writers to emulate closer to home, writers dealing with issues that affect him or her directly, that are in his or her personal realm of reality. Studying young adult novels can show students a wide variety of writing styles and subjects from which to draw inspiration. Reading stories to find your own stories is a perfectly valid way to approach writing and all writers do it. Reading and writing go absolutely hand in hand. Writers love books, they love words, they love stories more than they love the idea of being writers.

Any book that holds a young person's interest, that portrays the human condition with care and is well crafted, could and should be a young adult novel. The categories of books are more a marketing device than a limit to the appeal a book might have. If the characters and situations in a novel are relevant and meaningful to the teenager, that's the book he or she will read. The book without the reader has no life; it is static without the imagination and experience of another mind, the hand eagerly turning the page, the receiving heart.

I hope teenagers have good young adult books to read for many years to come. There are many already available which will be enjoyed by future generations looking for a "good read," and I expect more quality young adult books will be written if they continue to be taught in the classrooms, suggested for book reports, and made available in the libraries and class sets—in other words, if there continues to be a market. I don't think there'll be *Cliff's Notes* for them, though, and that's a blessing in itself.

Having been discovered by a teenage audience, I have come to treasure the bond between us. I expect the bulk of my future writing will be relevant to them, since their experiences continue to interest me. It is a young voice that I most often hear in my head.

I hope my books reflect the hopefulness I feel for young people as well as my seriousness about my work because I believe young adult books not only help young people grow emotionally but also contribute enormously to their becoming better readers and writers. These books make reading a recreational activity, setting the stage for years of adult enjoyment. At their finest, young adult books provide reading experiences kids never forget, moments they make their own. Imagine that.

6

Problem Novels for Readers Without Any

Richard Peck

When you write novels you hope young people will read, you do well never to invoke that fatal phrase: "When I was your age. . . ." However, give me a moment.

When I was a teenager, the world was run by adults. When you were out of sight of your parents, you were still within range of people who knew your parents well. My English teacher, who could have used some Christian charity, sat in the pew ahead of us at church—even Sundays weren't safe. My math teacher moonlighted in the suit department at Sears. You couldn't even go *shopping*, for Pete's sake. They had us outflanked.

In the 1950s, adolescents were an underclass with plenty of dues yet to be paid. The chief authority in a boy's life was the looming figure of the head of the local draft board, yet another adult in a world full of them. Back then adolescence didn't meld seamlessly with the lifestyle of the Yuppie. A boy knew when his adolescence was over. A notice to that effect came in the mail.

Like any normally paranoid teenager, I assumed I was behind an entire frame of eight balls all my own. I believed that if I didn't get straight A's, I wasn't going to win the necessary scholarship for college, assuming, always, the draft board would grant a college deferment.

I grubbed for grades, yearned for the scholarship, dreaded Korea, and feared the formless future. Moreover, I hadn't been born into the class of society that provided lemon-yellow Studebaker convertibles for their offspring. I managed to keep this genealogical outrage down to minor irritation somewhere on par with acne and two or three other afflictions that will remain nameless. Still, as a youth I was a worried man.

In writing to the young today, I spare them any hint of this exceedingly raw material. They've already heard these stories from their own parents, and they don't believe them.

When I was young, adults ran the world; when I became an adult, the young were running it. On darker days I figure that I lost out twice. Because I cannot replay my own youth for these very different beings, I must stay on their trail.

In the flossy suburbs where I was visiting schools recently, I was on familiar turf, one suburb being suspiciously like another, coast to coast. Here the children of the suburban successful sat limply in neat rows, perfectly groomed, handsomely dressed, and with the posture of the underemployed. Conditioned as critics and consumers, they were perfectly willing to watch one more adult account for himself if he could. But I wanted them to talk. They responded with the standard suburban litany: they felt pressured.

By whom, I wondered. The concept of both the part-time job and the draft board was surely beyond their grasp. They didn't mention scholarships, and as to cars, the parking lot was chock-a-block with late models. "By whom?" I asked. "Mother," they murmured. Then with sidelong glances, "Peers." But they were unwilling to expand.

Most young readers are growing up suburban. Reading remains a middle-class preoccupation, and readers are those with sufficient leisure to spend time with books. Oddly, in our young adult literature we've created for them a cast of outcasts and underdogs, from M. E. Kerr's intellectual misfits to S. E. Hinton's Okie underclass. In Robert Cormier's *The Chocolate War* the hero's position as solitary nonconformist in a parochial school nearly costs him his life. In Chris Crutcher's *Running Loose* a football star becomes a pariah in his senior year for confronting the corruption of the coach. The narrator of Bruce Brooks' *The Moves Make the Man*, a 1985 Newbery Honor Book, is a school's token black student during the integrating early 1960s.

We have a literature celebrating precisely the kind of people the reader tries not to notice around school. This marches in the proud Huck Finn tradition of fiction, for novels have always inclined to the biographies of survivors, of the wretched on the rise, of comers-from-behind. Let's hope there's value in providing a literature of nonconformity to a conformist readership, a literature of the under-valued for a readership of the over-praised. Books may well be the only alternative points of view our readers ever encounter. At our most optimistic, we can even hope the theme puts the readers' feelings of being pressured into some kind of perspective.

Only a very young writer or a crank believes his words will change readers in measurable ways. Not all of our novel's championing rebels, independent thinkers, nerds, even, seem to have won readers from their herd instinct and their social distinctions. Still, we know we've given a few isolated readers who feel rejected themselves some much-needed identity because we get heartfelt letters from them.

I want to do more novels to address the mainstream of readers more directly. Such books are harder to write, of course. How do we make role models of and for the conventional children of privilege and permissiveness?

We have at least one guidepost, Judith Guest's *Ordinary People*. It's a novel on the timeless, classless theme of the guilt of survivors. Yet it's told in terms of the emotional frigidity that exists within a center-hall colonial house in an over-manicured neighborhood of Lake Forest, Illinois. It's about a favored family who find themselves strangers to one another in the aftermath of a tragedy. It's about the price parents and their children pay for the habit of perfection.

We need more novels that don't trivialize the very real problems of people who aren't supposed to be having any. We live in an age in which both parents often work so their children may enjoy a higher standard of living than their own. There's guilt implicit in that. When parents function as your servants, you'll naturally patronize them, but you may not like yourself the better for it.

There's mounting doubt in the minds of young people who are drifting between the permissive home and the selective school. When parents' demands are only occasional, when teachers' standards are always negotiable, you may suspect there's no value in growing up to play such weak roles as these. You may even panic at the thought. This is the generation being pressed to be competitive and successful in adult life without the necessary stretched attention span, personal disciplines, and communication skills. This is a generation with new reasons to fear the future.

In my novel, *Remembering the Good Times*, a boy takes his own life. He's the son of the professional suburban class, self-motivated into a downward spiral. He's pressured by his own drive, by the unspoken expectations of his class, and he's nudged over the edge by a slack school and an aimless adolescence that aren't preparing him for the future. He's the quintessential adolescent suicide in that he appears to be living a far too-favored life to elicit anything but admiration. Even if he had an emotional vocabulary with which to cry out for help, he might not be heard.

In the 1980s and '90s, suicide is more than a metaphor among the young. It's an epidemic striking heavily at the suburban affluent for whom the permissive home, the elective course, and grade-inflation have, in some tragically ironic way, imposed unbearable pressure as slow-paced adolescence extends into graduate school and beyond.

The response from young readers to *Remembering the Good Times* inspired me in an unexpected way. A wonderful number continue to write back about that book with the blend of compassion and anger I'd hoped for from them. But there was a subtext in the early letters that troubled me and sent me off in the direction of another book. Too many letter-writers sympathized with a suicidal boy in the idea that what happened to him couldn't happen very near them.

It's only human to distance the self from the threatening, and the defenses of the young are higher than ours. Still, I wanted to try a book they couldn't deny. I called it *Princess Ashley*, and its about what I think is the ultimate challenge to the young now: peer-group conformity in an era when it has assumed the authority that once resided in parents and teachers. I wasn't tempted by autobiography. In my adolescence you could be a part-time conformist and get away with it; however, parents today who are pleased that their children are popular have no idea what that popularity costs.

Teachers know, and they helped me write the book. In recent years I've rarely visited a school in which a teacher didn't mention that most of the students come to school chiefly to see their friends. Anecdotes and settings and characters — both leaders and followers — were easy to find. The pitfall was that the young regard the peer group and its dictates less a problem than a solution. The result was a novel about a girl who believes her mother is never right and that the girl who runs her peer group at school is never wrong. It's a story of a protagonist who gets to go to all the right parties with the right people. A tragedy, of course.

When the book was about to be published, I went forth in my usual way to tell young people about it. In a visit to a well-to-do suburban school I got my ears pinned back on the first time out with *Princess Ashley*. I described its depiction of the powerful peer-grouping, augmented by parental defeat and youthful affluence, against a background of a school trying to keep everybody happy. I read passages. I summed up. I told them what was in my heart.

Then a boy spoke, and everyone in the classroom turned to him, and so he must have been their peer-group leader. "If you're so concerned about conformity," he said, "why don't you write a book about inner-city street gangs and leave our friendships alone?"

Even when you spend a lifetime in pursuit of them, adolescents remain the most mysterious of readers. Wherever they live, they regularly confuse the word for the deed, preaching tolerance and practicing exclusion. They are devoted, undependable friends to one another. They believe group identity will solve personal problems. They refuse to accept the consequences of their own actions, and they can project blame any distance. They believe passionately in surfaces — masks, uniforms, poses — and yet when you pierce their defenses, they seem relieved to see you.

We were like that, but less lonely. We weren't allowed to divorce our own families at puberty, demand the lock on the bedroom door and the elaborate sound system to screen out the possibility of a parental voice. We had less time on our hands to misuse, and less privacy in which to be isolated.

As a writer I had my first brush with suburban youth when I was researching the background for a novel called *Are You in the House Alone?* Through friendship with parents, I managed to find myself in a group of well-bred tenth-graders around a New Jersey dinner table. The other adults vanished discreetly in the way parents have nowadays. I came clean and admitted to the young people I was looking into their lifestyle for a novel. While true, it was far from an icebreaker.

"What do you want to know?" my young host asked. I wanted to know whatever they were willing to tell, but I said, "Books need authentic speech patterns. Let's start with your slang." My pen poised, but a ghastly pall descended.

At last one of the group said, "We don't use slang. We're gifted."

At the end of the long, informative evening, I read off the slang they had used in conversation. It ran to three pages. They laughed indulgently at the long list and enjoyed hearing their words handed back.

I learned more than language that evening. It came clear that these young people equated academic giftedness with suburban residence. By extension they didn't believe any language they used could be slang. It was standard speech because they spoke it.

They discussed the future with stolid certainty: college and grad school and the professions to follow. But they didn't touch on that authorial concern — setting. "Where do you think you'll be living and working?" I asked. "New York?"

Another terrible silence fell. "New York?" someone said. "Why would we want to live there? We'll be living and working here in Westfield. By then everything will be in the suburbs."

History may have already proved them right. But still I need to wring my hands a bit over the intense, stultifying provinciality of their conditioning. When you believe you're both academically gifted and socially superior because of the happenstance of your home address, surely your world is narrowed. The parents of this generation may believe they deserve utopia because they paid so much for the house, but it's worrisome when the young fall for the same fallacy.

It's worrisome because there's trouble in this paradise. Suburban schooling prepares the young for no other way of life, and the liberating subjects of geography and foreign language are far too elective now to serve as alternatives. In the pressures these favored young feel to compete with each other in their little realms, they reckon without their contemporaries elsewhere, in inner-cities and in foreign countries, who play by other rules and have their own reasons for winning.

We've given our mainstream readers a literature of nonconformity which they've accepted too calmly. We need a new one to question their provincial pieties without belittling the problems or telling them they don't have any. We need a literature that holds out hope to the children of parents who have become so successful in worldly ways that they seem impossible acts to follow.

The unearned advantages won from their parents and the happy endings these young people have promised themselves have edged them near despair. We've given them the success stories of outcasts and opportunities to champion underdogs. Now they need books that invite them to champion themselves, road maps pointing the way out of the subdivision.

7

What About Now?
What About Here?
What About Me?

Sandy Asher

Let me confess it up front: I was one of those elusive, often considered mythical, creatures known as "teenage readers."

No one ever seems to know quite what to do with teenage readers. They look fully grown. So why the indigestion when they're fed a steady diet of Great Books? They carry on like children. So why not serve them the bubblegum books they seem to enjoy?

When I was in school, in the fifties, the best a girl in a "teen" story could hope for was to get a boyfriend and grow up to become a nurse. That was the *best*. More often than not, it was just "get a boyfriend," with the clear implication that that was all the growing up she'd ever need to do. A teenage boy didn't need to grow up at all. He just had to be handsome and/or captain of a team.

Well, I got myself a boyfriend, and he was handsome. He was bright, too, and kind to old people, and lots of other things the books never even mentioned. But I still couldn't help thinking, "There has to be more to life than this."

When I ran out of teen fluff to read, I turned to the only alternative available at the time: books for adults. I gobbled up everything from Irving Stone's *Love Is Eternal* to Leo Tolstoy's *War and Peace*. Sure enough, there was more to life. But it was all for THEM, the grown-ups. Their intrigues, battles, affairs, and causes read like the fairy tale quests of my childhood. They were part of fascinating, exotic worlds far removed from my personal reality. Maybe someday I'd go there (right after I finally found the second star and flew straight on to

77

Neverland), but what about NOW? What about HERE? What about ME?

I couldn't find myself anywhere, not in what was passed off then as young adult literature and not in mainstream adult literature, either. Don't get me wrong. I loved reading all of it, the ridiculous and the sublime. I loved living inside of books. Even so, they often left me feeling excluded, insignificant, and lonely. And I was a reader by choice! It takes no great empathic skill to imagine how they might affect reluctant readers.

In the 1960s, writers for young adults ventured beyond teen dating rituals and began dealing with other concerns: death, divorce, alcoholism, child abuse. Anything happening in the real world became grist for the mill. YA novels, like everything else at the time, became relevant. And then, they became *Too* relevant. "Problem novels" put sensational issues ahead of literary concerns. And readers were given the impression that if there were no dead, divorced, drunken child abusers in their families, they weren't *normal*.

While I liked the new openness in young adult literature, I felt that many of the young people reading out there were still being left out of the picture. They were nice kids, as I'd been a nice kid, and they were being told they were too boring to write about. It was in response to this that I found my own place in young adult literature. I decided to center my work on nice kids, not reverting to the simplistic stories of the past, but involving them, as characters and as readers, in complex, sometimes humorous, sometimes unpleasant, examinations of their own reality. Egocentricity, after all, is a hallmark of youth, but it's not necessarily a fault at that age. Self-discovery is the work young people *must* do.

I feel I understand the private lives of nice kids — the ones who rarely give a teacher a minute's trouble, who would never confront a police officer except to ask directions, who might never attract the attention of social workers, sociologists, psychologists, journalists, and so on. I don't mean saints. I mean young people who are trying to figure out how to lead productive, meaningful lives. Who are asking, which end of the world is marked "this side up"? Which doors to life are marked "in" — and are you supposed to push or pull?

So far, my main characters have not resorted to alcohol, promiscuity, or violence to get through the day. This is not to say that their days are easy. I explore difficult situations in my books because my characters, like my readers, live in a world where such things do exist. Eighth graders in *Summer Smith Begins* come up against censorship and anti-Semitism. A teacher in *Things Are Seldom What They Seem* is accused of molesting his students. A failed athlete in *Everything Is Not Enough* batters his girlfriend — and she stays with him.

But center stage in my stories is reserved for nice kids. They learn to deal with grief, loneliness, fear, jealousy, anger, frustration, confusion, love — and the lack of it — because nice kids must, and nice kids do. And they need and deserve books that cheer them on, that encourage them to go with their own best instincts, and that assure them there is a cure for adolescence: equal parts of time, understanding, and laughter.

It's a rare day when a book changes the perceptions or value system of an adult. Generally, adults choose books that reflect and reinforce attitudes they already hold. Young adult readers, on the other hand, are actively searching for ideas, information, and values to incorporate into their personalities and into their lives. The books they read become a very real part of them.

Knowing how vital a part I may play in even one young person's life, I feel a heavy responsibility to be careful about what I say and how I say it. I'm not talking about censorship of my words or ideas, but about thoughtfulness: What do I really think about things, and what do I want to say to the next generation?

This becomes an even greater challenge when I consider the mixed messages young people receive daily from society. As we set men and women free from stereotypes, young people need more guidance than ever through what must seem a bewildering array of choices. The majority of readers of young adult fiction are girls, but that doesn't mean they all are. And the boys reading serious fiction along with them are bound to be those sensitive enough to realize they, too, are caught up in an exciting and terrifying time.

Let me define what I mean by serious fiction. It's not humorless fiction. I'm talking about stories that examine the human condition in a thoughtful way. Please note two important words here: *human* condition. Not male condition, not female condition. In serious fiction, there is no such thing as a boy's book or a girl's book, and I think I speak for all serious writers when I plead with librarians, teachers, and parents to stop labeling books that way. First of all, writers *have* to choose one gender or the other for their main characters. There are only two possibilities available, and characters are entitled to only one at a time! Writers do not choose one with the intention of turning their backs on the other half of the human race.

Second, how are the two halves ever to understand each other if they are encouraged to see the world only from the same-sex point of view? And finally, male and female, young people are searching for answers to basic questions about life. There really aren't and shouldn't be two mutually exclusive sets of answers.

Certainly there are many differences among human beings that add spice and more than a little frustration to our lives, but we travel common ground. In the words of eleven-year-old Paul Christakis, whose essay won national recognition from the Children as Peace-makers Foundation, "We are all people who have the same wants for food, shelter, families and fun." It is from the common ground that characters in serious literature, unique individuals all, draw their universality.

The questions young adult characters (and readers) must ask of themselves as they travel the common ground of growing up provide me with intriguing themes to explore. Those that most interest me fall into two categories: how to separate from other people and how to connect with them.

Much attention has been paid, in my own books and others, to the first and often most dramatic work of growing up: separation from parents. My writing for young adults began with my fascination with the problem of girls separating from their mothers. But with my first teenage male main character, Michael Paeglis in *Everything Is Not Enough*, I realized that boys and their fathers engage in the same struggle: To grow up, you have to become more like your same-sex parent. To be an individual, you have to become less like that parent. It's a tricky situation, and often an explosive one. How do you break free without destroying the relationship entirely?

This dilemma forms the basis for a variety of conflicts in my novels. In *Summer Smith Begins*, Summer attempts to separate herself from her highly competitive mother. Stephanie, the narrator of *Just Like Jenny*, struggles against her mother's perfectionism. Three teen-agers in *Missing Pieces* search for themselves in the rubble left behind by parents who are gone, either through death or divorce. In *Daughters of the Law* and *Everything Is Not Enough*, Ruthie and Michael are unfairly asked to make up for their parents' suffering and to live out their unfinished dreams.

"I'd like to say we lived happily ever after," Summer Smith muses, when she and her mother have finally confronted their differences. "But we didn't. Not exactly. We fought and made up and fought and made up again and again. But it was okay. It didn't kill us." Separation is an ongoing process. Necessary, even inevitable, it still poses a threat to the bond between parent and child and to self-esteem on both sides. A tense tug-of-war, it is often the central drama in young adult lives and novels.

There is a second, related, challenge young adults face: as they separate from and reorganize their relationship to the family, they must connect to the greater world. As they discover who they are, they must find out where they fit in.

Movies, TV, radio, magazines, and popular music suggest only limited ways of connecting outside the family: romance and sex, not necessarily in that order. The YA shelves of bookstores are increasingly stocked with fiction proclaiming and extolling the same limits, books similar to (and sometimes reprints of) those that left me hungry years ago.

This is particularly true of media images aimed at young women. There is a nod toward meaningful work as a way of connecting—a briefcase here, an American Express card there—but young women are still shown in an endless hunt for romance, for men who alone can complete and define them.

Certainly, romance and sex are important ways of connecting to the world beyond the families we're raised in; the survival of our species depends on them. And it's neither fair nor honest, it seems to me, to write for adolescents and ignore their sexuality. But I've also tried, in all of my books, to offer a third possibility for connecting outside the family: friendship.

Friendship. Pretty tame stuff, at first glance. But consider the cruelties young people inflict upon one another, from schoolyard bullies to fraternity hazing, from classroom cliques to sorority blackballing. In spite of rosy images of childhood pals, I don't think children know that much about real friendship. It's not their fault. They're new at it. They need practice, and they need role models.

If friendship appears at all in the media, it's usually superficial; friends are the other people in the party scene or at the game, faces in a crowd. And it's temporary—friendship is something to do until romance comes along. Crime and war stories have a curiously heart-warming aspect to them: warriors and crime fighters are allowed to have buddies—caring, supportive friends they can trust with their lives and most intimate thoughts and feelings—as they challenge death together. Under ordinary circumstances, girls compete with each other for guys, guys compete with each other for the fun of it, and romantic love is offered as the only alternative to loneliness.

Adolescence is particularly hard on friendship. Wanting to appear grown up, young people go to extraordinary lengths to mask their vulnerability. That doesn't make for the kind of open communication friendship requires. They also confuse friendship with being liked or being popular. The difference is critical. Being liked may be a result of conformity, of simply not being offensive; popularity has everything to do with quantity, but not necessarily anything to do with quality. People compete for popularity; there can be only one Homecoming Queen. They work together on friendship—yet it gains them no crown, no flowers, no applause. Is it any wonder values are skewed?

The friendships between Murray and Debbie in *Things Are Seldom What They Seem* and among a variety of characters in all of my books endure enormous hardships, undergo great testing strains, but they hold, and they grow. They're important, central to the characters' daily lives. That's my way of letting young people in on the big secret: a real life without friendship is emotional poverty indeed. But friendship doesn't come easily. It takes considerable effort. In making that effort, we grow — and we grow up.

Books, novels, stories, are one way we can reach out to one another without losing face, one way of saying: "We are not alone, not in our fears, not in our hopes, not in our nightmares, and not in our dreams."

A story that does that can be one of the best friends a young reader has. In a turbulent time of changes and choices, the characters in that story *understand* — and they never let you down. They're there whenever you need them; they don't smother you with attention when you don't need them. They never tell a living soul which parts of their story made you cry and which parts helped you to laugh. And they give you the words to explain yourself to yourself, words you can use to create your own life, to recognize your options and to make your choices, to separate as an individual and to reconnect as a member of the human race.

Serious literature for young adults speaks to a specific audience with specific needs. The hope is that teenage readers, be they avid or reluctant, will find that there is a place in books for *their* lives — for "now and here and me" — and a place in their lives for books.

Works Cited

Asher, Sandy. 1980. *Daughters of the Law.* New York: Beaufort.

———. 1987. *Everything Is Not Enough.* New York: Delacorte.

———. 1982. *Just Like Jenny.* New York: Delacorte.

———. 1984. *Missing Pieces.* New York: Delacorte.

———. 1982. *Summer Smith Begins.* New York: Bantam. (Originally *Summer Begins.* 1980. New York: Elsevier/Dutton.

———. 1983. *Things Are Seldom What They Seem.* New York: Delacorte.

Stone, Irving. 1954. *Love Is Eternal.* New York: Doubleday.

Tolstoy, Leo. 1942. *War and Peace.* New York: Simon and Schuster.

Part III
Teaching the
Young Adult Novel

8

Students and Teachers as a Community of Readers

Virginia R. Monseau

Teacher: I was so disappointed in this book. I just kept getting more angry. The more I read it, the more angry I became. I grew up on Pearl Buck, and when you grow up on Pearl Buck you expect . . . "Oh, I can't wait to get into a Chinese book!"

First student: Well, I *liked* this book because I like history. I like reading about old China . . . their customs and things.

Teacher: I like history, too. But, as I said, if you've ever read any Pearl Buck . . . she wrote about China back in the days of the dynasties . . . when they were put out of their homes, and the women were sold into slavery . . .

Second student: Are you saying she had more detail in her books?

Teacher: More detail, right. I cried and laughed with those people, but with *this* book . . .

First student: Yes, but you already know all that. You read about it before. Do you know what I mean? You already knew what was going on back then in China, so this book doesn't measure up. But this is all new to us.

Second student: You were spoiled, in other words.

Teacher: Yes. Yes. I was spoiled for this book. I expected great things of it. (Monseau 131–33)

This dialogue actually took place in a student-teacher discussion of Katherine Paterson's *Rebels of the Heavenly Kingdom*, a novel that depicts the struggle of a secret group of rebels to overthrow the Manchu Dynasty in China in the 1850s. Both the ninth graders and their teacher were reading the book for the first time. Though this was an informal after-school discussion rather than a classroom situation, it clearly indicates the value of student-teacher dialogue about literature — dialogue that encourages critical thinking and promotes examination of individual response to a work. That the examination here was prompted by the students rather than the teacher is significant, for it reveals a source of knowledge that is often ignored in the literature class.

Because literature classrooms are largely teacher-centered, students rarely have the opportunity for an exchange such as this; and even if they did, most would be reluctant to disagree with a teacher's opinion about a book, let alone try to show that teacher where she went wrong. Yet the classroom is the perfect place for this kind of community-building, and the young adult novel is an excellent vehicle for learning how to construct meaning together through student-teacher reaction to literature.

The idea of classroom as community is not new. It has been discussed frequently in relation to the writing class, where students read and respond to each other's work and collaborate on writing tasks. But this idea can just as effectively be applied to the study of literature, which ideally would be integrated with the teaching of writing.

Central to such a literature class is honest discussion — not one-sided, teacher-directed questioning, but true explorations of student and teacher response to a work. James Moffett emphasizes the importance of dialogue as cognitive collaboration:

> One of the unique qualities of dialogue is that the interlocutors build on each other's constructions. A conversation is verbal collaboration. Each party borrows words and phrases and structures from the other, recombines them, adds to them, and elaborates them. . . . Inseparable from this verbal collaboration is the accompanying cognitive collaboration. A conversation is dia-logical — a meeting and fusion of minds even if speakers disagree. (73)

Another look at the earlier conversation among students and teacher reveals the truth of Moffett's words. Because of the teacher's negative reaction to a book they liked, the students were prompted to speculate on the reason for that reaction. The teacher, in return, picked up on the students' use of words like "details" and "spoiled," using them as part of her own explanation of her response. In essence the students were helping her to understand why she reacted as she did to this particular novel. As an adult who brought years of reading experience to the book, she was disappointed that it didn't meet her expectations. As adolescents whose reading experience with historical novels was fairly limited, they found the book exciting and informative. The teacher-student hierarchy was put aside for a while as they all interacted as readers.

Emphasizing the role of language in the development of community, David Bloome tells us:

> Since reading and writing are inherently social processes, one way to think about literacy is in terms of community building. As people use language they signal their membership and participation in a community. Regardless of whether the community is a professional community, a neighborhood, a religious group, a children's peer group, or a classroom, people are expected to use language, including reading and writing, in ways consistent with that community. To do otherwise would signal that one was not a member of that community. (71–72)

Alan Purves goes further by connecting the idea of classroom community with the study of literature:

> Communities are in part held together by shared experiences, shared perceptions, and shared language ... Literature provides a major vehicle for creating communities, as witness the power of religious literature to hold together millions over time and space and language. (18)

The word "shared" is the key to connecting the concept of literature class as community to the response approach that is necessary to its success. In her classic text *Literature As Exploration* Louise Rosenblatt repeatedly reminds us that reading is an active process which aids in the development of social understanding as students and teacher work together to construct meaning in a text. Discussing the role of the teacher, she says:

> A much more wholesome educational situation is created when the teacher is a really live person who has examined his own attitudes and assumptions and who, when appropriate, states them frankly and honestly. He does not have to seem to possess "all the answers," which the students then need only passively absorb. ... The teacher needs to see his own philosophy as only one of the possible approaches to life ... Tolerance of other points of view is extremely important for the teacher—an attitude those who are insecure and fearful of challenges to their authority find most difficult to maintain. (130–31)

The sharing that is essential in a literature classroom community is inherent in a teaching approach that values all responses to a work, invites examination of those responses, and helps students find meaning in the literature they read. Teachers must become listeners and learners, refraining, as Rosenblatt says, from imposing their own ideas and interpretations on their students. This does not mean that teachers must relinquish classroom authority, only that they must share that authority with their students where literature study is concerned.

Robert Probst suggests that in designing a literature course teachers ask themselves this question: "What do we want the literature students to experience and learn in our classes?" If we don't do this, he says, "we assume that the goals of the professional literature student are also the goals of the secondary school literature student, though instinct, common sense, and brief experience in the classroom all tell us that this is not a safe assumption" (6). Most high school students will not become literary scholars, yet literature courses are commonly designed around objective analysis of classic texts. As Rosenblatt says, "In our zeal to give our students the proper literary training, we constantly set them tasks a step beyond their powers, or plunge them into reading that requires the learning of a new language" (1988, 215). She goes on to say that intensive analysis of the classics often forces students to work so hard understanding the language that the work loses its power to affect them. This kind of classroom encourages students to indulge in what Bloome calls "mock participation," where students employ deceitful behavior (72–73). In the literature class this may mean copying the answers to the study questions from a classmate, extracting an "interpretation" from *Cliff's Notes* and presenting it as one's own, or simply parroting information from lecture notes. None of these activities requires a true understanding of a literary work — or even a reading of it.

Contrast this with a classroom where engagement with literature is the primary concern, and where students are not only encouraged but expected to help each other find meaning in what they read. Listen as the same group of students quoted at the beginning of this chapter discusses an Arthurian fantasy — Susan Cooper's *The Grey King* — asking each other questions, trying to clarify mysteries of plot and character, helping each other understand the story. This particular discussion began with the villain, Caradog Prichard, and eventually led to questions about the identity of Guinevere:

First student: I hated him! [Prichard]

Second student: He was the dark ... The Grey King's servant.

Third student: But he didn't know it. He didn't know it until the end.

Second student: When he went mad, yeah, at the end.

First student: I was hoping Bran's mother would come back.

Second student: She was ... she was Guinevere, wasn't she? [Will] was told twice about Guinevere, wasn't he? Once by John Rowlands and once by somebody else? Who was the somebody else? One of the lords?

Third student: What was he told?

Second student: He was told ... about ... how Bran was brought into the future by Guinevere when he was a baby.

First student: It was Aunt Jen, wasn't it?

Second student: I don't know.

Third student: Owen Davies?

First student: No. Aunt Jen was telling Will, right?

Second student: Yeah.

First student: And then ... they had flashbacks while he [Will] was lying there with the dog.

Second student: Yeah, and towards the end John Rowlands told Will again. (Monseau 61−62)

This verbal-cognitive collaboration need not be confined only to students. In the following discussion, two teachers try to help each other make sense of the setting and cycle of events in *The Grey King*. At one point, the first teacher is confused about Guinevere's reasons for bringing her child Bran into the future:

First teacher: Bran was Arthur's son? Did they send him back because of her little affair with Lancelot?

Second teacher: She thought that the son was in danger.

First teacher: Did she feel that Arthur thought maybe it was Lancelot's son and not his, and that's why she came back with him?

Second teacher: [reading from book] "She betrayed her king, her lord and was afraid that he'd cast out his own son as a result." But even so, why would Prichard cause her to rush back [to the past]? Did I miss so much of that scene that I didn't know if that was enough motivation for her to flit back? I couldn't decide if that is just Davies' interpretation, or if that's the reason she went back.

First teacher: I was thinking all the way through that she went back because she just brought the boy, and she intended to go back all along.

Second teacher: OK, so that's just Davies' interpretation?

First teacher: That's what I think. I don't know if that's right or not. (Monseau 122−23)

Just as dialogue worked in these after-school discussions, it can also work in the literature classroom. Essential to success, however, is the establishment of an atmosphere of trust where readers can take chances without fear of being ridiculed for giving a "wrong answer."

And teacher attitude is crucial to the building of this trust. Reading a young adult novel together with students for the first time is a positive step in this direction. Instead of preparing a list of study questions for the students, why not invite them to bring a list of their own questions to class to be used as the basis for small group discussion? Representative questions from each group could then be shared with the entire class. When given the chance, students often come up with questions that relate to the very same material a teacher would cover in discussion. And since the questions emerge from their own curiosity about a work, the answers become much more meaningful to them. Another alternative is to divide the class into pairs of students, assigning each pair to "teach" a particular novel to the rest of the class. (This is where teacher modeling can really become apparent, as students will often "borrow" teaching techniques that they feel were effective.) This approach not only invites students to become responsible for each other's learning, but it also requires them to become extremely familiar with the text as they prepare for discussion, group work, writing assignments, etc. The atmosphere of sharing and trust created in such a classroom puts the students at the center, making them responsible for their own learning. The teacher's role is to create conditions conducive to this learning — to guide, encourage, and learn along with the students.

Because the successful classroom community is dependent upon a response approach to literature, we teachers must realize the importance of engagement to the development of literary appreciation in students. Reader response theorists have long believed that what a reader brings to a work of literature is at least as important as the work itself. In his book *Readings and Feelings* David Bleich says that readers can only view literature objectively by beginning with their subjective response. He points out, "Critical judgments are implicit in emotional reactions ... however, the process of making intellectual judgments is always conscious. ... There is a discoverable causal relationship between the conscious judgment and the earlier subjective reaction" (49).

The comments of the participants in the earlier dialogue show that teachers become as fully engaged with a work of literature as do their students, even when that literature is categorized as a "young adult novel." In the classroom, however, teacher engagement seems to become buried in an avalanche of objective analysis, which threatens to bury student engagement as well. Yet, as these conversations have shown, engagement is an element that is natural and necessary to the understanding of literature. That such an important factor is often overlooked in the literature classroom may be a major cause of student boredom and lack of interest. Perhaps it is a cause of teacher boredom as well.

But boredom need not reign in the literature class. One English teacher, tired of watching his students learn about literature through

Cliff's Notes, took charge of the situation. Having read Rosenblatt and Bleich, he set out to create a response-centered community of interpreters. On the first day of class he told his students:

> [S]tudent opinion is central to the curriculum here. Class participation counts big. I do not have the answers. If you hear me claim I do, you had better call me on this. You have the capacity to understand and argue forcefully about literary texts. You have an enormous amount of creative freedom in your interpretations. But be prepared to persuade us all that what you believe makes sense. (Athanases 46)

To train his students to be active, responsible interpreters, Athanases started out by discussing certain school issues about which the students felt strongly. He then moved to popular culture issues such as music and TV. On the third day he had his students looking at the texts of popular song lyrics as they listened to the songs on tape. By the fourth day they had moved to poetry: "accessible in theme (family problems) and in language (colloquial style)" (46). Athanases was now ready to move into more challenging literature — in this case, Salinger's *The Catcher in the Rye*.

Throughout his "training" he had encouraged controversy among his students, and when he happened to hear two of them arguing in the lunchroom about Holden Caulfield's sanity, he decided to use that as the basis for classroom discussion. Inviting the class to take sides, he presided over (but did not take a stand in) a debate that lasted three days. Students were expected to be clear and persuasive, supporting their claims convincingly. When the debate ended because of time constraints, some students were still dissatisfied that they hadn't been able to present all of their evidence. Reporting on the success of his venture, Athanases says, "Once the training and prodding and preparation have taken place, we need to relinquish some of the teacher control over discussion and to allow students to shape much of the meaning-making talk about literature" (48).

To create a student-centered literature class where the students are fully engaged with what they read requires carefully chosen selections, and this is where the young adult novel can play an important role. Bleich points out that adolescents are intensely preoccupied with themselves — physically, psychologically, and socially — and that teachers can make conscious use of this preoccupation (17–18). In creating an analogy between reading and playing a musical instrument, Rosenblatt observes that "in the literary reading, even the keyboard on which the performer plays is himself" (*Reader, Text, Poem* 14). These two statements make a powerful connection among transactional reading theory, young adult literature, and teaching. If adolescent readers are so preoccupied with themselves, and if they are both player and instrument, as Rosenblatt suggests, how much more intense is their reading experience with a work of young adult fiction? How much more potential exists for a meaningful learning experience? The reading of young adult novels can help students become equals (if not experts) in the literature class, making the idea of community possible. Yet the overall reaction of teachers to using young adult novels has been dubious at best. Some feel that these works are too simple and that high school students should read mature works of adult fiction. Others think that such novels should be used only in developmental classes. Still others believe that these novels speak only to the adolescent and do not address universal literary themes. (See Hipple's chapter in this volume for an extended discussion of universality in young adult novels.)

G. Melvin Hipps makes an important point about teachers who have been willing to use adolescent literature in their slow or average classes but have steadfastly rejected it for advanced students:

> What we often forget is that bright students are not necessarily more advanced socially or emotionally than other students their age. ...
> We also forget sometimes that conflicts that seem trivial or inconsequential to us are of earth-shaking importance to young people. Bright students, who may have more capacity for enjoying subtle vicarious experiences than slow ones do, may still have great difficulty becoming involved with the aging, impotent, cynical characters of Hemingway or Fitzgerald. (46−47)

G. Robert Carlsen makes a similar point: "Adults do not seem to realize that teenagers are still growing and changing in their literary tastes just as in their physical bodies," he says. "They assume that the teenager is ready to move into *great* literature. Nothing is further from the truth" (33).

In all fairness to teachers, however, skepticism about the literary value of young adult books may not be the only reason for their reluctance to incorporate them into the curriculum. Censorship fears are also very real. In discussing the young adult novel we must remember that many of the so-called "classics" have suffered the slings and arrows of the censors over the years. The most recent notable example is Salinger's *The Catcher in the Rye*, but history shows innumerable instances of attempts to remove Shakespeare and other literary masters from library shelves. Censorship concerns will always be a factor in book selection, but they must not turn well-meaning teachers away from the relatively new genre of young adult literature. It's important that we teachers come out from behind the protective wall of the classics and risk making some literary judgments of our own about the books we will use in the classroom, keeping the needs and interests of our students in mind. Since engagement is the first step toward literary appreciation, it's essential that we give our students literature in which they can become involved, if we hope to create an active literature classroom community.

In selecting books for our students to read as part of their literary community, it might be useful to give some thought to adolescent readers and what they expect of a literary work. Walker Gibson contends that there are two different readers distinguishable in every literary experience:

> First, there is the "real" individual upon whose crossed knee rests the open volume, and whose personality is as complex as any dead poet's. Second, there is the fictitious reader—I shall call him the "mock reader"—whose mask and costume the individual takes on in order to experience the language. (2)

Gibson feels that the term "mock reader" may be useful in recognizing reader discrimination and in providing a way to explain what we mean by a good or bad book. "A bad book," he says, "is a book in whose mock reader we discover a person we refuse to become, a mask we refuse to put on, a role we will not play" (5).

Keeping Gibson's idea in mind, we might ask ourselves some questions: How seriously do we take our students' evaluations of the literature they read in school? If they judge a book as "boring," can we assume that they are intellectually inferior or unable to appreciate good literature? If their opinion of a work differs sharply from our own, can we simply dismiss their view as immature or lacking in knowledge? If we accept Gibson's concept of the "mock reader," then it's natural to expect and accept reader discrimination, regardless of that reader's age or literary sophistication. The problem arises when a teacher must decide what to do about this discrimination, and this is where the classroom community works nicely. Instead of viewing student disagreement as hostile response, teachers might begin by looking at the reader's tendency to evaluate literature as a natural inclination which should be respected and capitalized upon. If a teacher feels that a book is worthwhile but a student considers it boring, the next step might be to examine the criteria each is using and the personal experience on which these criteria are based. This kind of examination might be done first in writing, as in a journal response, then in discussion, promoting both private and public exploration of how and why readers find meaning in a text. In this way, examining evaluative criteria can become an important part of literature study, as both students and teachers learn to trust each other and discover the "mock reader" in themselves.

Discussion of teaching approach in the communal literature class might also include the potential of the student reader as critic. Literature teachers work so hard to impart their literary knowledge to their students, yet it seldom occurs to them to capitalize on the knowledge those students may already possess. As one teacher pointed out, "We teach criticism of works we were taught to criticize in college, we say the same things our professors said, and we don't respond on our own level, nor do we allow our students to respond" (Monseau 184). Perhaps part of the reason we don't allow our students to respond on their own level is because we don't attach much importance to what they have to say. They don't usually talk directly about allusion, imagery, or symbolism; they want to discuss the plot, the characters' actions, and what it all means to them. Yet this kind of personal response is seldom valued in the classroom, where the focus is objective analysis. But if this subjective response is the root of the objectivity teachers seek, as Bleich and others say it is, then student readers do have a built-in critical resource that needs to be tapped and used, not stifled and ignored. Again we can listen as two students talk about the criteria they use to evaluate books.

First student: I generally base it on what I think of the characters, basically, and how they're built up. If you can tie yourself in with one character and relate to that person, it helps you become involved in the book.

Second student: Then again, it can be just the opposite. If it's someone that you have nothing in common with, you feel that you're learning something.

First student: It's like a magnet—opposite ends pulling in the same direction.

Second student: Yeah, telling you about something you don't know. Just like ... teen books about girls. They're all the same ... because you relate with them so much that you know what's going on, and most of them just tell you things you already know. Just ... a girl falls in love with a guy who's in a different crowd, and at the end she gets him, and that's all it is. (Monseau 42–43)

The students we met at the beginning of this chapter further discussed their reaction to Paterson's *Rebels of the Heavenly Kingdom*, revealing a sense of point of view, characterization, and irony:

First student: I learned something from this book. I learned that Chinese women have to get their arches broken. That made my feet hurt every time I read about it. It was a good book. I liked the idea of the whole thing—the Rebels being Crusaders and all.

Second student: It reminded me of ... cults.

First student: I thought they were brainwashing—doing something they shouldn't do.

Third student: This was like a book my brother would read. It's just ... I don't get into this war stuff ... this fighting with the Rebels. This book didn't invite you in too well. I thought it kept you ... like an outsider. You were only seeing what was going on. You weren't really there.

First student: In other words, it wasn't first-person narration.

Third student: I don't think she [Paterson] gave them much personality, as far as each character. I just don't think you got a chance to really know them.

Second student: I thought that Wang Lee was a good character. He was a peasant before, like his dad, and at the end he became a peasant again. What he was before, he ended up being the same thing, even though he fought with the Rebels.

First student: They reminded me of unmilitary geniuses.

Second student: The leaders of the Heavenly Kingdom were corrupt. Everybody wants more power. It's like in the eleven and twelve hundreds ... even the Church. They were fighting to see who had more power.

First student: What really bothered me was those people are supposed to be heavenly, and they're all yelling "Destroy!" "Destroy!" People use God's name ... they abuse religion so that they have an excuse for killing.

Second student: History has been shaped by war.

Third student: I have to reread this book. I can see that I missed a lot of things. From what I read, it's not my type, but you guys said a lot of things I didn't realize were in the book. (Monseau 49–50)

As these discussions illustrate, student readers do have a built-in critical resource—their subjective response. Though they approach elements like plot, theme, characterization, and irony indirectly, it's apparent that they have developed a certain critical judgment in themselves over the years as readers—and they don't even realize that it's there. What a wonderful opportunity the communal literature class affords to help students discover this ability in themselves.

The benefits of creating a literature classroom community are apparent. Perhaps the most significant of these is the dialogue that takes place among students and teachers, making teaching and learning an interactive process. Here we can go back to Moffett's idea of dialogue as verbal and cognitive collaboration. Moffett contends that thinking is "soliloquizing" and claims that "conversational dialogue exerts the most powerful and direct influence on the content and forms of soliloquy" (70, 72).

In relation to students, teachers, and literature, we can look at this dialogic interaction in two ways, using James Britton's concept of participant/spectator. According to Britton, the language of participation is language to get things done — informing, instructing, persuading, explaining. The language of spectatorship, on the other hand, is language from which we derive pleasure and enjoyment — storytelling, gossiping, day-dreaming aloud, reading fiction (122).

Student-teacher dialogue about literature is a participatory activity, establishing communication and fostering thinking on both sides. It is language to get things done. Students realize that they are being taken seriously by their teachers and that their input is welcome. Teachers realize that they can learn from students and possibly improve their teaching as a result. The thinking of both students and teachers can be altered by what each has to say.

Seeing the benefits of this kind of student-teacher interaction, then, we can go a step further and speculate on its value for the study of the young adult novel. Wolfgang Iser has said that "the manner in which the reader experiences the text will reflect his own disposition, and in this respect the literary text acts as a kind of mirror . . ." (56). In a small group of student readers the same mirror can reflect five or six different images, creating a potentially powerful learning situation, especially when that mirror is a young adult novel. Dialogue about this literature allows students and teachers to be both participants and spectators. On the one hand, they are taking an active part in a teaching/learning situation; on the other hand, they are contemplating their experiences with the literature, enjoying them, and perhaps reconstructing them as well.

The evidence indicates that a combination of responsive dialogue and young adult literature is essential to the successful creation of a classroom community in the secondary school; but curricular constraints, censorship worries, grading concerns, and accountability are real obstacles to the ideal. Though these obstacles can be dealt with and overcome, it takes unwavering conviction and commitment on the part of everyone involved. But if the discussions presented here are any indication, there is great potential for the use of responsive dialogue and the young adult novel in the classroom. While the dialogue exerts a powerful influence on thinking, the literature gives students an opportunity to exercise and develop their critical judgment through subjective response. All of these factors, combined with a view of teaching and learning as a back-and-forth process among students and teachers, lend even more significance to Moffett's statement that "interaction is a more important learning process than imitation, whatever the age of the learner" (72).

It seems appropriate to end the way we began, with the voices of students and teachers. This particular discussion focused on possible ways of changing content and method in the high school literature course.

First student: I like to talk to other people about what I read. Sometimes I pick up things I missed before. Then I go back and read over that part.

Second student: Yeah, you can find out what other people think about it. And like he said, if you missed anything, they might have spotted it.

First teacher: Wouldn't it be nice if you could do this and not be graded by tests?

Both students: Yeah!

First teacher: I suppose you could find a half dozen or eight adolescent novels to cover the course of the year ... and get writing assignments out of them, do some composition along the way ... and find some research work to do ...

Second teacher: But I have to spend eighteen weeks on grammar. I don't have any choice. My curriculum says I spend eighteen weeks on grammar.

First teacher: But we can *change* the curriculum. We can change whatever we want. We've done it periodically over the last few years anyhow. Wouldn't it be great to say, "All right, we've got nine months of school. We're going to read ... fourteen books. Go! Get done. Come back and discuss them, write about them, or whatever." Wouldn't that be ideal? Wouldn't that be great?

Second student: Yeah. Some people do. I think some people do that. Why couldn't we? (Monseau 138–39).

Works Cited

Athanases, Steven. "Developing a Classroom Community of Interpreters." *English Journal* 77.1 (Jan. 1988): 45–48.

Bleich, David. 1975. *Readings and Feelings: An Introduction to Subjective Criticism*. Urbana: NCTE.

Bloome, David. "Building Literacy and the Classroom Community." *Theory into Practice* 25.2 (Spring 1986): 71–76.

Britton, James. 1970. *Language and Learning*. Middlesex, England: Penguin Press.

Carlsen, G. Robert. 1980. *Books and the Teenage Reader.* 2nd rev. ed. New York: Bantam.

Cooper, Susan. *The Grey King.* New York: Macmillan, 1975.

Gibson, Walker. 1980. "Authors, Speakers, Readers, and Mock Readers." In *Reader-Response Criticism: From Formalism to Post-Structuralism.* Ed. Jane P. Tompkins. Baltimore: Johns Hopkins University Press.

Hipps, G. Melvin. 1973. "Adolescent Literature: Once More to the Defense." *Virginia English Bulletin* 23 (Spring): 44–50.

Iser, Wolfgang. 1980. "The Reading Process: A Phenomenological Approach." In *Reader-Response Criticism: From Formalism to Post-Structuralism.* Ed. Jane P. Tompkins. Baltimore: Johns Hopkins University Press.

Moffett, James. 1968. *Teaching the Universe of Discourse.* Boston: Houghton Mifflin.

Monseau, Virginia Ricci. 1986. *Young Adult Literature and Reader Response: A Descriptive Study of Students and Teachers.* Diss. University of Michigan. Ann Arbor: UMI.

Paterson, Katherine. *Rebels of the Heavenly Kingdom.* New York: Avon, 1983.

Probst, Robert E. 1988. *Response and Analysis: Teaching Literature in Junior and Senior High School.* Portsmouth, NH: Boynton/Cook.

Purves, Alan C. 1984. "Teaching Literature as an Intellectual Activity." *ADE Bulletin* 78 (Summer): 17–19.

Rosenblatt, Louise M. 1988. *Literature As Exploration.* New York: Modern Language Association.

———. 1978. *The Reader, the Text, the Poem: The Transactional Theory of the Literary Work.* Carbondale: Southern Illinois University Press.

9

Young Adult Novels in the Traditional Literature Class

Gary M. Salvner

We teachers have lots of explanations for what we do in our classrooms. We also have explanations for what we don't do. Given the bureaucracy of American mass public education and the long-established rituals through which such education is practiced, it is not hard to find explanations, even though they are more often based on our observations about schools themselves than on our understanding of how learning occurs.

What explanations do we offer for not using more young adult novels in our classrooms? Perhaps some of them do reflect reasoned thought. Young adult literature, after all, is still, as Robert Carlsen has observed, in its own adolescence as a genre (28). Since Dora V. Smith first split adolescent from children's literature nearly fifty years ago, we have been watching the growth of adolescent literature somewhat as parents observe a child's growth—curious about each new development, hopeful as a result of certain marked accomplishments, yet suspicious as to whether this youngster will ever fully grow up and become something. Maybe we don't use young adult novels because we are still not convinced that they have grown up and become something worthy of our students' attention.

Yet some of our explanations have little to do with a reasoned consideration of the issue. Many teachers, for example, have been convinced for at least a decade of the quality of young adult novels and of the appeal they have among adolescents, and yet those teachers still don't find ways to incorporate such works into their literature classes. Arthur Applebee's most recent study of high school literature programs confirms what we all suspect—what we have students read in our literature classes is what we have always had them read: a curiously formed but exceedingly durable "canon" of great works which contains very little minority or women's literature and relatively little of anything written in this century. The ten most frequently taught literary works in our classrooms today, notes Applebee, are nearly identical to the ten listed nearly thirty years ago in another national study of literature classroom practices (cited in "Teaching Literature in High School" 4–5). The more the world changes, the more our literature classes remain the same. And reasoned thought, in the end, has very little to do with it.

Why, then, are so few young adult novels found in English classrooms? Why, if we know and believe that adolescents will read young adult novels and if we recognize that examples of such works can be found which have substantial literary merit and quality, do we not make greater use of them? I know why. You know why, too. Time.

Curious quantity, time. Einstein taught us about its relativity, and our schools teach us about its preciousness. We all know that the customary schedules under which our secondary schools operate leave precious little time for teaching. Our usual 180-plus school days, carved down into 45- or 50-minute sessions with each group of students (minus interruptions for such priorities as office announcements, pep assemblies, and competency testing) come to look like moments when we teach. Parcel out those moments to address the conscientious English teacher's various responsibilities for composition instruction, language study, media, speech, and literature coursework, and they shrink further. Ask any English teacher why he or she doesn't do more. You'll most likely hear the answer "Time."

Time harrassess most English teachers, keeping us from all we know we should be doing and all we want to do. From September to June we all bustle about like Alice's White Rabbit, checking our watches and muttering, "I'm late!"

If limited time is our curse, then surely the most vivid reminders of that curse are those curious and altogether maddening school documents we call curriculum guides. "I might be able to elicit more and better student response to their reading if only the curriculum guide allowed more time for it." "There might be time for a young adult novel or two if only the literature course of study didn't contain all those objectives which seem to almost demand that we teach the classics."

The irony in all of this is that in most school districts, it is the teachers who create curricula—create them badly, perhaps, but still create them. Few district school boards dictate what will be taught and when. Teachers do that, usually by a process of cumulative compromise in curriculum meetings: you go along with *Romeo and Juliet* (which I really love to teach), and I'll agree to your *The Scarlet Letter* (even though I'm as uninspired by Hawthorne as my students are). You'd think we were pork barrel politicians. Look at curriculum guides sometime. Most are doorstop size, almost arbitrary, and filled with our own biases and compromises. The time that we don't have enough of is so precious because we have filled it (or allowed it to be filled) with matters which may have limited connection to what we know to be in our students' best interests.

If we can make overweight and out-of-balance curriculum guides, then certainly we can remake them. All of us need to become more insistent about our professional judgments; and if they include teaching Cormier's *The Chocolate War* instead of *Lord of the Flies* as an examination of humans' capacity to do evil, or Cynthia Voigt's *Homecoming* as a study of the journey motif in literature rather than Twain's *Huckleberry Finn*, then we must see that decisions to include these books get made. We are often reminded by our students that they will read if we work with them to find literature to which they can easily relate. We can no longer neglect those students by shaping our curricula around outmoded assumptions. Demands for stressing basic skills, along with testing pressures and state mandates, may be increasingly restricting our ability to make professional judgments, but we have not yet reached the point of mandated curricula. If young adult novels make sense to you, then find a way, during the next curriculum revision, to see that they become included in those guides.

In the meantime, of course, there is still much we can do to make better use of young adult novels in our classes ... which returns us to a consideration of time and how we use it. Perhaps time is preciously short in schools, but nearly all of us know from our own days in school (and, if we are honest, from our own teaching experiences) that time is also wasted. Time isn't only a fixed, quantitatively measured commodity; like teaching itself, it is qualitative as well.

As teachers of literature, then, our question might be, "How can we improve the quality of our classroom time?" As Thoreau went into the woods to "preserve the nick of time," how might we improve those moments we share with our students? The answer might not be in changing the objectives we have named for ourselves and our students in our curriculum guides; it might instead be in enriching the ways in which we address those objectives.

An example is in order. You're teaching a ninth grade literature class, and your curriculum includes instruction in those elements of narrative which so often occupy a first systematic course in literature: plot, character, setting, point of view, theme, and even (Lord help you) symbol, style, and figurative language. Conveniently, your literature anthology offers selections which highlight each of those elements: short stories by Poe and O. Henry, for example, and poems by Dickinson and Giovanni. You worry a bit about whether your students will enjoy Dickinson or, in the age of *The Terminator* and *Fatal Attraction*, still be surprised by O. Henry, but even more than that, you worry that by the time you've introduced each of those elements and read several illustrative examples of literature for each, Thanksgiving (or even year's end) will be upon you, and you'll already be racing toward the close of the first semester.

And so you head for the department storage room, looking for an alternative. On a shelf are several dozen copies of Natalie Babbitt's *Tuck Everlasting*, a slim little novel of 139 pages — hardly even a young adult novel (its protagonist is only ten, after all), and yet a book you remember being strangely moved by and one described by Jean Stafford in *The New Yorker*, you notice on the back cover, as a "fearsome and beautifully written book that can't be put down or forgotten."

Remembering the book, you realize how it will serve perfectly as a model of most of what you'd hope to get students to notice about various literary elements, and even more than that, about how those elements work together to create effect and engage readers. You recall the book's vividly drawn characters — characters like Angus, Mae, Miles, and Jesse Tuck, members of a family accidentally blessed (or perhaps cursed) with immortality, each member having a noticeably different reaction to that occurrence; like Winnie Foster, the protagonist, a girl who at ten already wants to do "something that would make some kind of difference in the world" (15); and like the mysterious and malevolent Man in the Yellow Suit, who seeks to use the secret of immortality for his own gain.

You also recall the vividness of the settings of *Tuck Everlasting*: the small town of Tree Gap and the Foster woods just outside of town; the small cabin where the Tuck family lives and the pond adjoining it; even the jail where Mae Tuck is imprisoned. You remember the almost casual reference to dates in the book's epilogue, which serves to set this book about timelessness and immortality in a certain (and revealing) time. Certainly, this brief novel reveals much about how setting is used deftly in a good story.

You also recall the suspense in the book (Will the Tucks' secret be preserved? Will Winnie join them as an immortal?), which helps to drive the plot forward, and you remember the brief references to a toad Winnie becomes enamored of and which, in a certain sense, foreshadows some of the changes which occur in Winnie. Of course, you can't forget the thematic implications of this slim novel — the far from simple explorations of the connections of death to life, the elegantly simple explication of the meaning of love in the attitudes of Winnie and the Tucks toward one another, even the exhilaration of escape and adventure which is thematically explored both in Winnie's wishes and in Jesse's actions.

After a brief rereading, you also discover *Tuck Everlasting*'s crafts-manship. Already in the prologue, for example, mystery and tension are established as Babbitt describes the early August days of the book's opening as those "strange and breathless days, the dog days, when people are led to do things they are sure to be sorry for after" (3). You also rediscover the novel's almost casual use of symbols, which even your hesitant ninth graders will undoubtedly understand and appreciate: the life force of water, not only in the "fountain of youth" discovered by the Tucks, but also in Angus Tuck's claim, "The pond's got answers" (59) as he takes Winnie out in a boat to explain his family's dilemma to her and in the renewing rain which begins falling just as Mae Tuck escapes from jail. You notice the wheels which appear in the book as symbols of the life cycle: the ferris wheel in the prologue, Angus Tuck's comment to Winnie that "everything's a wheel, turning and turning, never stopping" (62), even in the motions of Mae as she strikes out at the Man in the Yellow Suit to protect Winnie — "Her strong arms swung the shotgun round her head, like a wheel" (100).

This brief reminiscence about a slim novel reminds you that many of your course objectives about literary elements and devices can be achieved quickly and coherently with a slim book which even your reticent ninth graders can read easily in several hours. Using a book like *Tuck Everlasting* first to engage students in shared discussions of their feelings about what they have read and then to illustrate various literary elements allows you to quickly dispense with a whole fistful of objectives and still leaves time for other reading which students them-selves might choose. The literary terminology has been introduced and illustrated, and it's still only late September, not late December.

Other young adult novels might serve equally well for introducing students to what literature is and how it creates its impact and effect. Particularly useful might be those novels which have vivid characters and settings, and illustrate the interdependence of character and place in creating dramatic situations. Katherine Paterson, for example, is a master at characterization, creating such vivid portraits that characters such as Jess Aarons and Leslie Burke in *Bridge to Terabithia*, Gilly Hopkins, William Ernest Teague, and Maime Trotter in *The Great Gilly Hopkins*, and even Jiro in *The Master Puppeteer* (a book which takes place in feudal Japan) remain in one's thoughts long after the books have been read. Sue Ellen Bridgers' characters are also vividly drawn: Stella Willis and her family in *Home Before Dark*, Casey Flanagan and Dwayne Pickens in *All Together Now*, and Rob Dickson and his fatherly Uncle Fairlee and reclusive Aunt Coralee in *Permanent Connections*. So are those in many of Virginia Hamilton's books: Junior Brown in *The Planet of Junior Brown*, for example, and Teresa and Dabney Pratt in *Sweet Whispers, Brother Rush*.

Settings are equally memorable in many young adult novels. Students might learn a great deal about how effective settings are used in fiction to influence characters and affect events by examining the Great Smoky Mountain setting of Vera and Bill Cleaver's *Where the Lilies Bloom*, Kingcome Inlet on the Pacific coast of British Columbia in Margaret Craven's *I Heard the Owl Call My Name*, the Chesapeake Bay area of Voigt's Tillerman family cycle and of Katherine Paterson's *Jacob Have I Loved*, the Appalachian coal country of eastern Kentucky in Jenny Davis's *Good-bye and Keep Cold*, and even the fantasy world of Pern in Anne McCaffrey's *Dragonsong* and other dragon books.

Some adolescent (and even children's) books which depict basic human struggles which easily carry thematic and symbolic elements might also illustrate the ways in which literature is crafted to create certain effects. Madeleine L'Engle's *A Wrinkle in Time*, for example, a book whose simple messages about the nature of good and evil are made dramatic and complex through lively characters such as Meg and Charles Wallace Murry and through highly imaginative settings, might serve such a purpose well. So might books such as Lloyd Alexander's *Westmark*, a book whose complexity lies not in situation or event, but in the moral values placed upon those events as Theo seeks both to survive and to do what is right and finds that the two impulses are sometimes in conflict.

In *The Pigman*, Paul Zindel's use of different points of view provides not only a lively lesson on the importance of the narrator to a story, but also raises questions about reliability in point of view. Point of view is also crucial to the impact of Bruce Brooks' *The Moves Make the Man*, a story which reveals at least as much about its narrator, black teenager Jerome Foxworthy, as it does about the person he is supposedly writing about, his white friend Bix Rivers.

Time, then, can be saved in the literature class by replacing works in the literature anthology or other classics with more easily accessible and appealing young adult novels, rather than by attempting to add those works to an already extensive reading list. Books which engage adolescents and employ the rich array of literary devices found in more extended adult works will serve well as introductions to literary conventions and terminology.

Another common means for organizing literature study in the secondary school is historically, and one of our most common teaching objectives is to use literature to give students, through their reading, a history of the their own and others' cultures. By eleventh grade, history and chronology become a dominant means for organizing literary study. The eleventh grade American literature class and the twelfth grade study of English literature are as familiar to us as teachers as they were to us as students.

It would seem that adolescent literature has little place in such surveys, since young adult novels occupy only the most recent moments of our literary history and since none of them has yet attained the classic status of the masterpieces which fill most of the anthologies published today. Still, the range of subject matters of young adult books is so broad that there are titles which do fit nicely into such study.

Students reading the literature of various periods of our literary history are often limited in their appreciation because they know so little of the cultural and political histories surrounding those works. Chaucer, for example, is challenging to teach not only because of the language differences, but also because the political tensions between church and state during the Medieval Period and the customs and beliefs of the times are unknown to students and not likely to be appreciated on the basis of brief explanatory notes embedded in a text.

Malcolm Bosse's *Captives of Time*, however, might make that era better known to students. Set in the fourteenth century, Bosse's novel tells the story of Anne Valens and her mute younger brother, Niklas, who return home to see their parents being tortured and then killed by marauding soldiers and the mill that has provided their family's livelihood being pillaged. For their survival they set off to find their Uncle Albrecht in a distant town, and after an extraordinarily difficult journey, locate him and arrange to stay with him.

Albrecht is an ironworker and armorer, but his real obsession is to build a reliable clock. As Anne first observes his efforts and then assists him, she slowly begins to realize that without a reliable means for measuring time, the people of her age are captives to it. She also comes to understand the struggle between church and state about who will own the clocks when and if they are made. Those who control the timepieces control time itself, and thus control all those who will be regulated by its measurements.

Captives of Time is a violent book, containing graphic depictions of rape and murder as well as a chilling portrayal of the effects of the plague on a fourteenth century village. Yet it is a book of courage and determination as Anne overcomes one crisis after another to assert control over her own life. Most of all, *Captives of Time* is a memorable account of medieval life, one which dramatizes that period vividly for students.

Other literary periods are also captured effectively in young adult novels. Leon Garfield brings the eighteenth century to life in *Smith*, a novel about a London street urchin. Puritan America is dramatized in Elizabeth George Speare's *The Witch of Blackbird Pond*, and nineteenth century America comes to life in Joan Blos' fictional *A Gathering of Days: A New England Girl's Journal 1830–1832*. The conflicts between

Native Americans and white settlers during America's westward expansion are depicted in Conrad Richter's *A Light in the Forest*, and the evils of slavery become more fully understood upon reading Paula Fox's *The Slave Dancer*.

Many of the periods of literary history which we have students study, particularly those occupying the nineteenth and twentieth centuries, are periods marked by war, and the wars of our recent experience are dramatized amply in young adult novels. The American Revolution, for example, that period often associated in literature anthologies with the treatises of Franklin, Jefferson, and Thomas Paine, might be enriched with the reading of Esther Forbes' classic *Johnny Tremain* or with the more somber and perhaps more thought-provoking account Howard Fast gives of the beginning of the Revolution in his novel *April Morning*, about a young boy who loses his father on the green at Lexington.

Our Civil War, that struggle for national identity, brings to mind the anthologized works of Lincoln, Frederick Douglas, and even Twain and Sidney Lanier. It is a conflict often examined in the secondary literature class with Crane's classic *The Red Badge of Courage*, a work which still achieves intensity but which has come to seem in some ways as impenetrable as Shakespeare to many adolescents. Rather than reading literature of the Civil War period, perhaps students might be enriched by reading about the period in young adult novels such as Harold Keith's *Rifles for Watie* or in the 1987 Newbery Award-winning *Lincoln: A Photobiography* by Russell Freedman, an easy-to-read but moving portrait of a President caught in the struggles and dilemmas of war.

An entire unit, either historical or thematic, might be devised around the young adult novels of the Second World War, perhaps with individual students or groups reading separate titles and using those readings to compile both information and impressions of that global struggle. Students might read James Forman's nearly forgotten but stunningly moving *Ceremony of Innocence*, a novel based on historical accounts of a courageous but futile attempt by Munich students to publish an underground newspaper calling for the overthrow of Hitler's Third Reich. To extend students' understanding of the Holocaust beyond the instruction which might accompany the reading of Anne Frank's diary, students might read Aranka Siegal's autobiographical *Upon the Head of the Goat*, the story of the experiences leading up to Siegal's family being taken to a concentration camp, or Marietta Moskin's *I Am Rosemarie*, also an autobiographical novel about life in a concentration camp.

Other facets of World War II are depicted in John Hersey's famous *Hiroshima*, about the dropping of the first atomic bomb (the 1986 edition contains an account of Hersey returning to Japan forty years later to learn of the bomb's continuing effects); in Theodore Taylor's

The Cay, a novel of racial acceptance which opens on the Caribbean island of Curacao in 1945 as German submarines have crossed the Atlantic to cripple the oil refineries there; in Fred Uhlman's *Reunion*, which tells how a childhood friendship between two German boys is destroyed by the War; and in Jeanne Wakatsuki Huston and James D. Huston's *Farewell to Manzanar*, about the government-ordered internment of orientals living in the United States during the war.

Though few young adult novels treat the wars of our own generation, there are several that illuminate those times of conflict. Walter Dean Myers' *Fallen Angels* examines the Vietnam War, while Sue Ellen Bridgers' *All Together Now* tells the story of Casey Flanagan, who comes to a small southern town to spend the summer with her grandparents because her father is "off in Korea fighting his second war" (4). Several times during the events of the novel, Casey reflects upon the impact of that "unofficial war" on herself and on those around her, and the result is that the novel provides a portrait of those left behind during a war.

Certainly, then, there are young adult novels which fit the curricular patterns of many traditional literature classes—by illustrating various literary devices and elements, for example, or by extending students' awareness of various important periods in literary history (or by examining various themes which are commonly found in literature, as discussed in Ted Hipple's chapter in this book). Furthermore, young adult novels meet those needs in a way which may save the teacher time—both because the books are often relatively brief and because their closeness in experience and insight to teenagers today suggests that they might be read with less resistance and more efficiency.

Something more needs to be said about these advantages of economy and effectiveness, for if change is ever to come to our English classes, it must be built upon a re-evaluation of our aims in the light of such benefits. Certainly an obvious advantage young adult novels have in secondary English classes is that, on the average, they are short enough to be read in a relatively brief time period. In this case length is both a function of the number of pages in a work (and young adult novels typically have fewer pages than adult works) and of difficulty, since the challenges of a text will influence greatly the time required to read it.

In his comments about reading instruction in general, Frank Smith discusses this factor of difficulty, suggesting that we have typically tried to coax students into becoming readers by giving them materials that are too difficult for them to comprehend. The result, says Smith, is that reading for them becomes "nonsense," and young readers deal with that nonsense by becoming bored or by giving up (90).

The same principle, certainly, applies to the reading of literature. If we are seeking to have students understand the elements of fiction, it makes no sense to use as models of those elements a work so impenetrable or imposing that students aren't able to even perceive the model. Just as Smith says we help students learn to read by keeping reading simple and manageable, so we help students understand the way literature works by using selections which are accessible to them. And, because of their economy and relatively simple structures, young adult novels are accessible.

But there is a second reason why young adult novels might be particularly effective as a means of teaching about literature, and that reason has to do with the relationship between such texts and many adolescents. One of the problems which plagues many literature classes is that of authority, in which students see themselves as subservient to, and controlled by, both the text being read and the teacher who chooses the text and directs the reading. Of course, the very nature of the teacher's role creates part of the problem, and teachers in all subjects struggle with the authority vested in their positions. In discussing the writing class, for example, James Moffett describes how authority eventually interferes with teaching:

> Although younger children often want to write to a "significant adult," on whom they are willing to be frankly dependent, adolescents almost always find the teacher entirely too significant. He is at once a parental substitute, civic authority, and the wielder of marks. Any one of these roles would be potent enough to distort the writer-audience relationship; all together, they cause the student to misuse the feedback in ways that severely limit his learning to write. (193)

If we agree with Rosenblatt that "no one else can read a literary work for us" (278), or with Purves, Rogers, and Soter that "the mind as it meets the book ... is the center of a curriculum in literature" (15), then it is easy to see why authority such as the kind described by Moffett can undermine the literature class. Certainly, as teachers, we inherently hold an authority which cannot be (and perhaps should not totally be) neutralized. Inevitably, teachers can and do inhibit student response by imposing their own readings upon the texts being studied.

Yet it isn't always teacher authority that causes the problem. Literary texts themselves also carry authority, particularly when they have been accepted into a recognized canon of great works. How many students would openly challenge Henry James as being tedious (even though many of them find his writing insufferable), or how many would argue with conviction that Melville is trivial because Ahab's obsession with the great white whale seems silly and illogical? (It seemed silly to me when I first waded through *Moby Dick* as an eleventh grader, but I never dared to tell anyone that.)

In discussing the authority of texts, Dennie Palmer Wolf refers to a student who once observed, "What is the point of analyzing the things in the anthology? They already made it into the book, so we know they are supposed to be good; so what are we taking them apart for?" "Deference ...," suggests Wolf herself, "deadens the senses. We cheat literature when we treat works as masterpieces rather than as experiences or questions" (52).

While young adult novels can be vested with as much authority as the classics, there is a chance, at least, that students will not so immediately defer to that authority because their experiences equip them with some knowledge they can use to talk back to those books. Since young adult novels are typically about young adults and their experiences, students inherently hold the authority to say, for example, "Yes, the relationships among the swimming teammates in Chris Crutcher's *Stotan!* are 'true' adolescent friendships. They are like friendships among teens which I know or imagine." Likewise, they might say, "The reaction of sixteen-year-old Anne Cameron to her mother's death in Zibby Oneal's *A Formal Feeling* doesn't ring true to me," even though it may ring true to many other adolescents in the class, and to the teacher.

It remains to make some concluding comments about the methods we use in our literature classrooms, for method is closely related both to the issue of choice I have been discussing and to the matter of time which has initiated many of my claims about young adult novels. Louise Rosenblatt's comments about the importance of the reader to the literary transaction lead her eventually to a discussion of what ought to go on in the literature class. "In the *teaching* of literature, then," she suggests, "we are basically helping our students to learn to perform in response to a text" (279). If young adult novels lend themselves to student performances because of their closeness to adolescent understanding and experience, then what methods will help the teacher to orchestrate student performances?

A number of methods being discussed today capture the spirit of Rosenblatt's performance metaphor. Dennie Wolf, for example, suggests that students be taught to "hold a conversation with a work" as they "make use of their experience to fill out the meaning of a work and to raise questions about it" (53). Virginia Monseau, in her essay in this book, suggests that the classroom become a "community of readers" whose individual conversations with works become shared openly.

In a previous essay, I have claimed that literature games, activities "in which students accept the constraints of an invented world" ("Readers as Performers" 137) and interact with a book within that world, have promise for generating "performed" responses to literature. One such game, for example, might tell students that a character they have read about has become a popular singer and has written an album of songs based on various experiences in the book (songs/poems that the students themselves will then write). Another might propose something as outrageous as characters from various books joining together to form a baseball team and then suggest that the students, as team promoters and managers, prepare a scouting report and baseball cards of team players. Such gamelike scenarios are promising not because they are gimmicks, but because they allow students to inquire about books within familiar contexts — to make connections between the new experiences of a book and elements of their own expertise and background. The juxtaposition of these new experiences with those things they have authority over can create stunning insights. (If you're not convinced of this, try another game: ask students to transfer the key conflicts of a novel into a plan for a video game — which is nothing more than a visual representation of conflict. You may be surprised not only by their ingenuity in doing so, but also by the insightful comments they are able to make afterwards about conflict and plot structure in the novel.)

Regardless of the specific methods we employ, our aim in teaching literature should be for students to avoid falling into the misconception Flannery O'Connor once described about books: "The fact is, people don't know what they are expected to do with a novel, believing, as so many do, that art must be utilitarian, that it must do something, rather than be something" (quoted in Wolf 26–27). Young adult novels help to achieve that aim by keeping our priorities straight. Because they are about adolescents and for adolescents, they put our students at the center of the learning experiences we devise. Because they illustrate for young readers what literature can be (moving them and revealing to them how literature builds knowledge and perspective), they use our time effectively. Time well spent with young adult novels may not eliminate our temptation to say "I'm late!" on occasion, but it will eliminate our anxiety about wasting time with literature that fails to speak to our students.

Works Cited

Alexander, Lloyd. 1981. *Westmark*. New York: Dell.

Babbitt, Natalie. 1975. *Tuck Everlasting*. New York: Farrar, Straus, and Giroux.

Blos, Joan. 1982. *A Gathering of Days: A New England Girl's Journal 1830–1832*. New York: Macmillan.

Bosse, Malcolm. 1987. *Captives of Time*. New York: Dell.

Bridgers, Sue Ellen. 1980. *All Together Now*. New York: Bantam.

———. 1985. *Home Before Dark*. New York: Bantam.

———. 1987. *Permanent Connections*. New York: Harper and Row.

Brooks, Bruce. 1987. *The Moves Make the Man*. New York: Harper and Row.

Carlsen, G. Robert. 1984. "Teaching Literature for the Adolescent: A Historical Perspective." *English Journal* 73.7: 28–30.

Cleaver, Vera, and Bill Cleaver. 1969. *Where the Lilies Bloom.* New York: Signet.

Cormier, Robert. 1974. *The Chocolate War.* New York: Dell.

Craven, Margaret. 1973. *I Heard the Owl Call My Name.* New York: Dell.

Crutcher, Chris. 1986. *Stotan!.* New York: Dell.

Davis, Jenny. 1987. *Good-bye and Keep Cold.* New York: Dell.

Fast, Howard. 1962. *April Morning.* New York: Bantam.

Forbes, Esther. 1969. *Johnny Tremain.* New York: Dell.

Forman, James. 1970. *Ceremony of Innocence.* New York: Dell.

Fox, Paula. 1975. *The Slave Dancer.* New York: Dell.

Freedman, Russell. 1989. *Lincoln: A Photobiography.* New York: Clarion Books.

Garfield, Leon. 1987. *Smith.* New York: Dell.

Hamilton, Virginia. 1971. *The Planet of Junior Brown.* New York: Macmillan.

———. 1982. *Sweet Whispers, Brother Rush.* New York: Avon.

Hersey, John. 1986. *Hiroshima.* New York: Knopf.

Huston, Jeanne Wakatsuki, and James D. Huston. 1973. *Farewell to Manzanar.* Boston: Houghton Mifflin.

Keith, Harold. 1987. *Rifles for Watie.* New York: Harper and Row.

L'Engle, Madeleine. 1962. *A Wrinkle in Time.* New York: Dell.

McCaffrey, Anne. 1976. *Dragonsong.* New York: Bantam.

Moffett, James. 1983. *Teaching the Universe of Discourse.* Boston: Houghton Mifflin.

Moskin, Marietta. 1981. *I Am Rosemarie.* New York: Dell.

Myers, Walter Dean. 1988. *Fallen Angels.* New York: Scholastic.

Oneal, Zibby. 1982. *A Formal Feeling.* New York: Fawcett Juniper.

Paterson, Katherine. 1987. *Bridge to Terabithia.* New York: Harper and Row.

———. 1978. *The Great Gilly Hopkins.* New York: Harper and Row.

———. 1980. *Jacob Have I Loved.* New York: Avon

———. 1975. *The Master Puppeteer.* New York: Avon.

Purves, Alan C., Theresa Rogers, and Anna O. Soter. 1990. *How Porcupines Make Love II.* New York: Longman.

Richter, Conrad. 1953. *The Light in the Forest.* New York: Bantam.

Rosenblatt, Louise. 1988. *Literature as Exploration.* New York: Modern Language Association.

Salvner, Gary M. 1987. "Readers as Performers: The Literature Game." *Children's Literature Quarterly.* 12: 137–39.

Siegal, Aranka. 1983. *Upon the Head of the Goat.* New York: Signet.

Smith, Frank. 1985. *Reading Without Nonsense.* 2nd Edition. New York: Teachers College Press.

Speare, Elizabeth George. 1958. *The Witch of Blackbird Pond.* New York: Dell.

Taylor, Theodore. 1969. *The Cay.* New York: Avon.

"Teaching Literature in High School: 'The More Things Change ...'" In *Council-Grams.* NCTE 52.2 (1989), 4–5.

Uhlman, Fred. 1971. *Reunion.* New York: Farrar, Straus, and Giroux.

Voigt, Cynthia. 1981. *Homecoming.* New York: Fawcett Juniper.

Wolf, Dennie Palmer. 1988. *Reading Reconsidered: Literature and Literacy in the High School.* New York: College Entrance Examination Board.

Zindel, Paul. 1968. *The Pigman.* New York: Dell.

10

The Young Adult Novel Across The Curriculum

Jeanne M. Gerlach

The movement for writing in the content areas, which is also referred to as writing across the curriculum, has become one of the most visible educational concepts and curricular developments in American schooling today. Following the lead of James Britton and his colleagues in the London schools, a number of schools, colleges, and universities in this country have initiated and developed schoolwide writing programs. Part of this initiative has been the recommendation that teachers in all content areas include writing as a part of their courses. Just as we have recently come to appreciate and understand the value of writing across the curriculum, we need to recognize the opportunities for learning offered by reading literature across the curriculum, especially adolescent literature.

Seemingly, the idea that reading literature should be the concern of all secondary educators should be attractive to both English and non-English teachers. Yet, as I talk with teachers and listen to teachers talk among themselves, I am confronted with predominantly negative attitudes concerning the teaching of literature, particularly adolescent literature, in the content areas. There is evidence from these conversations that content teachers don't perceive reading literature to be an important activity in their courses. Many content teachers feel that this responsibility belongs solely to the English department; they argue that they have enough trouble just trying to cover the content of their respective courses. Many believe that the added pressure of teaching literature would only increase their already heavy workloads. In regard to adolescent literature, some think that it is oversimplified and written to accommodate students with low-level reading skills; others see it as

113

a didactic, anti-adult genre that dwells on taboo topics and features only white middle-class protagonists. Some teachers honestly admit that they have no idea what reading literature in the content areas is or should be; and some admit that they have never read an adolescent novel. The fact remains, however, that reading literature can, like writing, enhance content area learning.

Obviously, teachers will need assistance if reading young adult literature in the content areas is to expand. Many teacher preparation programs don't include a literature component for all education majors; course enrollment is usually limited to English education majors. Moreover, while some school systems do provide their faculty with quality inservice programs on literature and the teaching of literature, many do not.

The purpose of this chapter, then, is to determine what secondary content area teachers need to know about the relationship between reading adolescent literature and learning and to suggest ways that English teachers might encourage their colleagues to make use of young adult novels in their classes. While sections of the chapter discuss classroom practice, the emphasis is on providing teachers with a theoretical framework which explains why particular practices and activities are more important than others. Equally important, the theoretical framework is crucial in determining what it is that secondary content area teachers need to know about literature, adolescent literature, the teaching of literature, and the teaching of adolescent literature as a prerequisite to teaching it in the particular content area. This knowledge will provide a rationale for using adolescent literature as learning in all content area classrooms.

Literature and Learning

Literature in the content areas assumes that reading and responding to literature is a meaning making activity and a way of learning content material in all disciplines in the secondary school curriculum. Investigations into the processes of reading and responding to literature have produced evidence that the skills approach to teaching literature is inadequate. Simply put, teaching that emphasizes dates, names, places, histories, and critical analysis is an ineffective way to teach literature (National Assessment of Educational Progress; Petrosky 1970; Purves and Beach). Reading and responding to literature is more than an atomistic process of memorizing facts about a work. Instead, as Sternglass indicates, reading and responding to literature is a powerful instrument for thought which, when unified with composition, encompasses the full range of mental traits that comprise critical thinking. According to Lazere, reading literature helps the readers to unify and make connections in their experiences; to follow an extended line of thought through propositional, thematic, and symbolic development, to engage in mature moral reasoning and to form judgements of quality and taste; to be attuned to skepticism and irony; and to be perceptive of ambiguity and meaning (literal and figurative language, syntactic and structural complexity, etc.). (2)

As Wolfgang Iser tells us, reading literature is more than receiving information from a printed page; it is a way of inventing and discovering knowledge (19). According to Louise Rosenblatt, "Literature makes comprehensible the myriad ways in which human beings meet the infinite possibilities that life offers," (1968, 6). She argues that the reading of literature is distinctive not only because of the content of the text, but because of the readers' approach to it. She has distinguished two kinds of reading approaches, efferent and aesthetic:

> In nonaesthetic [efferent] reading, the reader's attention is focused primarily on what will remain as residue after the reading — the information to be acquired, the logical solution to a problem, the actions to be carried out . . . . In aesthetic reading, in contrast, the reader's primary concern is with what happens during the actual reading event. In aesthetic reading, the reader's attention is centered directly on what he is living through during his relationship with that particular text. [1968, 23; 24; 25]

Rosenblatt notes that there is not a hard-and-fast separation between the efferent and aesthetic stances; rather, she likens the distinction to a continuum, with most reading being a mixture of the efferent and aesthetic. It is where the reader stands on the continuum that determines the extent to which the experience of a particular text will be literary. For example, while a poem might suggest an aesthetic stance and a biology text an efferent stance, a reader could choose to approach the poem efferently and the biology text aesthetically. Thus, most literature can be approached from both efferent and aesthetic stances. The classroom teacher can direct the students' approach according to the task at hand.

While content teachers need to be concerned with both approaches to reading literature, they need to place a high value on aesthetic reading. This is important because it helps readers to personalize the literature and reflect upon the work in light of their past experiences — to discover and make meaning for themselves. The meaning, therefore, does not reside in the text, but in the mind of the individual reader.

The profession has the works of Louise Rosenblatt (*Literature as Exploration*, 1938, 1968 and *The Reader, the Text, the Poem*, 1978), Alan Purves (*How Porcupines Make Love*, 1972) and Arthur Applebee (*The Child's Concept of Story — Ages 2–17*, 1978), to help us understand readers' interactions with and responses to literature. These works tell us that those responses proceed from personal, prior knowledge and must be developmental, self-expressive, and self-concerned before they can be outward looking and self-effacing. In spite of this knowledge, many teachers continue to center their instruction on the ready-made knowledge that literature provides one with. This type of instruction encourages student responses that demonstrate the student's mastery of facts to teacher-given assignments. Robert Probst describes this method of literature teaching:

> If literature is instead the domain in which we develop basic skills, then we may teach it simply as practice material, the exercises in which we teach skills of decoding, using context clues, identifying techniques of characterization, and so on. We are likely to be concerned about measuring progress and about reading levels, and we may plan our teaching around specific skills, probably phrased as behavioral objectives, rather than around intellectual content or some other organizing principle. (1986, 60).

This is not the teaching of literature intended for use in the content areas. The content teacher using literature to learn is concerned with how students make sense of a literary work and how the reading helps to shape student thinking. Literature for learning is based on the knowledge that students learn by integrating their prior knowledge with new information; by making connections between, for example, the body of knowledge in a content area and the expression of that knowledge in a young adult novel; and by being personally engaged in their learning. According to Rosenblatt, the student must be "free to grapple with his own reaction" to a literary work and "given the opportunity and the courage to approach literature personally, to let it mean something to him directly" (1978, 6). In this way, students come to understand what they are reading about and integrate that knowledge into their own learning.

For example, one can consider Robert Newton Peck's young adult novel *Fawn*. The story centers on Fawn, a wilderness boy whose father is a French Jesuit and whose mother was an outcast Mohawk. Young Fawn, in his quest to find himself, becomes caught up in the turmoil of the French and Indian Wars.

Students who are encouraged to read Peck's novel and respond to it in terms of their own feelings will be better able to understand why Fawn considered himself to be an American, not a Frenchman or a Mohawk. Teachers might suggest that the students discuss what it means to be an American, a Russian, a Chinese, etc. This kind of activity encourages students to explore their personal reactions to a work and share them with others in an effort to both clarify past knowledge and discover new meaning. It is an activity which helps each student to come to know self in terms of response to the assigned readings, while at the same time coming to appreciate the historical and cultural issues raised by the book.

Teachers who would have their students read *Fawn* and respond to such teacher-made test questions as (1) What was the year in which the story took place? (2) What was Fawn's mother's name? and (3) What was the name of the French fort? are merely testing students' memory skills and emphasizing facts.

Teachers have traditionally viewed literature in this way—as a body of information to be read and recalled for evaluation/assessment rather than as experiences to be enjoyed and reflected upon. Researchers Taba, Hoetker, Squire and Applebee, Purves, and Applebee have found that most of the school-sponsored teaching of literature for the last thirty years has, as reported by Johannessen, Kahn, and Walter, "relied on lecture, recitation, and short answer discussions, which may preclude students engaging in the kind of extended inquiry necessary to interpret, analyze, and write about the literature they read" (3). From the research that we have, it may be possible to make the claim that we have not yet put literature as learning into practice.

At this point it might be useful to note that debate about learning in the schools is often based on two broad views of knowledge. One view concentrates on the teacher's role as the initiator of knowledge; teachers transmit or deliver knowledge, a collection of facts and ideas, to the students through lectures and course readings. Students passively receive the information and store it for later use on examinations and term papers. The ability to recall information and ideas is emphasized. Thus, learning means receiving information. Knowing is the condition of having received information, which can be measured by evaluating students' responses to exam questions.

The other view of learning focuses on knowledge as an activity or process that the school is charged with developing in each student. Here, knowing implies the making of connections; and both the teachers and students are learners. Teaching involves creating contexts for learning, not for reporting facts. Learning, according to Britton, is the process of an individual mind making meaning from the materials of its experience. This is the essential connection between reading, writing, and learning.

One of the primary values of teaching literature to learn is that it requires mental activities that are also employed in learning—discriminating ideas one from the other and relating them to each other. According to Probst, reading and responding to literature entails the search for connections and "enables each of us to shape knowledge out of our encounter with it. It is personal knowledge, knowledge of how we relate to the world, how we feel and think and see" (1987, 27).

The key concept linking subject learning and reading and responding to literature is meaningfulness. Through reading and responding to literature, students in all subject areas are able to make meaning from new information by identifying it, selecting from it, reconstructing it, organizing it, and relating it to what they already know. The conditions for learning content material as identified by McKeller require the same skills: identifying new information, reconstructing knowledge in other terms, creating associations with that knowledge, applying the knowledge to other contexts, and subjecting the new knowledge to analysis and comparison. The making of meaning is, according to Rosenblatt, the most important reason for having adolescents read literature. She says:

> There is an even broader need that literature fulfills, particularly for the adolescent reader. Much that in life itself might seem disorganized and meaningless takes on order and significance when it comes under the organizing and vitalizing influence of the artist. The youth senses in himself new and unsuspected emotional impulsions. He sees the adults about him acting in inexplicable ways. In literature he meets emotions, situations, people presented in significant patterns. He is shown a causal relationship between actions, he finds approval given to certain kinds of personalities and behavior rather than to others, he finds molds into which to pour his own nebulous emotions. In short, he often finds meaning attached to what otherwise would be for him merely brute facts. (1968, 42)

Adolescent fiction—literature that is realistic and contemporary that young adults and mature readers find aesthetically, artistically, and thematically pleasing and that is both implicitly and explicitly written for adolescents—is a significant genre for helping students to learn and must have an important place in the curriculum. For the most part, young adult novels depict protagonists who move through two stages of growth and development: childhood-adolescence (11–14 years) and adolescence-adulthood (15–21 years). Therefore, they deal with issues that young readers are likely to be confronting; thus, the novels encourage the reading and learning encounters of which Rosenblatt speaks.

The literature that draws upon the author's sense of adolescent development strives for relevance by mirroring societal attitudes, issues, and concerns to young readers. In this way, the fiction creates for the readers a sense of reality to which they can relate. It addresses topics, including parental relationships, values conflicts, broken families, sex, handicaps, runaways, drugs, moving, school and teachers, racism, etc.; i.e., it addresses issues and raises questions which directly relate to and affect the lives of young readers. The student responses are likely to be significant because the literature offers an honest and important perspective about the nature of adolescent development. Thus, the transactions the adolescents have with the fiction are as important as the work itself. Probst concludes,

> We must not judge the literature solely on criteria of worth that deal only with features of the text. We must instead judge it on the likelihood that the students' transactions with it will be of high quality — that is, committed, interested, reasoned, emotional, personal. It is of little significance that students remember twenty years from now the distinction between metaphor and simile — far more significant that they have felt the shaping effect of metaphoric language and they have profited by it. (1987, 28)

Again, let us consider Peck's novel *Fawn* in an effort to understand the power of language in helping adolescents shape and make meaning of their world. Peck writes:

> Tight against the wet moss of the lakeshore, Fawn felt the drum of his heart as it beat upon the earth itself. It was this way with every deer. For until today every deer that Fawn had stalked had fled its arrows. But the taut gut of his bent bow pulled tighter, until Fawn could hear the wind strum into music and the gut bit into his fingers, and sang . . . not this deer. (16)

By reading this passage, students may learn more than that Fawn was a hunter; they may also feel through figurative language the excitement and intensity that Fawn feels. The students can understand Peck's language, because it creates a sense of reality for them.

This same passage elicits other transactions for the reader. It awakens one to the world hunters live in and thus raises questions concerning the moral aspect of hunting and killing animals. Additionally, it provides adolescent hunters with an experience that they might compare and relate to their own hunting expeditions.

What Is Young Adult Literature in the Content Areas?

The movement to teach young adult literature in the content areas challenges traditional attitudes about the teaching of literature. Young adult literature in the content areas implies that literature should be included in all courses in the curriculum, including English; it recognizes the expertise of the science teacher, the art teacher, the history teacher. Traditionally teachers have thought of literature as a way of preserving cultural heritage, a way of developing basic reading skills, a way of teaching moral lessons. By contrast, the emphasis of young adult literature across the curriculum is on learning content.

As we have learned, reading and responding to literature is more than a skill of memorizing facts about a work to be recalled later for evaluation purposes. Rather, reading and responding to literature is a process fundamental to the lifelong course of connecting and integrating thoughts and ideas.

In *Literature as Exploration*, Rosenblatt emphasizes literature's connection to other disciplines when she asks, "Is not the substance of literature everything that man has thought or created?" (5). In fact, she contends that "whatever the form — poem, novel, drama, biography, essay — literature makes comprehensible the myriad ways in which human beings meet the infinite possibilities that life offers" (6). She contends that literature's value across the curriculum is that it has the potential to help the student make meaning and discover knowledge:

> Certainly to the great majority of readers, the human experience that literature presents is primary. For them the formal elements of the work — the style and structure, rhythmic flow — function only as a part of the total literary experience. The reader seeks to participate in another's vision — to reap knowledge of the world, to fathom the resources of the human spirit, to gain insights that will make his own life more comprehensible. Teachers of adolescents, in high school or in college, know to what a heightened degree they share this personal approach to literature. (7)

If the literature is to have any meaning for the readers, then they must reconstruct it and order it for themselves using their cognitive, emotive, linguistic, imaginative, and psychological resources. Readers must bring to the text their knowledge about the world, as well as their attitudes, beliefs, interests, and their emotional and intellectual maturity. Young adult literature, which deals honestly with adolescent growth and development, equips students to manage their own growth and learning through literary experience.

From what has just been said, we can begin to sense the importance of literature across the curriculum. If the literature is to have meaning for readers, the readers must construct it and order it for themselves. They must respond, analyze, synthesize, organize, apply, and evaluate — all of which are tools of learning — in order to make meaning and demonstrate an understanding of literature as it applies to their own lives. Through reading and responding to young adult literature, readers come to search for and make knowledge of their worlds.

To illustrate, let me give several examples of how young adult literature can help learning in the content areas. When a group of students has studied about family relationships in a sociology class, instead of testing their textbook knowledge about these relationships with fill-in-the-blank, true/false, or multiple-choice tests, the teacher could suggest that the students extend their understanding of family relationships by reading, and perhaps writing about, young adult novels such as Cynthia Voigt's Tillerman books and Sue Ellen Bridgers' *Notes for Another Life* and *Permanent Connections*. In these books students can experience strong cross-generational family relationships and perhaps truly learn what an extended family is. A different sort of relationship is found in Virginia Hamilton's *Sweet Whispers, Brother Rush*, where an absentee mother indirectly forces her fifteen-year-old daughter to confront a painful and frightening past as she struggles to care for her retarded older brother. Reading such books can help students to better understand different kinds of family relationships by putting into a dramatic context those facts learned from a textbook.

Equally important, reading and responding to young adult literature promotes exploration and discovery and allows the students to interact with and respond to the work being read. In a like manner, when students have trouble understanding facts about slavery in history class, their teacher can encourage them to read *The Slave Dancer* by Paula Fox. A Newbery Medal winner, the story offers a view of slavery as seen through the eyes of a young white boy who is shanghaied on a slave ship and forced to make music for its cargo. The novel offers young readers an opportunity to experience slavery from the perspective of characters who are near the readers' ages and who think at the readers' level.

In her science fiction novels Mildred Ames presents young adult readers with issues that stimulate creative thinking. Science teachers who want to get their students thinking about whether or not technology is dehumanizing might have them read Ames's *Is There Life on Another Planet*? The story is about eleven-year-old Hollis, who changes places with a lookalike doll-robot. At first Hollis is thrilled because the robot does all the things Hollis hates to do — go to school, take ballet lessons, and deal with people Hollis doesn't like. Hollis, of course, is free to play all day. Changing places seems like such a good idea, but eventually Hollis becomes more like a machine, while the robot becomes more human. The novel challenges young adult readers to consider what they know about humans and machines and extrapolate that knowledge to a further degree. In *Anna to the Infinite Power* Ames presents the reader with yet another ethical dilemma. Anna, the protagonist, discovers that she is more than a self-centered twelve-year-old girl; she is a clone with an identity crisis. Who is she? Who was she cloned from? Science teachers might use science fiction novels such as these to help students think about the world, as it exists and as it may exist in the future. Examining these issues in fiction will enhance what students learn from textbook fact.

In a slightly different vein, students in a botany class might benefit from reading Vera and Bill Cleaver's *Where the Lilies Bloom*. Here they will see how orphaned fourteen-year-old Mary Call Luther and her siblings make a living by wildcrafting—gathering medicinal plants and herbs to earn money for food and clothing. This fictional work nicely complements a textbook unit on flowers and plants that have more than aesthetic value by adding an extra dimension to the students' learning. While it is one thing to know about and be able to identify such plants, it is quite another to see enterprising young people use them as a means of survival.

Even the health class can be a stimulating environment for the young adult novel. M. E. Kerr's *Night Kites*, for example, can help students understand the conflicting emotions involved when a family is forced to deal with the AIDS virus, as well as the degree of responsibility placed on young adults who choose to have premarital sex. Chris Crutcher's *Stotan*! is another novel that may help achieve the goals of a health class. Here student readers experience the strong bonds of loyalty, friendship, and teamwork forged among four members of a high school swim team; they feel the pain and frustration of watching as those bonds are tested by the tragic, terminal illness of one of the team members. Using such works of young adult fiction in the health class can assure that the human element will not be overlooked in the study of diseases and bodily functions.

Just as young adult novels can help readers in sociology, science, and health classes to discover and make meaning for themselves, it can help math classes learn how to use deduction and inference to draw logical conclusions and solve problems. For example, Ellen Raskin's whodunit novel, *The Westing Game*, involves the reader in a play-along game to solve a murder. While the characters in the novel all have clues which will help lead them to the murderer, the reader is the only one who has all the clues. The object of the game is for the readers to solve the mystery before the characters do, using a process akin to that employed in mathematical proofs to crack the case.

Similarly, young readers of Isaac Asimov's classic short story collection, *I, Robot*, might use the book to explore the implications of mathematical logic in the creation of artificial intelligence. Three simple robot laws—that robots may not harm humans, that robots must obey humans, and that robots must protect themselves—govern the logical actions of Cutie (QT) and other robots in the book. In trying to work through conflicts and ambiguities in those seemingly simple laws, however, Asimov's robots become as torn by moral dilemmas as humans are. Part of Asimov's lesson is clear: even precise mathematical reasoning eventually has to come to terms with human ambiguity.

Mysteries like *The Westing Game* and science fiction stories like *I, Robot* require students to think about how new ideas are related to one another and, more particularly, about how mathematical reasoning is related to the seemingly more subjective processes of human decision-making. Math teachers, then, might want to use mysteries and science fiction stories to help students understand more about the act of thinking. Other subject areas are also enriched by the use of young adult literature. Music teachers, for example, who wish to promote critical thinking about their subject can encourage students to read young adult works in which characters become involved with music. One such work is William Sleator's *Fingers*, a novel about a wonder-child pianist, Humphrey, and his brother Sam. Although Humphrey was once a child prodigy, he appears to be losing his musical talent. In an effort to maintain Humphrey's reputation, his mother devises an elaborate plan to have Sam write music to play during his concerts. The scheme becomes even more complicated and hoax-like when his mother tells the public that Humphrey is receiving messages about how to compose music from the dead gypsy composer Laszlo Magyar.

While Sleator's work is clearly a supernatural fantasy, it raises issues that some young musicians have to confront. For example, Humphrey played the piano and gave musical performances because his mother forced him, not because he wanted to. What kind of encouragement should young musicians be given? If they have substantial talent, are parents and other adults justified in pushing them to improve? How might young people in general be encouraged to enjoy music? These and other questions might be raised by music teachers whose objectives include developing music appreciation in their students.

Other young adult novels which introduce students to the musical world and to young musicians might accomplish the same purposes. These include Nat Hentoff's *Jazz Country*, in which the main character, Tom Curtis, must decide whether to pursue his dream of becoming a jazz musician or to begin college; D. Manus Pinkwater's fanciful children's story, *Lizard Music*, in which an eleven-year-old boy named Victor hears music from a mysterious lizard band on late-night television and is led on a series of exciting adventures as a result of being captivated by that music; and Virginia Hamilton's *The Planet of Junior Brown*, the story of another child prodigy pianist, Junior Brown, who is following his insane music teacher Miss Lynora Peebs into madness.

The Hamilton novel might also be used by art teachers who are interested in raising questions about the value of art. Junior Brown, his music taken away from him by Miss Peebs and by a sick mother who can't bear listening to his "noise," turns to art to express his troubled emotions. Using his paints, he creates a primitive, terrifying creature called the Red Man, who acts out all the power and passion that Junior sublimates within himself.

Carrie Stokes in Zibby Oneal's *The Language of Goldfish* also draws, using art to keep hold of reality, just as Jess Aarons in Katherine

Paterson's children's novel *Bridge to Terabithia* secretly draws to create a world more kind than the one he inhabits. Jamal Hicks in Walter Dean Myers' *Scorpions* draws to create a world more beautiful than the frightening Harlem in which he lives; and young characters Chip Becker in Cynthia Rylant's *A Kindness* and Ellery Collier in Sue Ellen Bridgers' *Permanent Connections* learn from their mothers, both artists, what art contributes to the world.

These books illustrate only a few of the many ways in which teachers can facilitate reading as a way of discovering knowledge in their subject areas. The examples reveal how reading literature can provide reinforcement for learning when students read about content which they can relate to and enjoy. Mayher reminds us that no matter how the curriculum is organized, learning takes place only when learners make active connections between what they need to learn and what they already know, understand, and believe. Reading young adult novels in the content areas encourages learners to synthesize and organize their own ideas with the view presented in the novels and thus discourages teachers from using literature as a way of testing memorized facts.

What Teachers Must Do

If teachers believe that the goal of education is to develop informed, thinking citizens capable of participating in world affairs, then they must recognize that this development depends on the essentials of education as noted in the following statement:

> The interdependence of skills and content is the central concept of the essentials of education. Skills and abilities do not grow in isolation from content. In all subjects, students develop the ability to reason; they undergo experiences that lead to emotional and social maturity. Students master these skills and abilities through observing, listening, reading, talking, and writing about science, mathematics, history, and social sciences, the arts, and other aspects of our intellectual, social, and cultural heritage .... Such a definition calls for a realization that all disciplines must join together and acknowledge their interdependence. (ASCD 6, 7)

Reading, talking, and writing about young adult novels that realistically and accurately depict adolescent lives can be a powerful way for students to extend and integrate their content area learning in all disciplines. With this is mind, let us examine some matters content area teachers can attend to in order to successfully implement reading young adult novels to learn in their classrooms.

Reading/Responding Activities to Encourage Content Learning

Talking

Teachers should encourage students to engage in expressive talk before, during, and after they read and respond to literature. Britton explains that "it is by means of talking it in speech that we learn to take it in thought" (14). He contends that by explaining their ideas to others orally before they respond in writing, students strengthen their knowledge which can be reexamined and extended during the writing process. For example, students who are discussing divorce and its implications on society might choose to read Judy Blume's *It's Not The End of the World*, Norma Klein's *Taking Sides*, Norma Fox Mazer's *I, Trissy*, or John Neufeld's *Sunday Father*, novels which examine the fears, frustrations, hopes, and actions of young protagonists who are children of divorce. If after reading the novels students are encouraged to talk with their peers about the impact of divorce on young adult lives, they will gain other perspectives and thus be able to connect various views to their own thinking in order to clarify meaning and make new knowledge for themselves.

Just as students in a social studies class can read and talk about young adult literature to enhance content learning, students in English classes can do the same. For instance, today many English teachers are requiring their students to keep journals. While most teachers take time to explain the reasons for keeping a journal, many students don't see the value of such a task. To help clarify and further explain the reasons for writing in a journal, teachers can ask their students to read novels like Gary Paulsen's *The Island* and Eleanora Tate's *The Secret of Gumbo Grove*. The young protagonists in both novels value journal writing as a way of learning. After the students have read Paulsen's and Tate's works, they can talk about their personal reactions to the texts. Through the sharing of ideas, students may see more clearly why they are asked to keep journals.

In addition to talking with their peers, students need to talk to their teachers. Student talk reveals what students do and don't know so that the teacher can determine what guidance or instruction the student needs.

Writing About Literature

A powerful way to help students understand their transactions with literature is to have them write about what they read. Petrosky explains that writing about reading is one of the best ways to get students to unravel their transactions so that we can see how they understand and, in the process, help them learn to elaborate, clarify, and illustrate their responses to the associations and prior knowledge that inform them. (1982, 24)

Petrosky carries his point even further when he argues that

our comprehension of texts, whether they are literary or not, is more an act of composition — for understanding is composing — than of information retrieval, and the best possible representation of our understandings of texts begins with certain kinds of compositions, not multiple choice tests. (1982, 19)

James Squire contends that comprehending what is read and writing about what is read are inextricably linked. He states that teaching students to compose and comprehend are "what the teaching of higher thought processes is all about" (582). If all this is true, then students need appropriate opportunities to read literature and then explore their reactions to it through written responses which will reinforce and help them clarify their learning.

For example, students in a social studies class may be learning about marriage, parenthood, and adolescent pregnancy. As a way of enhancing learning, the teacher may ask students to read a young adult novel which explores one of these topics and to record their responses to the work in a journal. The students may choose to read one of the following books: *Too Much in Love* by Patty Brisco, *Love Is Never Enough* by Bianca Bradbury, *Phoebe* by Patricia Dizenzo, *Mr. and Mrs. Bo Jo Jones* by Ann Head, or *For All the Wrong Reasons* by John Neufeld. The authors of these books portray young couples' initial relationships, the ways the relationships change as a result of pregnancy, and how the characters feel about themselves as individuals at both the beginning and end of the novels. Readers see how some of the protagonists grow and discover their own identity as a result of the problems they are forced to face in an "adult" world. After reading one of the novels, students can be encouraged to make a written journal response concerning their feelings about young couples who become involved in premarital sex. The students might choose to discuss the fears and frustrations that young adults face as a result of sexual encounters, or they might decide to write about why some of the relationships survive, while others do not. In either instance, the students have the opportunity to bring their personal experiences to the writing activity. Through their writing, they may find that sexual relationships involve moral and practical considerations and that responsibility for pregnancy that sometimes results from sexual intercourse belongs to both the young man and young woman. If asked by the teacher, students could use their journal entries as a beginning for a formal paper on how adolescent pregnancy can affect the lives of those involved. This kind of reading-writing activity helps students to see that reading and writing are the processes of learning and not only a means for giving back to the teacher information that he or she included in a lecture or that the student memorized from the textbook.

When students use writing to reflect on their own experiences, the writing becomes a way of exploring the subject matter by connecting old ideas to the new material in order to reach an understanding of the concepts involved in the study. Teachers who use a writing-to-learn approach are concerned with how the students present ideas, make connections, and draw conclusions about the content to be studied. In this way, writing to learn enhances instructional content and does not take instructional time from teachers, who will still provide ways for their students to learn the content they are teaching. As James Britton brings to our attention:

> What we mean by language across the curriculum is getting teachers who are teaching history and biology and social studies and so on to think more about the role of language in their lessons. In history, we learn to get historical perspectives on the world we live in; in geography and science, we get an organization of our experiences of the environment in different sorts of ways. These are all concerned with organizing the objective aspects of our experience. We have to show them that this isn't basically a concern for language. It's a concern for the quality of learning in all subjects. The quality of learning in all subjects might well benefit if teachers took more into account the actual talking and writing process as learning process. (89)

During the reading/responding-to-learn process, the teacher's function is to guide the students in their reading and responses. Teachers identify, understand, and encourage students' natural learning inclinations to use reading and responding to promote self awareness within the reading/responding context. The reading and responding can be personal, speculative, and exploratory; it is done primarily to benefit the student. If, however, students are required to read and respond to demonstrate how much they know to a teacher who looks for right or wrong answers, the reading/responding can inhibit learning because it isolates what is to be learned from the vital learning process—that of making links between what is already known and the new information. Teachers, then, may provide students with opportunities for making personal responses that focus on ideas rather than on correctness.

As we have seen, the teaching of young adult literature across the curriculum should include reading/responding activities that are based on the students' personal growth. The activities will provide the students with experience to help them discover knowledge by enabling them to learn through involvement. Simply, the students will learn by doing. In a like manner, if the teacher evaluation is concerned with completeness, logic, and clarity of thought, students will not be overly concerned with the memorization of facts where they interfere with clear transmission of thoughts and ideas.

This chapter has attempted to clarify what is meant by "Young Adult Literature Across the Curriculum" and to offer suggestions for implementation. Any attempt to use young adult literature in cross-curricular learning must begin with the acceptance of *four* vital ideas:

1. Reading and responding to young adult literature is a meaning-making activity and is a way of learning content material in all disciplines in the secondary school curriculum.

2. Young adult fiction helps young readers to discover knowledge and make meaning, because it provides students with realistic experiences that deal with their "here and now." It treats seriously and respects adolescent problems, values, issues, and concerns.

3. Reading and responding to young adult literature is related to and reinforced by other language skills including talking, writing, and listening. All language skills are closely related and vital to the learning process.

4. Reading young adult literature to learn involves responding, analyzing, synthesizing, and organizing ideas into meaningful content. Therefore, students need to read and write often about their thoughts and ideas rather than simply to concentrate on the mastery of facts and concepts in a given subject.

Works Cited

Ames, Mildred. 1987. *Anna to the Infinite Power*. New York: Scholastic.

———. 1987. *Is There Life on Another Planet?* New York: Scholastic.

Applebee, Arthur N. 1974. *Tradition and Reform in the Teaching of English: A History*. Urbana, IL: National Council of Teachers of English.

———. 1978. *The Child's Concept of Story — Ages 2–17* Chicago: University of Chicago Press.

———. 1981. *Writing in the Secondary School: English and the Content Areas. Urbana, IL: National Council of Teachers of English.*

Asimov, Isaac. 1950. *I, Robot*. New York: Doubleday.

Association for Supervision and Curriculum Development (Producer). 1982. *The Essentials of Education*. Filmstrip. Alexandria, Virginia: ASCD.

Ausubel, D. P., and F. G. Robinson. 1969. *School Learning: An Introduction to Educational Psychology*. New York: Holt, Rinehart and Winston, Inc.

Blume, Judy. 1972. *It's Not the End of the World.* New York: Bantam.

Bradbury, Bianca. 1971. *Love Is Never Enough.* New York: Scholastic.

Bridgers, Sue Ellen. 1981. *Notes for Another Life.* New York: Knopf.

———. 1987. *Permanent Connections.* New York: Harper Keypoint.

Brisco, Patty. 1979. *Too Much In Love.* New York: Scholastic.

Britton, James, T. Burgess, N. Martin, A. McLeod, & H. Rosen. 1975. *The Development of Writing Abilities (11–18).* London: Macmillan Education.

Cleaver, Bill, and Vera Cleaver. 1969. *Where the Lilies Bloom.* Philadelphia: Lippincott.

Crutcher, Chris. 1988. *Stotan!* New York: Dell.

Dizenzo, Patricia. 1975. *Phoebe.* New York: Bantam.

Duncan, Lois. 1979. *Daughters of Eve.* New York: Dell.

Fox, Paula. 1974. *The Slave Dancer.* New York: Dell.

Fulwiler, Toby. 1982. "Writing: An Act of Cognition." In C. Williams Griffin (Ed.), *Teaching Writing In All Disciplines* (pp. 15–26). San Francisco: Jossey-Bass.

Hamilton, Virginia. 1979. *The Planet of Junior Brown.* New York, NY: Laurel Leaf.

———. 1982. *Sweet Whispers, Brother Rush.* New York: Avon.

Head, Ann. 1968. *Mr. and Mrs. Bo Jo Jones.* New York: Signet Books.

Hentoff, Nat. 1965. *Jazz Country.* New York: Harper & Row.

Hoetker, James. 1968. "Teacher Questioning Behavior in Nine Junior High School English Courses." *Research in the Teaching of English 2*: 99–106.

Iser, Wolfgang. 1978. *The Act of Reading: A Theory of Aesthetic Response.* Baltimore: Johns Hopkins University Press.

Johannessen, Larry R., Elizabeth A. Kahn, and Carolyn Calhoun Walter. 1984. "The Art of Introducing Literature." *The Clearing House 57*: 263–66.

Kerr, M. E. 1986. *Night Kites.* New York: Harper & Row.

Klein, Norma. 1974. *Taking Sides.* New York: Avon.

Langer, Susanne. 1960. *Philosophy in a New Key* (3rd ed.). Cambridge, MA: Harvard University Press.

Lazere, Donald. 1987. "Critical Thinking in College English Studies." New York: ERIC.

McKellar, P. 1957. *Imagination and Thinking: A Psychological Analysis.* London: Cohen and West.

Mayher, John, et al. 1983. *Learning to Write: Writing to Learn.* Portsmouth, NH: Boynton/Cook.

Mazer, Norma Fox. 1971. *I, Trissy.* New York: Dell.

Myers, Walter Dean. 1990. *Scorpions.* New York: Harper.

National Assessment of Educational Progress. 1981. *Reading, Thinking, and Writing: Results from the 1979—80 National Assessment of Reading and Literature*. Denver: National Educational Commission of the States.

Neufeld, John. 1974. *For All the Wrong Reasons*. New York: Signet.

————. 1976. *Sunday Father*. New York: New American Library.

Oneal, Zibby. 1980. *The Language of Goldfish*. New York: Fawcett Juniper.

Paterson, Katherine. 1977. *Bridge to Terabithia*. New York: Avon.

Paulsen, Gary. 1990. *The Island*. New York: Bantam.

Peck, Richard. 1989. *Close Enough To Touch*. New York: Avon.

Peck, Robert N. 1975. *Fawn*. New York: Dell.

Petrosky, Anthony R. 1977. "Response to Literature." *English Journal* 66 (October): 96—98.

————. 1982. "From Story to Essay: Reading and Writing." *College Composition and Communication* 39: 19—36.

Piaget, J. 1967. *Six Psychological Studies*. New York: Random House.

Piaget, J., and B. Inhelder. 1969. *The Psychology of the Child*. New York: Basic Books.

Pinkwater, D. Manus. 1976. *Lizard Music*. New York: Bantam Skylark.

Polanyi, Michael. 1958. *Personal Knowledge: Toward a Post-Critical Philosophy*. Chicago: University of Chicago Press.

Probst, Robert. 1986. "Three Relationships in the Teaching of Literature." *English Journal* 75 (January): 60—68.

————. 1987. "Adolescent Literature and the English Curriculum." *English Journal* 76 (March): 26—32.

————. 1981. *Literature and the Reader*. Urbana, IL: NCTE.

————. 1981. *Reading and Literature: American Achievement*. In *Perspective*. Urbana, IL: NCTE.

Purves, Alan. 1972. *How Porcupines Make Love*. New York: John Wiley & Sons.

Purves, Alan C., and Richard Beach. 1972. *Literature and the Reader*. Urbana, IL: NCTE.

Raskin, Ellen. 1978. *The Westing Game*. New York: Avon.

Rosenblatt, Louise M. 1968. *Literature as Exploration*. New York: Noble and Noble.

————. 1978. *The Reader, the Text, the Poem: The Transactional Theory of the Literary Work*. Carbondale, IL: Southern Illinois University Press.

Rylant, Cynthia. 1988. *A Kindness*. New York: Dell.

Sleator, William. 1983. *Fingers*. New York: Bantam.

Squire, James R. 1983. "Composing and Comprehending: Two Sides of the Same Basic Process." *Language Arts* 60: 581—89.

Squire, James R., and Roger K. Applebee. 1968. *High School English Instruction Today*. New York: Irvington Publications.

Sternglass, Marilyn S. 1983. *Reading, Writing, and Reasoning*. New York: Macmillan.

Tate, Eleanora. 1988. *The Secret of Gumbo Grove*. New York, NY: Bantam.

Voigt, Cynthia. 1981. *Homecoming*. New York: Fawcett.

———. 1986. *Izzy, Willy-Nilly*. New York: Fawcett.

———. 1985. *The Runner*. New York: Fawcett.

11

Cultural Diversity and the Young Adult Novel

Lois T. Stover
Eileen Tway

As our classrooms become increasingly populated with recent immigrants from other cultures, as more students born in the United States find themselves living temporarily in other countries, as we find more and more that "the minority" population is becoming the majority, and as barriers which formerly acted to keep peoples separated are broken down, it becomes increasingly important that teachers and their students search for means of understanding our coinhabitants of this country—and this earth. Gonzales cites Waggoner, who notes, "In principle, the United States is a monolingual country where English is indisputably the language of all major institutions. In reality, it is a multilingual, multicultural country where one person in seven speaks a non-English language at home or lives with family members who do" (16). Gonzales then goes on to make several specific recommendations for English teachers, including "that curriculum content and approaches to that content reflect the histories, values, and languages of the student population" (18–19).

One method English teachers can use to help students break down barriers of culture and ethnicity is to use young adult novels by and about minorities, by and about recent immigrants to the U.S., and even by authors from other countries who write literature for adolescents about the adolescent experience in other lands. Donelson and Nilsen state that through reading good literature, the unique qualities of individuals can be celebrated at the same time as the similarities of human experience which cross cultural boundaries can be explored (403). They also note that good literature written for and about adolescents is an especially valuable tool to use when seeking to help adolescents connect with the larger world of human experience because the characters are immediately accessible to younger readers due to the similarities of age and concerns between the reader and those who populate young adult books. As Romero and Zancanella explain, "It is important for students to explore the literature of various cultures they are fortunate enough to have around them so that they can better understand the diversity of American society" (29) and, of the society of the world as a whole.

For students who represent minority cultures within the larger U.S. society, young adult literature from those cultures provides validation of their own experience. Romero and Zancanella state that students need "to know that authors and artists of substance and value come from their culture" (29). Hence, teachers and librarians need to be aware of new materials such as Harcourt, Brace, Jovanovich's recent *Mexican American Literature* anthology, and should provide access for all students to young adult books by authors such as Yoshiko Uchida, who writes about the Japanese immigrant experience; Nicholassa Mohr, whose characters are Puerto Ricans living in the U.S.; Maureen Crane Wartski, who provides a vivid picture of the Vietnamese refugee experience; Gunilla Morris, who writes about the experience of Scandinavians living in the U.S.; Rudolfo Anaya, who depicts Chicano life in the United States, as do Danny Santiago and Sandra Cisneros; Virginia Hamilton, Mildred Taylor, Walter Dean Myers, Joyce Carol Thomas, June Jordan, Sharon Bell Mathis, Rosa Guy, Eloise Greenfield, or Eleanora Tate, all of whom detail the lives of Black Americans from various periods of U.S. history; Laurence Yep, who describes the Chinese immigrant experience; or N. Scott Momaday and Jamake Highwater, whose books allow readers to learn about life from the Native American perspective.

It is also true that through reading and vicariously experiencing life from a different cultural perspective, young adults from the mainstream of U.S. culture can and will develop the beginnings of increased tolerance for and appreciation of the ways of life of people from other countries, as Ehle points out in a review of research about the influence of literature on readers. Before starting to read a young adult novel from Russia, eighth grade students in a Carroll County, Maryland, middle school were asked to write an imaginary letter to their best friend describing their reactions upon learning that their families were being transferred to Moscow for an indefinite period. Sam's response is indicative of all of them. He wrote, "Dear Ben, You'll never guess what awful thing is going to happen to us. My dad's being transferred and we have to move to Russia. I think I'll probably just die. How do people survive over there? ..." After reading *Shadows Across the*

Sun, a young adult novel published originally in Russian by Albert Likhanov, students were asked to reflect on their initial letter and to identify what parts of it they would change now that they had a better understanding of what daily life in Russia is like and how they are both alike and different from their Russian peers. Sam again captured the essence of all thirty-six responses when he stated, "I'd change the part about 'I'll probably die' because reading the book I see that it's not all that hard to adjust to the Russian way of life, especially with friends like Fedya and Lena [the two main characters in the novel]."

Sam's reflections indicate that he was able to identify with Fedya and Lena. Thus, he was able to revise his initial perceptions of Russia and was able to feel the kind of personal connection with young adults from that country which allowed him later to feel comfortable in reaching out to Russian students when he visited the school run by the Russian Embassy in Washington, D.C.

There are also many good young adult books about segments of the American population which are culturally diverse but about whom students may have little knowledge. Jane Yolen (*The Devil's Arithmetic*), Fran Arrick, and Chaim Potok (*Chernowitz! The Chosen*) have written novels about being Jewish. Gary Paulsen (*Dogsong*) and Jean C. George (*Julie of The Wolves*) develop characters who must come to terms with the Eskimo heritage. Vera and Bill Cleaver and Robert Newton Peck present daily life and its hardships for young adults growing up in very rural environments such as Appalachia (*Where The Lilies Bloom*), Vermont, (*A Day No Pigs Would Die*) and Florida (*Arly*) while George Ella Lyon describes the differences between life in the coal-mining regions of Kentucky and life in the city of Memphis in *Borrowed Children*. And Kathryn Lasky in *Beyond The Divide* writes about an Amish father and daughter who experience the custom of shunning. They must leave their community and so must deal with the tensions involved in preserving their beliefs while fitting into a larger society than they had previously experienced.

The point is that in our multicultural society and increasingly interconnected world, we need to emphasize certain goals of the literature program. Through their reading, students should be able to explore 1) issues of self-identification, 2) their relationships between themselves and others, and 3) the relationships between and among cultures. The inclusion of young adult novels about adolescents from diverse cultural backgrounds in the literature curriculum should help accomplish these goals.

Writing about the history of young adult literature dealing with diverse cultural experiences, Hugh Moir notes of the period from 1960–1980:

As our social structures and institutions were shaken during the 60s, books for children and young adults changed forever. *Real* problems of *real* kids told in *real* language were fair game for a nation of readers who watched much of the Vietnam War and the Civil Rights Movement on their television screens. Such topics as racial conflict, divorce, substance abuse, sex and sexuality, death, and child abuse were and are discussed with greater candor and realism.

Minority authors, so long silenced by a cynical publishing industry and uncaring society, found new audiences among white and minority readers demanding that books be relevant (8).

Moir also points out that, unfortunately, there has been a recent decline of minority writers and themes "that illuminate the cultural diversity in a country enriched by its multicultural heritage. . . . There is a paucity of new books by minority writers or [about minorities] themes, especially those by Hispanic, Asian-American, and native American writers" (9). On a more positive note, there has been a recent increase in the number of books available in translation from other countries which can be used to complement books about minority and immigrant experience, and which can help students become more globally literate and aware of the similarities and differences among cultures on a global scale. If teachers conscientiously seek to include many of the good works which *do* exist, even if they are hard to find, and which do reflect the themes and issues of concern to young adults from diverse cultures, perhaps we can begin to counter the negative social perceptions that children of minority subcultures have of themselves or that society has of them (Gonzales 19). At the very least, using novels by young adult authors such as Laurence Yep, Nicholassa Mohr, Mildred Taylor, Max Martinez, or Yoshiko Uchida may help our adolescents become aware of the issues of racism, ethnocentricity, and resulting prejudices and stereotyping.

Finding and Selecting Young Adult Novels Representative of Cultural Diversity

As teachers seek to select young adult novels that represent the experiences of adolescents from culturally diverse backgrounds, there are several criteria which should be considered. Most importantly, we need to avoid "tokenism." As Gonzales states, "Token representation of the histories and literatures of culturally different children are inadequate attempts at engaging and inspiring students' participation in the educational process. One piece of literature or one chapter in American history cannot counter the negative social perceptions that children of minority subcultures have of themselves or that society has of them. A significant proportion of the curriculum must be dedicated to positive ethnic histories and literature and the many contributions that all groups have made to American life" (18–19).

How can tokenism be avoided? Curriculum workers developing courses and librarians creating displays would have to first agree to accept as goals for the literature program the three broad goals of 1) exploration of self; 2) exploration of the relationship between the self and others; and 3) exploration of the relationships among cultures — and between a culture and the novels which grow from it. Organizing by themes representative of issues that cross cultural boundaries might better allow for these goals to be met than organizing the literature program by chronology or by genre. If the focus of the unit is on an issue, individuals from diverse cultural backgrounds can respond to that issue as well as to the literature, sharing their own experiences — as shaped by culture — with death or friendship as they also respond to the text and its presentation of the issue as shaped by the cultural background of the author. By exploring themes such as "Courage," "The Nature of Childhood or Adolescence," "Peer Relations," "Who Am I?," "Death and Dying," "The Frontier Experience," or "Ways of Knowing" through young adult novels reflective of many kinds of experiences, students could examine the nature of the theme in general — and could investigate how various cultures approach these issues. For instance, Nicholassa Mohr's older but still timely novel *Nilda* could be included in many of the thematic units mentioned above. *Nilda* is about a young Puerto Rican girl who lives in New York City. Her experiences provide an excellent starting point for discussing issues such as the place of the female in a male-dominated society, the nature of adolescence within the Hispanic culture, or the issue of language and how language determines a sense of self. Nilda is shunned by a young woman from Spain who, as a speaker of the "pure" Castilian Spanish, feels that Nilda's language reflects a lack of culture and education. Caught between her Catholic mother and her Communist father, Nilda also explores the place of religion as she attempts to define herself and answer "Who am I?" And, the *barrio* could be discussed as an example of frontier; how it limits the world of Nilda and her family, and how she attempts to go beyond these limits into new, uncharted territory. The frontier as experienced by Nilda is quite different from that explored by Daniel Boone, of course. His was a mostly empty space into which the pioneers could escape from society's restrictions and in which they survived through courage and a combination of intelligence and common sense. On the other hand, the barrio is surrounded by a well-organized society, many of whose members have a vested interest in keeping Nilda locked out. However, if the focus of the unit is on "frontier," the experiences of Nilda and Daniel Boone could be compared and contrasted, students could talk about the meaning of "frontier" on an individual basis and about its nature as perceived by members of various cultures, learning more about themselves and others as a result.

John Rowe Townsend, author and literary critic, speaks of the need to look at literature for young people broadly — not just to regard books as useful if they deal with contemporary issues or attitudes and views, but also to consider their literary worth (8). This, too, is a good caution. Otherwise, adults might force didactic books down young readers' throats. Instead, instructors, teachers, librarians, and parents must search out the best of the books reflective of cultural diversity. Searching for such novels and using them in genre-oriented units is another possible way to avoid the problem of tokenism. In a unit focused on the discussion of the novel, for example, students could compare and contrast *A Hero Ain't Nothin' But a Sandwich*, by Alice Childress, about a black youth dealing with drug addiction in an inner city setting, with *The Pigman*, by Paul Zindel, since both novels effectively use alternating points of view in unfolding the plot line. At the same time, differences in character perspective in this novel might be related to differences in cultural background as students read other works. In such a unit, the Childress book would not just be a token work, thrown in to appeal to a certain segment of the student population; rather it would be viewed as an exemplar of the genre as a whole.

It might be wise, however, to reflect again on the implications of avoiding tokenism as it relates to the overall goals of the literature program. There are school districts in the United States serving students from more than thirty different cultural and ethnic groups. To provide novels reflective of each student's background would require *many* different titles to be available. We could allow one novel about an Oriental culture to represent them all, but to do so would be more damaging than token. We need to select books to help students understand diverse points of view and understand people from other times and places while also providing them access to novels to which they can realistically relate. Balance must be achieved — balance between students' need to feel validated through the experiences they read about in books and their need to learn about other worlds and perspectives; balance between teacher-made selections and student-made selections; and balance between novels selected because of the authors' excellent craftsmanship and those selected primarily because they appeal to students' interests.

Another set of criteria that may be useful in selection is found in *Reading Ladders for Human Relations*, edited by Tway. The compilers suggest that teachers look for certain qualities in selecting books to promote better human relations. Their guidelines argue for books that

1. contain the essentials of all good literature. For fiction these are: well-developed plot, characterization, setting, theme, and style;

for nonfiction: clear, logical writing and accurate information; for poetry: lyrical beauty of language or poetic statement of truth.

2. are positive and fair in their presentation of people, both in text and illustration, and that belittle no people either through condescension, deprecatory statements, or ridicule.

3. are natural and convincing instead of contrived and suggesting superficial treatment in solving difficult problems human beings face.

4. offer illustrations to supplement the text, adding content or contributing to the mood.

5. help prevent the carrying forward of old prejudices and stereotypes into the new generation.

6. recognize minority groups' participation in and contributions to history and culture of our country.

7. help each reader to a realization of identity, an appreciation of individuality, and a respect for heritage.

8. contain subject matter appropriate to the age levels given.

9. avoid sex role stereotyping of women or men.

10. contain an honest and authentic portrayal of the human condition, including different stages in the life cycle, different life styles, and life in different cultures. (5−6)

Teachers and librarians might also do their best to find and stock young adult novels in which characters from diverse backgrounds interact realistically, reflecting both the prejudices of our society and the ability of individuals to overcome these, interacting in a more positive way and learning from each other. For instance, in Voigt's *The Runner*, Bullet Tillerman must face his prejudices against blacks head-on as he learns that one of his best friends is of mixed racial heritage and as he comes to respect a new member of the school track team who happens to be black. Craven's *I Heard the Owl Call My Name* describes the ways in which a white priest comes to value the Native American approach to nature and to death as he himself faces dying. In *The Moves Make the Man*, Brooks explores a variety of issues such as parent/child relationships, the importance of sportsmanship and of doing one's best, and friendship while describing the relationship between two young men, one white and one black. The British novel *My Mate Shofiq* by Jan Needle provides a powerful description of interracial prejudices — and then provides hope by focusing on Bernard and his developing ability to overcome the prejudices he has learned from his family and peers because of his developing friendship with the Pakistani boy, Shofiq. Or, the Russian novel *Playing the Game* by Irina Strelkova describes the coming of age of a group of male friends who all represent various segments of the Russian population, and who must deal with their stereotypes about members of other cultures as they struggle to remain friends. On a lighter note, in *It's an Aardvark-Eat-Turtle World*, Danziger's main character deals with the fact that she is of mixed cultural heritage.

These works are useful in promoting discussion about significant social issues because while the characters may be less than perfect in their abilities to interact with others in ways free of prejudice, the authors present realistic individuals who must wrestle with their limitations — and who provide a mirror in which readers may examine their own behaviors — but the effect of the books in their entirety is not to deprecate systematically any particular group or race. It is important that teachers selecting novels for use with students avoid selecting those which may either reinforce negative stereotypes or which may cause discomfort to some students because of the demeaning portrait of characters from diverse cultural backgrounds. For example, Frank's *Alas, Babylon*, a novel written in the 1950s, may have been "progressive" in its treatment of relations at that time, but in today's society the patronage system described, the relationship of domestic to employer, is out of date. This novel is still often read because it deals with the timely topic of nuclear war, but there are more current novels, ones with more ability to provoke reader response and with more ability to provide food for discussion of literary craftsmanship, which could be used — and which would not reinforce outmoded ways of interacting.

Obviously, much "classic" literature contains stereotyping reflective of the historical context in which it was written, and many contemporary figures in well-written young adult novels do interact with others based on their prejudices and negative stereotypes. For example, Hamilton's *White Romance* often provokes anger in readers because of the stereotyping and prejudices the black characters have of some of their white peers. Or, in *Kindred* by Octavia Butler, the love Rufus feels for Alice, a freeborn black woman, is destroyed because of his inability to see her as an equal instead of through the eyes of a slave holder. Books which provide "an honest and authentic portrayal of the human condition" (Tway 6) will be full of characters who are condescending and deprecatory. Students need to be exposed to such characters who do reflect current and historic realities, however uncomfortable those realities might be, and then they need to examine why those stereotypes exist and to confront their own stereotyping behaviors as a result.

Those responsible for selecting novels for adolescent readers should be aware that there is a growing body of young adult literature from other countries. For instance, Pribic (1983) discusses the "blue jeans fiction of Yugoslavia," Osa (1986) describes "the new Nigerian youth literature," and Finch (1984) defines "the Caribbean bildungsroman." Because many of these works are now available in translation, teachers, parents, and librarians who are selecting books to which young adults will have access should include novels by young adult authors from foreign lands. Students like Sam and his peers, participants in the Sykesville Middle School research project on *Shadows Across the Sun*, are intrigued by the thought of living elsewhere, are interested in other countries even when they may not be curious about the lives of their peers in the U.S. who come from diverse cultural and ethnic backgrounds. These novels provide insight for readers about both the commonalities of the adolescent experience and about how the cultural milieu in which a person acts affects decisions and life choices. Some of the common concerns of adolescents which seem to transcend cultural boundaries include:

- the need to define oneself outside the realm of the family.
- the need to come to terms with new visions of one's parents as "less than perfect."
- the need to determine an individual set of moral, ethical, religious, or political principles.
- the need to come to terms with a developing sexuality and with the physiological changes brought on by puberty.
- the need to begin to develop positive relationships with the opposite sex.
- the need to begin to think about the future, about career options and job possibilities, about whether to marry or remain single.
- the need to forge a niche in the larger society.

For instance, in *The African*, Conton tells the story of Kisimi, who moves upward in society as a result of his scholastic endeavors, which win him a scholarship. As he pursues his studies, he must make important decisions about how to use his gifts, and he decides he can make a contribution to his country as a politician. *The River Sumida* (Nagai Kafu) captures the confusion of Chokichi as he seeks to decide what the future holds for him. Will he follow the path to the university outlined for him by his mother, or will he follow his heart and become an actor? Irina Korschrunow's Christopher is almost a German twin of the Japanese Chokichi, except that he finds the tensions involved in making such decisions about the future so intense that he decides life is not worth living in *Who Killed Christopher?*

Any student who has read and enjoyed Blume's *Are You There God? It's Me, Margaret* and has related to Margaret as she tries to figure out what her twelve-year-old body is doing would also appreciate the Russian *Shadows Across the Sun* by Albert Likhanov. Fedya, the main character, is at that age when his body is growing and maturing, leaving him feeling gangly and awkward. Also, he feels the first stirrings of sexuality as he becomes friends with Lena. She, too, is coping with the awkwardness inherent in puberty, but her situation is complicated by the fact that she is wheel-chair bound, a result of polio. Shell, in *Green Days by the River* (Michael Anthony), is fifteen when he must contend with changes in his family situation compounded by his developing feelings of sexuality, which confuse and trouble him. His confusion in the face of awakening sensations of physical desire can easily be compared to those of Pennington, the working class British hero in *Pennington's Seventeenth Summer* (K. M. Peyton), or to the Russian Dima, whose dedication to the clarinet suddenly must take a back seat to his interest in a young woman as portrayed in the delightful *My Brother Played the Clarinet* (Anatoli Aleskin). And Janine Boissard, in the French novel *A Matter of Feeling*, beautifully captures the same feelings from the female point of view as she describes Pauline's experiences with first love.

It would seem that the questions "Who am I?" or "What is the meaning of my life?" are asked by young people all over the world. In *Balloon Top*, Kana is on a quest to determine who she is, a quest complicated by conflicts between her traditional Japanese family values and her sense of the world as colored by her participation, in a limited way, in the political uprisings of the 1960s, as well as by conflicts between her desire for others to tell her who to be and her frustration at not being allowed to determine this for herself. She experiments with political activism, with the theater, with various kinds of relationships with young men, and she even seeks answers through a sexual encounter to the question of what it means to be a liberated woman. *Balloon Top* isn't easy to read or to summarize. The characters and the setting in which they are growing and changing are complex and the author does not, in the end, provide Kana with any definite solutions. But the ending is hopeful. Kana promises her father that she will listen to his advice: "Never to attempt to be someone other than yourself, a great pitfall of the impressionistic young" (111). *Balloon Top* is an outstanding portrait of the confusion and search for answers experienced by young adults, and its setting in another country reminds us that this quest is common to emerging adolescents in many cultures.

Just as these novels from other countries point out the similarities of developmental tasks and issues which exist in many cultures, they also can be used as a springboard for discussing the role of one's cultural heritage in making decisions and for pointing out differences that exist among cultures. When young adult novels from Russia were used in a rural Maryland middle school, the students felt safe to explore topics such as racism, prejudice, the role of religion, and gender stereotyping because of the distance between them and the characters created by differences in cultural backgrounds. Thus there was free discussion of these issues. These novels seemed to provide useful bridges into books by authors from the United States who wrestle with such concerns in settings more familiar, and so perhaps less comfortable for students to discuss. Possible topics for discussion include differences in:

- school systems and philosophies of education.
- the role of the state/government in the life of the individual.
- perception of family.
- the nature of the prevailing religious orientation.
- perceptions of history.
- the perception of the role of the adolescent in society.
- the routines of daily life.
- the perception of time.
- the nature of language use.

For example, in *The Bride Price* (Buchi Emecheta), the devaluation of women and their rights in Nigeria is heartbreakingly portrayed. *Hiroshima No Pika* (Toshi Maruki), through the illustrations which accompany the text, visually presents a different view of the afterlife. The main character in *Totto Chan: The Little Girl in the Window* (Tetsuko Kurayanagi), initially experiences problems because she is a divergent thinker in a very regimented Japanese school, and *Balloon Top* by Albery presents a very clear picture of the Japanese educational system. *Beka Lamb* by Edgell could be used to discuss differences in the place of adolescents in society, and the British *Handles*, by Mark, includes a wonderful glossary which could be used to discuss differences in the use of language. In fact, any novel from another country will convey something about the differences in the routines of daily life.

Also, students can examine whether or not their own cultural background influences in any way their response to a novel from another country. One of Sam's peers in the eighth grade class which read *Shadows Across the Sun* acknowledged that she was put off by some of the words the author used and by the fact that Fedya raises pigeons as a hobby, birds known to her only as "vile, dirty things." In her reflections on her responses, kept in a dialogue journal format, she states, "I think I have these responses because of our culture and the way we live." She later wonders, "How would Lena and Fedya react to *Bridge to Terabithia*? What would puzzle them about it?" thus showing her growing awareness of how the individual's experience and perceptions color the way in which he or she reacts to a text. This same student, along with several others in the class, spent a small group discussion session wrestling with the pigeon issue. They ultimately decided Fedya's pigeons represented the freedoms for which he was longing, an interpretation which worked to enhance other aspects of the plot line—and one at which they may not have arrived had they not been aware of the cultural divide which separated them from the characters.

One final comment on selection. As Townsend writes, "... any line which is drawn to confine children or their books to their own special corner is an artificial one. Whenever the line is drawn, children and adults and books will wander across it" (9). In selecting books for use in the classroom we must pay attention to what students tell us they find appropriate and stimulating. Thus novels such as Chinua Achebe's *No Longer at Ease*, James Baldwin's *Go Tell It on the Mountain*, or Gloria Naylor's *The Women of Brewster Place*, or novels by authors such as Alice Walker, Toni Morrison, and Ntoshake Shonge may be the books students choose to explore issues related to differences in cultural and ethnic heritage. Donelson and Nilsen, writing about this point—that young adult literature includes, basically, whatever young adults can and will read—note that the selection process can be supplemented by the use of "current reviewing sources and annual lists of recommended titles compiled by *School Library Journal*, *Booklist*, the Young Adult Division of the American Library Association, the *New York Times*, and the University of Iowa Books for Young Adults Poll published in the *English Journal*" (unpaged introduction). The *English Journal* often publishes, too, "Booksearch" columns on the theme of cultural diversity. Also, once a year, *Social Education* publishes a list of young adult novels useful for inclusion in the social studies classroom, many of which deal with issues of cultural diversity in an historical context.

In summary, teachers, librarians and others selecting novels for use in the classroom or guiding students' independent reading should consider the following selection principles:

1. Avoid tokenism.

2. Avoid didacticism. Choose books that are valuable for their literary merit.

3. Select books in which characters from diverse cultures interact in realistic ways.

4. Select books that deal with minority experiences, recent immigrant experience, and with the experiences of young adults growing up in other countries in order to provide as much diversity as possible.

5. Listen to young adults as they describe books which stirred them and promoted their thinking.

Teachers, instructors, and librarians also have an obligation to make these works easily accessible to students. Students can't read what they can't find. If money isn't available for class sets, an individualized reading program can be established that would allow students to read books of their own choosing and then come together in both small and large groups to share their new insights and perceptions.

Some Strategies for Using the Books Once You Find Them

Given the complexity of adolescence, what are some classroom activities teachers can use in conjunction with reading young adult literature about adolescents from diverse cultural backgrounds? Here are a number of possible teaching strategies, grouped by their usefulness as prereading, reading, and post-reading strategies. Note, too, that many of the activities can be done either by individuals or by groups of students.

Pre-Reading

1. Cubing—from Cowan and Cowan, *Writing*. Write for one to three minutes from each of the following perspectives, moving from one to the next without pausing to think: When you think of a Russian (or Japanese or German or Puerto Rican or Jew, etc.), a) describe; b) compare/contrast to someone from the U.S.; c) analyze (kind of thinking, beliefs, historical events which shaped current behavior, etc.); d) argue for or against knowing about the culture, knowing individuals representative of that culture. This might be useful as an initial activity to assess level of knowledge and stereotypes as well as for an ending activity.

2. Individual and class brainstorming on initial impressions, on characters in the book (prior to writing comparison papers between characters and self), on other aspects of the book. Again, collecting impressions at the beginning of the unit, then at the end, should provide evidence of how the unit changes perspectives.

3. Predictions: Knowing the book is about a young female/male from *X* culture, what plot tensions might you anticipate?

4. Asking questions as readiness before reading: What do you want to know about the location (the country, the *barrio*, the hills of Kentucky) in which the story is set?

During Reading

1. Dialectical journals/reading response logs.

2. Pen pal exchanges with students in the country in which the book is set—or with U.S. students attending American schools in the country. Pen pal exchanges with students from a different part of America—inner city Baltimore and rural Vermont, for example.

3. Comparison writing: essays about how students perceive themselves to be alike and different from the characters in the books, cinquains which start with the character and move to the self, cinquains about the character at the beginning of the book reflecting growth throughout the book.

4. Independent reading outside of class while reading a novel in common from the same country or culture or minority experience to compare information gleaned about schools, shopping, clothing, parent/child relationships, special occasions, housing, etc.

5. Role-playing significant plot events or alternative endings.

6. Selecting the most illustrative quotation from the chapter; discussing with the class why you chose it.

7. Pointing to two strong images from the reading, and discussing their significance to the work.

8. Creating character charts for main characters; adding to them as you read and learn more about each one.

9. Creating a dictionary of important terms reflective of the other culture with translations for future readers to use. Students might explore terms used to label certain ethnic and cultural groups, try to order those terms chronologically, and discuss the connotations associated with variations.

They might also discuss whether name calling hurts and whether the language we use colors our view of reality.

After Reading

1. Make a collage of initial perceptions, of characters, of settings, of themes, of ending vs. initial impressions.

2. Compare and contrast the books by authors from other countries or cultures to books for young adults written by authors such as Judy Blume, Katherine Paterson, S. E. Hinton, or M. E. Kerr—for theme, treatment of parents, language usage, etc. (Such discussions might also occur during the reading of a novel about characters from diverse cultural backgrounds.)

3. Analyze other media (TV, movies) for popular stereotypes and perceptions of the other culture. (This might also be done during the reading of the novel. Students might keep a special log in which they record such examples as homework.)

4. Imagine that you've been selected to make a play out of this book, but you have a very limited budget and can afford only one prop. What will you choose and why?

5. Create timelines of the major events in the work and discuss why you included those events you did.

6. Create a class newspaper based on the work.

7. Do a forced debate; ask those students who think the main character is a hero to stand up and move to one side of the room and tell those who do not share that perception to move to the other side. Hold the discussion as students are standing, and then ask those who'd like to do so to move to a middle ground at the end.

8. Create interview questions about the culture and individuals from the culture represented in the story and then conduct interviews of parents, peers, older citizens, and younger children and compare and contrast views held with students' own perceptions both before and after reading.

(The book *Multicultural Teaching: A Handbook of Activities, Information and Resources* by Tiedt and Tiedt (1986) provides a wealth of suggestions for teachers interested in promoting multicultural studies with students of all ages.)

Teachers can promote students' desire to read books about adolescents from culturally diverse backgrounds by using book talks (and by allowing students to share books with each other); by providing annotated bibliographies (several useful sources, such as those by Bracken, Corson, Davis and Davis, Dorney, Duran, Finch, Frankson, Martinez and Lomeli, Osa, Schone are provided in the references at the end); by surrounding students in the classroom with many and diverse books; by using and exploiting connections with the media center and its director (for instance, if a student has read a book about growing up in the inner city, he or she might view the filmstrip, with tape, of *The Me Nobody Knows*, based on the book of poems by the same name edited by Stephen M. Joseph and then create a media event); by volunteering to develop independent reading lists of novels about diverse cultural experiences that social studies teachers can use to supplement history, geography, and other social studies lessons; and by providing time for students to browse and read.

Also, it's important that teachers themselves be honest with their students about their feelings related to issues of cultural diversity. Teachers need to educate themselves about cultural differences through extensive reading. It will be pointless to celebrate cultural diversity in literature if we don't respect cultural differences in our students and teach in ways that show we value all students and their cultural heritages. We need to read books such as *Intercultural Theory and Practice: Perspectives on Education, Training, and Research* (Davey, Editor) or *Intercultural Sourcebook: Cross-Cultural Training Methodologies* (Hoopes). We need to read articles such as Delpit's "The Silenced Dialogue: Power and Pedagogy in Educating Other People's Children" or Steele's "On Being Black and Feeling Blue." We need to read books such as Heath's *Ways with Words: Language, Life and Work in Communities and Classrooms*, Highwater's *Many Smokes, Many Moons: A Chronology of American Indian History through Indian Art*, or Richard Rodriguez's *Hunger of Memory: The Education of Richard Rodriguez*. We need to read reference works such as Houston Baker's *Three American Literatures: Essays in Chicano, Native American, and Asian Literature for Teachers of American Literature*, Geneva Gay and William Baber's *Expressively Black: The Cultural Basis of Ethnic Identity*, or James Banks's *Education in the 80s: Multiethnic Education*. We need to read Friere's *Pedagogy of the Oppressed* and then take a hard look at what we believe should be the goals of the literature program — what it is we are trusting and hoping the study of literature will accomplish, and how to involve students in the creation of their curriculum. In a community of readers, where the teacher is but one member, discussion can center about questions such as:

1. When you meet someone who is different from you in customs, appearance, or in some other way, are you uncomfortable? Frightened? Repelled? Why or why not?

2. Can you learn to be interested in or to appreciate the likenesses and differences in the human family? How? Do you think it is important to do so?

3. What book have you read that sensitized you to another's background and way of life?

4. Just how different is it possible to be, in looks and behavior, before being perceived as dangerous rather than merely eccentric? Just how far can and should society go in telling its members how to think and act?

We need to implement the reading workshop approach outlined by Atwell in her book *In the Middle* as one means to accommodate differences in interest, motivation, and need while still developing the feeling of a community of readers in which each person, student and teacher alike, has something of value to contribute and important perceptions to share. We need to reconsider, too, our heavy emphasis on across-the-board reading assignments. Mike, a student from the

Sykesville Middle School project, received an A for the quarter the students read *Shadows Across the Sun*. But, when asked his overall impression of the unit, he said, "I hated it." Elaborating on why, he noted that he didn't mind the book, though it was not his favorite novel, but "hated" reading "anything when it's assigned" because "then I read for the teacher and not for me." We would violate the whole reason for including novels reflective of cultural diversity in the literature program if students feel, like Mike, that they are not reading for themselves but are only meeting the teacher's requirements.

Conclusion

After reading *Shadows Across the Sun*, the Russian novel used in the Sykesville Middle School, one eighth grader said, "If Fedya and Lena were called Jack and Jill, I wouldn't have known this was a Russian book." In fact, that assessment is not quite true. The setting, the food, the clothing, the influence of the state on day-to-day life, the treatment of the handicapped within the society—are all quite different from that which students from the majority culture in the U.S. experience. What this student seems to tell us as teachers is that he is willing to see the commonalities rather than the differences. There are similarities of concern and experience among young adults from varied backgrounds which may help our students, as they read about their peers from other cultures, develop a tolerance and appreciation for those whose cultural trappings and day-to-day behaviors set them apart. Through reading such novels, they may be exposed to the effects on society of prejudice, ethnocentricity, or cultural stereotyping and may begin to wrestle with their own values and related behaviors as a result. For instance, reading novels about the Native American experience should help students begin to think about their own attitudes toward the environment. Wilson and Hughes cite Jamake Highwater, a scholar of cultural anthropology and an author of books for young adults of Cherokee/ Blackfoot heritage. Highwater describes how, at times, he felt

> alienated by the ways ideas find their way into English words. For instance, when an English word is descriptive—like the word "wilderness"—I am often appalled by what is implied in that description. After all, the forest is not "wild" in the sense that it is something that needs to be tamed. For Blackfeet Indians, the forest is the natural state of the world; it is the cities that are wild and need taming. ... Indians do not believe in a "uni-verse," but in a "multiverse." Indians don't believe that there is only *one* truth, but think there are many truths. (223)

The hope is that by reading such literature we can help the "shadows across the sun" caused by a lack of understanding of others dissipate and so lay the foundation for a more tolerant and peaceful world. Perhaps Eloise Greenfield, author of *She Come Bringing Me That Little Baby Girl* and *Sister* best describes the goal of using young adult novels reflective of diverse cultural experiences in the classroom:

> I want to encourage children to develop positive attitudes toward themselves and their abilities, to love themselves ... I want to write stories that will allow children to fall in love with genuine Black heroes and heroines who have proved themselves to be outstanding in ability and in dedication to the cause of Black freedom ... I want to be one of those who can choose and order words that children will want to celebrate. I want to make them shout and laugh and blink back tears and care about themselves. They are our future. They are beautiful. They are for loving. (quoted in Tiedt and Tiedt, 148)

Works Cited

Achebe, Chinua. 1960. *No Longer at Ease*. Greenwhich, CT: Fawcett.

———. 1988. *Things Fall Apart*. Portsmouth, NH: Heinemann.

Albery, Nobuku. 1978. *Balloon Top*. New York: Pantheon.

Aleskin, Anatoli. 1975. *My Brother Plays the Clarinet*. New York: Henry Walck.

Anaya, Rudolfo. 1972. *Bless Me, Ultima*. Berkeley, CA: Tonatuiuh-Quinto Sol International.

Anthony, Michael. 1987. *Green Days by the River*. Portsmouth, NH: Heinemann.

Arrick, Fran. 1981. *Chernowitz!* New York: Bradbury.

Atwell, Nancie. 1987. *In the Middle: Writing, Reading, and Learning with Adolescents*. Portsmouth, NH: Boynton/Cook.

Baker, Houston (ed.). 1982. *Three American Literatures: Essays in Chicano, Native American, and Asian American Literature for Teachers of American Literature*. New York: Modern Language.

Baker, Houston, and Patricia Redmond (eds.). 1989. *Afro-American Literary Studies in the 1990s*. Chicago: University of Chicago Press.

Baldwin, James. 1953. *Go Tell It on the Mountain*. New York: Dell.

Banks, James (ed.). 1980. *Education in the 80s: Multiethnic. Education*. Washington, D.C.: National Education Association.

Blume, Judy. 1972. *Are You There, God? It's Me, Margaret*. New York: Dell.

Boissard, Janine. 1977. *A Matter of Feeling*. Trans. Mary Feeley. Toronto: Little, Brown.

Borland, Hal. 1984. *When the Legends Die*. New York: Bantam.

Bracken, Jeanne. 1981. *Books for Today's Young Readers: An Annotated Bibliography of Recommended Titles*. Old Westbury, NY: The Feminist Press.

Brooks, Bruce. 1984. *The Moves Make the Man*. New York: Harper Junior.

Butler, Octavia. 1981. *Kindred*. New York: Pocket Books.

Bykov, Vasil. 1981. *Pack of Wolves*. Trans. Lynn Solataroff. New York: Crowell.

Childress, Alice. 1977. *A Hero Ain't Nothin' But a Sandwich*. New York: Avon.

Cisneros, Sandra. 1988. *The House on Mango Street*. Houston, TX: Arte.

Cleaver, Vera, and Bill Cleaver. 1969. *Where the Lilies Bloom*. New York: Lippincott.

Conton, William. 1982. *The African*. Portsmouth, NH: Heinemann.

Corson, Carolyn. 1987. "Young Adult Afro-American Fiction: An Update for Teachers." *English Journal*. 76.4: 24—27.

Cowan, Gregory, and Elizabeth Cowan. 1980. *Writing*. Glenview, IL: Scott, Foresman.

Craven, Margaret. 1980. *I Heard the Owl Call My Name*. New York: Dell.

Danziger, Paula. 1986. *It's an Aardvark-Eat-Turtle World*. New York: Dell.

Davey, William (ed.). 1979. *Intercultural Theory and Practice: Perspectives on Education, Training and Research*. La Grange Park, IL: Society for International Education, Training and Research, Intercultural Network.

Davis, James, and Hazel Davis. (eds.). 1988. *Your Reading: A Booklist for Junior High and Middle School Students*. Urbana, IL: National Council of Teachers of English.

Delpit, Lisa. 1988. "The Silenced Dialogue: Power and Pedagogy in Educating Other People's Children." *Harvard Educational Review*. 58.3: 280—98.

Donelson, Kenneth, and Alleen P. Nilsen. 1980. *Literature for Today's Young Adults*. Glenview, IL: Scott, Foresman.

Dorney, Jaculine M. 1987. "Booklists on Young Adult Literature." *Journal of Reading*. 31.2: 182—85.

Duran, Daniel Flores. 1979. *Latino Materials: A Multicultural Guide for Children and Young Adults*. New York: Neal Schumann.

Edgell, Zee. 1987. *Beka Lamb*. Portsmouth, NH: Heinemann.

Ehle, Maryann. 1982. "The Velveteen Rabbit, The Little Prince, and Friends: Postacculturation through Literature." Paper presented at the Annual Meeting of the Professional Clinic of Association of Teacher Educators, (Phoenix, AZ, February 13—19), ERIC Document ED 221 881.

Emecheta, Buchi. 1976. *The Bride Price*. New York: Braziller.

ERIC Clearinghouse on Reading and Communication Skills. 1983. Urbana, IL. *Literature, Literary Response, and the Teaching of Literature: Abstracts of Doctoral Dissertations Published in "Dissertation Abstracts International" July through December*. ERIC Document ED 238 013.

Finch, J. B. 1984. *The Carribbean Bildungsroman: Notes on a Culture*. Paper presented at the National Council of Teachers of English Conference, Detroit, MI, November. ERIC Document Ed 254 865.

Flores, Juan. 1985. "Let's Discuss Chicano Adolescent Literature." *Reading Horizons*, 25.2: 127–32.

Frank, Pat. 1976. *Alas, Babylon*. New York: Bantam.

Frankson, Marie Stewart. 1990. "Chicano Literature for Young Adults: An Annotated Bibliography." *English Journal*. 79.1: 30–35.

Freire, Paulo. 1970. *Pedagogy of The Oppressed*. New York: Seaburg Press.

Gannon, Susan R., and Ruth Anne Thompson (eds). 1987. *Cross-Culturalism in Children's Literature: Selected Papers from the 1987 International Conference of the Children's Literature Association*. (Ottawa, Canada, May 14–17). ERIC Document ED 311 465.

Gay, Geneva, and William Baber (eds.). 1987. *Expressively Black: The Cultural Basis of Ethnic Identity*. New York: Praeger.

George, Jean C. 1973. *Julie of the Wolves*. New York: Harper and Row.

Gonzales, Roseann Duenas. 1990. "When Minority Becomes Majority: The Changing Face of the English Classroom." *English Journal*. 79.1: 16–23.

Greenfield, Eloise. 1974. *She Come Bringing Me That Little Baby Girl*. New York: Lippincott.

———. 1974. *Sister*. New York: Crowell.

Guy, Rosa. 1986. *The Disappearance*. New York: Dell.

———. 1983. *The Friends*. New York: Bantam.

———. 1989. *The Ups and Downs of Carl Davis III*. New York: Delacorte.

Hamilton, Virginia. 1976. *Arilla Sun Down*. New York: Greenwillow.

———. 1985. *Junius over Far*. New York: Harper and Row.

———. 1987. *A White Romance*. New York: Philomel.

Heath, Shirley Brice. 1983. *Ways with Words: Language, Life and Work in Communities and Classrooms*. New York: Cambridge University Press.

Highwater, Jamake. 1985. *Ceremony of Innocence*. New York: Harper and Row/Zolotow.

———. 1978. *Many Smokes, Many Moons: A Chronology of American Indian History through Indian Art*. New York: J. B. Lippencott.

Hoopes, David S. 1979. *Intercultural Sourcebook: Cross-Cultural Training Methodologies*. Chicago: Intercultural Press of Chicago.

Joseph, Stephen M. 1972. *The Me Nobody Knows*. New York: Avon.

Jordan, June. 1971. *His Own Where*. New York: Crowell.

Kafu, Nagai. 1965. *The River Sumida*. In *Kafu the Scribbler: The Life and Writings of Nagai Kafu* by Edward Seidensticker. Stanford, CA: Stanford University Press.

Korschrunow, Irina. 1978. *Who Killed Christopher?* New York: Collins.

Kuroyanagi, Tetsuko. 1981. *Totto Chan: The Little Girl in the Window*. Trans. Dorothy Britton. New York: Kodansha International.

Lasky, Kathryn. 1983. *Beyond the Divide*. New York: Macmillan.

Likhanov, Albert. 1983. *Shadows Across the Sun*. New York: Harper and Row.

Lyon, George Ella. 1988. *Borrowed Children*. New York: Bantam.

Mark, Jan. 1985. *Handles*. New York: Atheneum.

Martinez, Julio A., and Francisco A. Lomeli, (eds.). 1985. *Chicano Literature: A Reference Guide*. Westport, CT: Greenwood.

Martinez, Max. 1988. *Schoolland: A Novel*. Houston, TX: Arte.

Maruki, Toshi. 1982. *Hiroshima No Pika*. New York: Lothrop.

Mathis, Sharon Bell. 1972. *Teacup Full of Roses*. New York: Viking.

Mitchell, Arlene Harris. 1988. "Black Adolescent Novels in the Curriculum." *English Journal*. 77.5: 95–97.

Mohr, Nicholassa. 1986. *Going Home*. New York: Dial.

———. 1973. *Nilda*. New York: Harper and Row.

Moir, Hugh. 1989. "Current Trends and Lasting Values: A Five-Year Retrospective on Children's Books." *Ohio Media Spectrum*. 41.4: 5–11.

Momaday, N. Scott. 1969. *House Made of Dawn*. New York: Signet.

Morris, Gunilla. 1967. *A Feast of Light*. New York: Alfred Knopf.

Myers, Walter Dean. 1975. *Fast Sam, Cool Clyde, and Stuff*. New York: Penguin.

———. 1987. *The Outside Shot*. New York: Dell.

———. 1987. *Sweet Illusions*. New York: Teachers and Writers Collaborative.

———. 1988. *Won't Know Till I Get There*. New York: Penguin.

Naylor, Gloria. 1982. *The Women of Brewster Place*. New York: Viking.

Needle, Jan. 1978. *My Mate Shofiq*. London: Deutsch/Armada.

Osa, Osayimwense. 1986. "The New Nigerian Youth Literature." *Journal of Reading*. 30.2: 100–104.

Paterson, Katherine. 1977. *Bridge to Terabithia*. New York: Avon.

Paulsen, Gary. 1985. *Dogsong*. New York: Bradbury Press.

Peck, Robert Newton. 1972. *A Day No Pigs Would Die*. New York: Dell.

———. 1989. *Arly*. New York: Walker and Co.

Peyton, K. M. 1972. *Pennington's Seventeenth Summer*. New York: Crowell.

Potok, Chaim. 1978. *The Chosen*. New York: Fawcett.

———. 1972. *My Name is Asher Lev*. New York: Alfred Knopf.

Pribic, R. 1983. "Blue Jeans Fiction of Yugoslavia." *Journal of Reading*. 26: 430–34.

Richter, Conrad. 1966. *Light in the Forest*. New York: Knopf.

Rochman, Hazel. 1989. "Booktalking: Going Global." *Horn Book*. 65.1: 30–35.

Rodriguez, Richard. 1982. *Hunger of Memory: The Education of Richard Rodriguez*. New York: Bantam.

Romero, Patricia Ann, and Dan Zancanella. 1990. "Expanding the Circle: Hispanic Voices in American Literature." *English Journal*. 79.1: 24–29.

Santiago, Danny. 1983. *Famous All Over Town*. New York: New American Library.

Schone, Isabel. 1988. *A Hispanic Heritage: A Guide to Juvenile Books About Hispanic Peoples and Cultures, Series III*. Metuchen, NJ: Scarecrow.

Sleetor, Christine E. 1988. *Making Choices for Multicultural Education: Five Approaches to Race, Class, and Gender*. Columbus, OH: Charles Merrill.

Steele, Shelby. 1989. "On Being Black and Feeling Blue." *American Scholars*. 58: 4977–5012.

Stover, Lois, and Rita Karr. "The Effects of Reading a Young Adult Novel from the U.S.S.R. on U.S. Adolescents' Perceptions of their Russian Peers." Unpublished research study sponsored by Towson State University and Sykesville Middle School conducted during the 1989–1990 school year.

Strelkova, Irina. 1983. *Playing the Game*. Trans. J. C. Butler. Chicago: Imported Publications.

Tate, Eleanora. 1987. *The Secret of Gumbo Grove*. New York: Bantam.

Tatum, Charles (ed.). 1990. *Mexican American Literature*. Chicago: Harcourt Brace Jovanovich.

Taylor, Mildred. 1983. *Let the Circle Be Unbroken*. New York: Bantam.

———. 1976. *Roll of Thunder, Hear My Cry*. New York: Dial.

———. 1983. *Song of the Trees*. New York: Bantam.

Tiedt, Pamela L., and Iris M. Tiedt. 1979. *Multicultural Teaching: A Handbook of Activities, Information, and Resources*, 1st ed. Boston: Allyn and Bacon.

Thomas, Joyce Carol. 1986. *Water Girl*. New York: Avon.

Townsend, John Rowe. 1979. *A Sounding of Storytellers*. New York: J. B. Lippencott.

Tway, Eileen (ed.). 1981. *Reading Ladders for Human Relations*, 6th ed. Urbana, IL: National Council of Teachers of English.

Uchida, Yoshiko. 1984. *The Best Bad Thing*. New York: Atheneum.

———. 1982. *A Jar of Dreams*. New York: McElderry.

Voigt, Cynthia. 1985. *The Runner*. New York: Atheneum.

Wartski, Maureen Crane. 1981. *A Boat to Nowhere*. New York: New American Library.

———. 1980. *A Long Way from Home*. New York: Signet Vista.

Wilson, Roy, and Darlene Hughes. 1981. "Appreciating Different Cultures." In *Reading Ladders for Human Relations*, 6th ed. Ed. Eileen Tway. Urbana, IL: National Council of Teachers of English. 223–313.

Yep, Laurence. 1977. *Child of the Owl*. New York: Harper Junior.

———. 1975. *Dragonwings*. New York: Harper Junior.

Yolen, Jane. 1988. *The Devil's Arithmetic*. New York: Viking/Kestrel.

12

Gender Issues and the Young Adult Novel

Patricia P. Kelly

If we believe that literature can make us rethink or resee or reevaluate our ideas about others and ourselves, then the portrayal of male and female roles in adolescent fiction is an important classroom consideration. If adolescent literature provides an environment for young adults to experience vicariously the situations they may someday encounter, to see the results of decisions made by characters, and to evaluate their ideas and behaviors, then how males and females interact in those fictional situations can shape thinking by reinforcing stereotypes or by promoting alternative views. Because adolescent novels are written by as many female as male writers and because the stories generally reflect a modern setting with male and female protagonists, young adult novels provide excellent opportunities to look at the way gender roles are played out. Of course, any novel is much more than the gender issues embedded within the story line, but for that very reason it is an important consideration. Because readers get swept up into the story, they may not consciously note stereotyped behaviors yet unconsciously process the information.

Any consideration of gender during the act of reading is further complicated because it involves not only the gender of the characters but also the gender of the reader. In the early years of the young adult novel, Carlsen described the reading preferences of early adolescents. He said that by eighth grade boys' and girls' reading interests differ sharply, and the difference continues even in mature adult readers. Boys want the main character to be male; girls will read books with either sex playing a major role. Boys prefer a large cast of characters in an action-packed plot with subplots, taking place over a long period of time and in many locales with lots of dialogue and description of action. On the contrary, girls like few characters in a more direct plot taking place in a specific locale, a school or a town, and covering a discrete period of time, a summer or a year for example, with descriptions of inner thoughts and emotional reactions. Carlsen pointed out that it is not unusual for girls and women to read and enjoy a "masculine" story, but boys and men rarely enjoy a "feminine" one (23–24).

Other research of reading preferences and responses has generated similar findings. Beaven's study, for example, found that girls could identify with both male and female characters, though they listed more males than females, but boys identified with male characters only (60–61). To further complicate the process of looking at gender through literature, Symmonds found that as "male students get older, they seem less able to identify with characters that are not male. Conversely, as females get older they seem to relate equally if not better with male characters" (19). Muted group theory, where "language and the norms for its use are controlled by the dominant group" (Crawford and Chaffin 21), may explain this occurrence. Specifically, in our male-dominated literary curriculum, females have grown up reading literature from the male perspective and in a male voice and, therefore, may have learned to value that literature more highly than the fiction that reflects their own experiences and feelings.

Preferences in reading and differing responses to characters make it difficult to select for classroom use literature that reflects a variety of gender relationships. The content of many adolescent novels, however, makes it equally difficult to find good gender roles. This chapter first contains a discussion of gender issues of girls in selected young adult novels, then gender issues in romance novels, followed by gender issues related to boys in selected young adult novels, concluding with a description of two adolescent novels particularly suited for gender study.

A Girl's Relationship with Her Own Body

Girls' acceptance of their own bodies as they grow and change is a theme of many novels and of particular importance when looking at young adult literature from a gender standpoint. There appears to be no exact corollary to this theme when boys are the protagonists. Although there is an occasional boy who is not as tall or athletic as others, he is usually a minor character. For boys the visible characteristics of puberty are positive: they get taller, stronger, hairier. Conversely, for girls the visible signs of puberty make them vulnerable: breasts are noticeable and the entire body begins to change shape as it moves from an androgynous child's form to a woman's form. This change, even when easy, is a distinct demarcation in a female's life, but when difficult can result in any number of behaviors, among them eating disorders and acute dissatisfaction with one's body.

In recent years a number of novels have been published about anorexia nervosa, a problem of primarily young females in affluent, industrialized countries. Sometimes it is the onset of puberty with the accompanying body changes that triggers the intial diet, an effort to meet some ideal shape promulgated in the media. Then it becomes a matter of exercising control over one's life as a way to enhance self-esteem. A particularly effective novel is Deborah Hautzig's *Second Star to the Right* because the first-person narrator, Leslie Margolee Hiller, leads the reader insightfully through the entire experience from the initial diet and her desire to be thin and happy to her hospitalization when she has reached 76 pounds and is eating only three cottage cheese curds per day.

A different but related eating problem is bulimia. Primarily associated with females, bulimia stems from a need similar to that causing anorexia, the need to gain control over some element of one's life. With bulimia, the feeling of control comes through purging after binge eating. In Patti Stren's book *I Was a 15-Year-Old Blimp* Gabby Finkelstein uses a combination of crash diet and purging to begin losing weight. Even at a camp designed to help her lose weight sensibly, she continues purging. Her parents, a mother who is thin and exercises extreme control, and a father who is understanding, realize the need for therapy when Gabby says, "... no matter how thin I get, I still feel fat inside. ... I have a hard time liking myself" (146). Unfortunately, the end of the book leads a female adolescent reader to believe that a special boyfriend, not a therapist, is the answer. As Gabby dances with Mel, she thinks, "I finally, *finally*, liked myself, and it felt right" (156). To conquer bulimia, Gabby has to learn to like herself without Mel, and only a therapist can help her in that struggle.

Reflecting the psychological ramifications of being overweight, Sheema in Virginia Hamilton's *A Little Love* eats to fill the emptiness inside her, the need for the love of a father who deserted her. Also to fill this void, she meets the boys who come around late at night: "It was nice to hold somebody. ... She didn't know why people made so much out of a little love" (14). Forrest sees beyond Sheema's bulky exterior; he treats her gently and with respect. With him, Sheema feels tiny and pretty inside, but he cannot convince her that she is pretty on the outside. She sees herself in the words of others: mumpy fat, ugly baby, slow-motion melons. After Forrest takes her to find her father, Sheema realizes that her father will never love her; but strangely now that the quest is over, she no longer has the appetite she had, the need for food to ease the pain. She says, "Don't long for no food now"

(200). There is, of course, no simple solution for such psychological scarring, but Sheema has taken the first step toward gaining control of her own body. With yet a different physiological problem, fifteen-year-old Grace Schmidt in *Monday I Love You*, by Constance C. Greene, has endured countless humiliations because of her size 38D breasts and a thin mother who says to Grace when she first develops in fifth grade, "What will they think, a great big girl like you with a dainty little person like myself for a mother?" (13). Grace is saving her babysitting money for a breast reduction operation. In the meantime, several girls hold her down in the restroom and strip her clothes off, revealing the two bras she always wears. Ms. Govoni, the physical education teacher, enters, for the moment saving Grace even more humiliation. She then helps Grace learn to exercise, watch her eating, and buy good bras. Grace's improved appearance begins to enhance her self-esteem, an important step toward the time when she can make an adult decision about surgery.

Girls' Relationships with Other Girls

Generally in adolescent novels written for early middle school grades, the plots, regardless of the other twists, center on girls as friends. Novels appealing to girls in late middle school and early high school frequently include a female protagonist who knows a boy or dates a boy, thus making her female friends secondary characters. Even during the time the girls spend together, they tend to discuss boys. Ironically, the audience for these books is girls, yet the subtle message being communicated to them, however positive, humorous, or mysterious the rest of the plot may be, is that girls are second best, less significant. The underlying message in these novels for a female audience is that having a boyfriend is more important in a girl's life than having girl-friends. Girlfriends are there to listen, to plan, to console when the relationship goes awry, and to spend time with when a boy is not around.

One positive example of girlfriends in an early middle school situation is Judy Blume's *Are You There God? It's Me, Margaret*, which chronicles the emergent adolescent antics of Margaret and her friends as they wait for their periods, and their vicious insults to Laura, who has matured two years earlier. Every adolescent female reader sees her own experience through Margaret's story, wearing a bra she did not need or needing a bra before anyone else wore one, having the burden of being first to begin menstruation or dreading being last, needing the approval of the group and fearing being different. Talking, sharing, spending time together — young girls use each other as a baro-meter, a measurement for what is right, wrong, good, and bad.

Although early adolescent girls as friends are depicted frequently, one topic rarely portrayed in the young adult novel is a lesbian relationship. In *Ruby*, Rosa Guy treats the subject with honesty and sensitivity. Her mother dead, her father tyrannically strict, Ruby Cathy is desperately lonely. She is beautiful but not particularly intelligent, so Daphne Duprey, tall, confident, smart, and stylish, offers to help. Daphne's mother unquestioningly allows her daughter complete privacy. The relationship continues until Ruby, rather than confronting her father, allows Daphne to risk her life. That choice is the turning point. Leaving for college soon, Daphne, always in control, breaks none too gently with Ruby, who declares she cannot live without Daphne, not realizing their relationship is fulfilling a temporary need. Their talks and plans, their love and hurt are similar to the heterosexual relationships described in other adolescent novels.

Girls and Their Mothers and Fathers

The teenager's world in fiction does not include parents to any great extent. At best, fathers are seen driving girls and their friends somewhere or commenting on various behaviors, such as grades, lateness, or clothing, although occasionally a father is portrayed as the nurturer, the one who understands. Gabby's father in *I Was a 15-Year-Old Blimp* is the consoler, the confidante; her mother does not know how to communicate, although she tries. Whatever the father's role in adolescent novels, however, it is rarely anything but minor.

On the other hand, young adult literature reflects many variations of the ageless mother-daughter theme. Because this relationship is such a difficult one for a teenage girl, most books that include a mother and daughter have at least some reference to conflict even in the best of circumstances. For instance, Margaret Mahy's *The Catalogue of the Universe* portrays a strong mother in a supportive mother-daughter relationship. Unmarried, Dido May has struggled to feed and clothe her daughter Angela, and in order to foster Angela's self-esteem has constantly talked about the loving father Angela has never known but sets out to find. Because Dido has helped her daughter feel good about herself and her capabilities, Angela is not devastated when she discovers the truth, that her father had rejected her mother when she became pregnant. Dido lives her life by her own standards high on a mountaintop, encouraging Angela to become her own person making her own decisions.

A totally different woman in Sue Ellen Bridger's *Notes for Another Life* is Wren Jackson's mother, who has left her children with their grandmother to pursue a career but breezes in for occasional visits. Here Bliss, the grandmother, functions as the mother: listening, caring, encouraging. Although fourteen-year-old Wren has vowed never to be like her mother, she begins to see the choices women sometimes have to make. Wanting to be a pianist, she wonders whether she has room within her for anything but music; however, she does not want to have only her music. At this point she is beginning to understand not only the choice her mother made but also her own dilemma as a talented female.

Gender Issues in the Romance Novel

The romance novel is not new, but the recent proliferation of adolescent romance novels is somewhat disturbing. Young adult romances, such as those in the *Silhouette First Love* series, have many of the same characteristics as adult romance novels. The heroine is in some way vulnerable — a condition brought on by a move to a new environment, an illness, or some secret flaw; she meets a handsome hero, who is initially drawn to her; some type of conflict occurs that separates them or causes a misunderstanding; in the final resolution they are happily together (Radway 134). In the teen versions there is always a great deal of description about clothes, hair, makeup, figures, long looks, and touching hands. People are beautiful, houses are decorated, and love scenes are dramatic as in Dorothy Francis' *Special Girl*: "... he took her in his arms and kissed her slowly and tenderly. He kissed her the way she had imagined he would kiss her and she was reluctant to see the kiss and their evening end. She felt as if she had been looking through a kaleidoscope, watching their relationship fall into a different and more pleasing pattern" (128). This scene with slightly different wording appears in every romance novel. Like the adult versions, the adolescent heroine's happiness depends on her having the love of a man. Her identity is tied to "coupleness."

Carlsen suggests that girls' interest in the romantic novel peaks around ninth or tenth grade (38). However, in Symmonds' study, high school girls through twelfth grade prefer novels of love and romance (18). Although more studies may need to be done to state that finding with certainty, it is clear that sales of these books indicate a substantial market. Ironically, at a time when teens should be reading to find direction for their lives, to develop personal values, and to picture themselves in an adult world, many female adolescents are receiving one message: a woman has value only if she is with a man.

Even books that are not strictly in the romance genre often paint the same message. For example, a book like *All for the Love of That Boy* by Linda Lewis makes a good statement about peer pressure to drink, and the fifteen-year-old protagonist Linda is intelligent, attending a special high school for technology. However, her major interest in life is Lenny, who hangs out and drops out of school. She wants to graduate early, not to go to college but to marry Lenny, despite their on-again, off-again relationship. Linda sees herself as important only with Lenny: "I stood next to him the whole time, thinking how glad I was to be Lenny's girlfriend. He was so full of life and had so much personality" (45). Because this type of novel has realistic settings with characters who are less than beautiful and contains some type of social commentary, the gender messages may be more "dangerous." A romance novel sets itself forth as a fairy tale, making it easier perhaps to separate oneself from the stereotypical view of male/female relationships. When those same messages are conveyed in a more realistic format, it may be difficult for a teenager to avoid internalizing such views of herself.

Other Boy-Girl Relationships

Even in novels other than romance, boy-girl relationships in books targeted toward female readers tend to be stereotyped. A girl's happiness depends on having a boyfriend. Books for boys have a different perspective; they fit girls into their other activities where appropriate. They talk things over with girlfriends, party with them, and occasionally fall in love. But usually this relationship does not result in turning their lives upside down or occupying their thoughts throughout their waking hours. Often they are even ambivalent about their feelings, as Walker is in Chris Crutcher's *Stotan!* He dates Devnee, a prettily stereotyped, nurturing female, but he wants to break off with her because he likes Elaine, a nontraditional girl who is also a friend. Walker eventually decides to stop dating Devnee, even though Elaine has let him know that they will be friends only. Such decisions would be rare in a book written for a female audience.

Generally, fictional accounts of boys and girls as true, long-lasting friends are also rare. An excellent example of such a relationship, however, is in Julie Reece Deaver's *Say Goodnight, Gracie*, where Jimmy Woolf and Morgan Hackett have been like brother and sister since birth; they are friends almost to the exclusion of others. They share similar interests—Jimmy's is dancing and Morgan's is acting; they support each other emotionally; and they thoroughly enjoy each other's company. When a girl from acting class asks who Jimmy is, Morgan says, "He's just a friend. My best friend." To which, the girl replies, "Your best friend's a *guy*? ... Definitely weird" (106). But when a drunk driver kills Jimmy, Morgan must learn to face life without her alter-ego. There are few examples in either adolescent or adult fiction of such a compelling male-female relationship.

Boys' Relationships with Other Boys

In realistic adolescent fiction boys may be high achievers or athletes, but just as frequently their characters are troubled or in trouble, are rebels or at least testing the boundaries of societal expectations, and appear to be without ambition or at least do not perform well in school. Although not all male characters fit this description, many of them do. And even though the culminating messages of the novels are usually appropriately positive, the image subtly conveyed to the male teenager is that of the man alone with his inner feelings, depending primarily on his own resources. Extremely popular with boys, these books do encourage them to read, but perhaps the stereotyped portrayal is as invasive of their self-perceptions as romance novels are of girls' self-perceptions.

Stotan! is an unconventional story of athletes which not only describes four realistic adolescent male characters but also a variety of male relationships. Central to the story is the commitment, care, and understanding shared by Walker, Nortie, Lion, and Jeff, who are members of the swim team as well as best friends. Together they go through Stotan Week, a grueling training period set up by Max, their coach, to give them an inner reserve to draw on. During Stotan Week they share Stotan stories, times they endured pain. Nortie tells of life with his abusive, drunken father and of finding his thirteen-year-old older brother hanging in the garage because he could not endure any more. The portrait of the abused mother and children is a textbook case, even to Nortie's saying he still loves his father and tries to please him. With Jeff dying of leukemia, the boys must tap the strength they found during Stotan Week. Max is the father figure in these boys' lives. Walker's father is very old; Lion's father is dead; Nortie's is abusive; and Jeff's father is alive but somewhat protective. Ironically Max is a father to them but not to his own young daughter, whom he rarely sees since being divorced. He is the man alone, the Stotan — part Stoic, part Spartan — the role model for his four athletes, the grownup version of many young adult male protagonists.

Although there are more young adult novels dealing with homosexuality of males than females, there are still relatively few, with one of the earliest, *Sticks and Stones* by Lynn Hall, not confronting the issue directly but treating the subject obliquely. Tom Naylor, who plays classical piano, has not been accepted well in his new school. The only people who want to be his friend are Floyd Schleffe, a fat misfit, and Amber Showalter, who looks upon him as a happy addition to a school with fewer boys than girls. Tom makes the mistake of avoiding both of them. Instead, when Ward Alexander moves back to town after being medically discharged from the armed services, Tom finds he is attracted to this intellectual, sensitive man. Together they repair a shack on the Alexander family property, making a place for Ward to write and for them to spend time talking. Floyd spreads the rumor because he thinks "there are worse things than being fat and dumb" (52). Eventually the principal tells Tom that some parents do not want a homosexual traveling to compete in the state music finals. Over and over again he relives his feelings and actions, looking for the truth about himself. Concentrating is impossible, and Tom's school work suffers to the point that he slips from honor status to failing, which puts him on a par with Floyd, who knows all about failure. After a car accident which kills Floyd, Tom realizes with clarity: "There was nothing wrong with me at all, until I started listening to their whispers. . . . They brought me down, and I let them. . . . There's probably nothing wrong with my masculinity, only with my stupid head, for not being surer of myself" (187). And he welcomes Ward to his hospital bedside, welcomes back a valuable friendship he almost lost for fear of public finger-pointing. At issue is not whether Ward or Tom is homosexual but whether society at large can accept the depth of such a relationship.

Boys and Their Mothers and Fathers

In many adolescent novels written for boys, mothers, if not totally absent, play minor roles. The limited interaction between mothers and sons makes it difficult to picture the women as characters. They say hello and goodbye, serve meals, and occasionally express an opinion, which the son views as criticism. Of course, there are exceptions, such as Mrs. Woolf in *Say Goodnight, Gracie*. Though she is portrayed as a conventional, middle-class woman, Mrs. Woolf supports Jimmy in his desire to be a dancer, has good communication with him when he is alive, and exhibits strength after his death.

Providing an extensive depiction of a mother as a major character, *A Kindness* by Cynthia Rylant portrays an unusual mother-son relationship. Anne Becker, a divorced artist and mother of fifteen-year-old Chip, becomes pregnant by Ben, her longtime friend and an art dealer. Chip, who is brighter and handier than his mother, has for years run the household, assembling his own toys, fixing appliances, filing income taxes, and shopping for groceries because he knew how to save money. He is aghast when his mother decides to have the baby because he knows he will have even more to do. The irony is that Anne does not recognize that Chip has taken care of things for years. He has feared that he might die, leaving her alone and unable to cope. Anne admits she has let the boundaries in their relationship get blurred:

> I need to have this baby and I'd like to keep your love. I don't need
> your help in taking care of it and I don't need your presence to keep

me happy or safe. I have no expectations of you. I just ask that you not punish me for the way I have to live. (53)

Hoping to involve Chip with the baby's arrival, Anne lets him name the baby, Dusky Anne. But despite Anne's promise that she will ask nothing of Chip, the baby's presence changes their home to chaos as only a baby can. Slowly, Chip begins to love his little sister and cannot imagine life without her. Giving new meaning to both their lives, the baby has helped Chip and Anne forge a different but stronger relationship.

Father-son relationships in adolescent literature, however, are as varied as they are in real life: absent fathers, abusive fathers, single-parent fathers, supportive fathers, or mentally ill fathers, as in *Notes for Another Life*. For years, Kevin has not been able to accept his father's mental illness but in the end assumes a caretaker's role as he bathes and dresses his catatonic father as a father would bathe a child. Once Kevin can love his father as a human being, even though he is not functioning as a father, and once he realizes his mother left not because there was something wrong with him but for her own needs, he is ready to begin the healing process. The complexity of the family interactions makes this novel a particularly rich vehicle for examining gender implications, including those already discussed in mother-daughter relationships.

Yet a different father-son relationship is integral to the plot of Robert Cormier's *After the First Death*. Mark Marchand, a general in Inner Delta, has knowledge of his son Ben that no father should have. Ben's classes are monitored to provide behavioral data, and home telephone conversations are taped and checked. Ben's weakness and failures are noted; he is studied like a lab specimen. When terrorists hijack a bus of children, the General offers his son as the courier. Knowing Ben will be tortured for information, his father has let him overhear an incorrect plan of attack but one he wants the terrorists to believe. Theirs is a general-soldier relationship: they shake hands "stiffly"; the general "resists" reaching for his son and holding him in his arms (196). Ben is devastated by his failure to withstand the torture; he tells the false plan and the children are rescued. He is even more devastated when he learns that he was sent because he was expected to fail: "To find out that I not only betrayed my country but had been expected to do it. To find out that I was expected to act as a coward, unable to take a little pain" (226). His father is not without feeling; his son's screams never leave his head and he asks Ben's forgiveness. The remorse, however, is too late to save Ben.

A novel in which the father-son conflict fairly bristles is Richard Peck's *Father Figure*. Jim Atwater's father left when Jim was nine. After his mother commits suicide, Jim, then seventeen, and his eight-year-old brother Byron must spend the summer with their father. Jim thinks of himself as Byron's protector, his substitute father for all these years, and he resents his father's efforts to establish a relationship with Byron. But most of all Jim is angered by his father's desertion of him. When Jim sees himself in his father's face and they talk about the past and the future, they begin taking the first steps toward mending their relationship. There have been too much pent-up anger and too many angry words to effect a complete reconciliation, but for Byron's sake these two men begin to understand each other.

A twist on the father-son conflict is in Katie Letcher Lyle's *Dark But Full of Diamonds*, where Scott Dabney is in love with Hilah Brown, his English teacher and former swim coach, but discovers his father is dating her and intends to marry her. Scott changes from a communicative son to a vengeful, unlikable person. Both care about Scott's happiness to the point they decide not to marry. It is when he becomes sick while searching his mother's past and Hilah takes care of him that he sees his selfishness in depriving his father and her of the happiness they deserve.

Two Books with Good Gender Models

Symmonds found that both boys and girls like adventure and science fiction (19). Consequently, a selection like Robert C. O'Brien's *Z for Zachariah* used for in-common class reading would be a way of getting male readers involved with a particularly strong female character who is the product of a male writer. As a survivor of a nuclear holocaust, sixteen-year-old Ann Burden has established a routine for surviving alone on her family's farm. Ann, who had wanted to be an English teacher, knows how to use a gun, fish, and operate the farm equipment. Into that space comes Mr. Loomis, a former chemist who has the world's only radiation-proof suit, but he becomes gravely ill from nuclear poisoning when he foolishly bathes in a contaminated stream. Ann nurses him back to health and maintains the farm. But Mr. Loomis acts like an overseer, telling her what to plant and checking on the quantity and quality of her work. Even though the farm is Ann's, Mr. Loomis, as a man, assumes the boss's role. She remains wary of Mr. Loomis as a stranger, but she also initially reacts to his masculinity: she fixes better meals and she is "ashamed to have him see me ... dirty, hot, and sweaty" (57). Ann, who has had only one date at age thirteen, later fantasizes that she and Mr. Loomis might get married at apple blossom time next year when she is seventeen.

But these romantic dreams of a young girl give way to the harsh reality of attempted sexual assault. Thinking Ann is asleep, Mr. Loomis quietly comes into her room one night. Alert, Ann feels his hand searching for her:

> Then, suddenly, both his hands were over me, not roughly, but in a dreadful, possessive way that I had never felt or imagined. His breathing grew faster and louder. He was not going to go away. ... I knew what he was planning to do as clearly as if he had told me. One hand brushed my face, and then came down hard on my shoulder to pin me to the bed. (133–134).

Ann desperately fights back and flees to the cave, where she had lived when Mr. Loomis came. She realizes that not only must she again live alone but also she must contend with an aggressive enemy. Late when Mr. Loomis shoots her in the ankle, Ann knows, "He wanted to maim, not to kill me. So that he could catch me" (168). In this battle of wills and strategy, she continually outwits him. Knowing she will die there or become his prisoner, Ann steals the "safe-suit" so that she can try to find another place to live. Before she goes, she confronts Mr. Loomis but cannot shoot him even in self-defense. In the end he begs her not to leave him alone, but Ann cannot trust him; and though she cannot kill him, she does hate him. Despite the stereotyped themes of female nurturing and male dominance, Ann's actions are not those of a submissive, dominated female. Quite the contrary, she is a self-sufficient, self-reliant, daring protagonist, who takes control of her own life. If her character were male, very little would have to change in the story.

Permanent Connections, by Sue Ellen Bridgers, offers even more possibilities for discussing gender relationships within a tense, coming of age novel. The male protagonist, Rob Dickson, is enough of an outsider, a rebel, to interest boys. Dabbling in drugs and generally not doing well, Rob is sent to a family farm in North Carolina to help an injured uncle, Fairlee. There he must assume some caretaking responsibility, a new role for Rob. The male relationships are complex. Rob's relationship with his father is distant; it is Uncle Fairlee who acts the father, advising Rob, standing up for him, and paying for a lawyer when he gets into trouble. Even Rob's grandfather, who never understood his own son, Rob's father, becomes a father-protector. The female relationships are equally unique. Having rejected an upper-middle class life, Ginny, a weaver who lives with her daughter on a mountaintop, gently coaxes Aunt Coralee, an agoraphobic who is ignored by her family, back into society. Theirs is a quiet, lovely friendship. The two boy-girl relationships are diametrically opposite. Leanne, Rob's cousin, dates Travis, the football star. In many ways they act married, settled into traditional roles. Rob occasionally dates Ellery, Ginny's daughter, who like him feels different in this small town but who also is intelligent and independent, not needful of a relationship in which she cannot function as her own person. Interestingly, Ellery battles her mother, who in turn functions as a mother for Rob, whose own mother does not know how to communicate with her son. Even minor characters are well drawn in this tale of complex interpersonal relationships.

These are but two books that a classroom teacher might use to generate a realistic discussion about gender roles and gender relationships. It seems time to consider gender as an issue when selecting books for class study and recommended independent reading, for a look at much adolescent fiction from a gender perspective shows that girls are likely to be stereotyped as dependent in their relationships with boys, that mothers and fathers play fairly insignificant roles at best and detrimental roles at worst, and that boys are also frequently stereotyped as athletes or loners. There are, of course, notable exceptions, and those books can appeal to young people as they struggle with defining themselves in relation to others.

Works Cited

Beaven, Mary H. 1972. "Responses of Adolescents to Feminine Characters in Literature." *Research in the Teaching of English* 6: 48–68.

Blume, Judy. 1970. *Are You There God? It's Me Margaret*. New York: Dell.

Bridgers, Sue Ellen. 1982. *Notes for Another Life*. New York: Bantam.

———. 1987. *Permanent Connections*. New York: Harper & Row Junior Books.

Carlsen, G. Robert. 1967. *Books and the Teen-age Reader*. New York: Bantam.

Cormier, Robert. 1979. *After the First Death*. New York: Pantheon.

Crawford, Mary, and Roger Chaffin. 1986. "The Reader's Construction of Meaning: Cognitive Research on Gender and Comprehension." In *Gender and Reading*, Elizabeth A. Flynn and Patrocinio P. Schweickart, Eds. Baltimore: The Johns Hopkins University Press, 3–30.

Crutcher, Chris. 1986. *Stotan!* New York: Dell.

Deaver, Julie Reece. 1988. *Say Goodnight, Gracie*. New York: Harper & Row Junior Books.

Francis, Dorothy. 1981. *Special Girl*. New York: Silhouette Books.

Greene, Constance C. 1988. *Monday I Love You*. New York: Harper & Row.

Guy, Rosa. 1976. *Ruby*. New York: Bantam.

Hall, Lynn. 1972. *Sticks and Stones*. New York: Dell.

Hamilton, Virginia. 1984. *A Little Love*. New York: Philomel Books.

Hautzig, Deborah. 1981. *Second Star to the Right*. New York: Greenwillow.

Lewis, Linda. 1989. *All for the Love of That Boy*. New York: Pocket Books.

Lyle, Katie Letcher. 1981. *Dark But Full of Diamonds*. New York: Bantam.

Mahy, Margaret. 1986. *The Catalogue of the Universe*. New York: Antheneum.

O'Brien, Robert C. 1974. *Z for Zachariah*. New York: Dell.

Peck, Richard. 1978. *Father Figure*. New York: New American Library.

Radway, Janice A. 1984. *Reading the Romance*. Chapel Hill: The University of North Carolina Press.

Rylant, Cynthia. 1988. *A Kindness*. New York: Dell.

Stren, Patti. 1985. *I Was a 15-Year-Old Blimp*. New York: New American Library.

Symmonds, Andrea. 1990. "High School Students, Gender Identification and Literature." Idaho English Journal: 18–19.

13

Censorship and the Young Adult Novel

James E. Davis

We literature and reading teachers are bombarded with criticism from all directions. If it is not the governor or the president criticizing us and blaming us for the world's ills, it is some censor or another fearing that books might corrupt the young — with ideas. This bombardment causes schools to resemble battlegrounds at times. In 1989, for example, the People for the American Way tallied 172 censorship attempts and other challenges to public education. That is fifteen more than in 1988. That 172, of course, is incomplete, including only confirmed incidents and not even touching on closet censorship.

The conservatives' habit of trying to censor practically anything under the charge of "secular humanism" during the first part of the 1980s has changed. Their new targets, among other things, are satanism, witchcraft, and the occult. Some young adult novels touch on, or even center on, all of these subjects. And the liberals are still objecting to Bible readings and instruction, sexism, racism, ageism, and a number or other -isms including conservatism, all of which are sometimes subjects of books for and about young adults.

But tactics really have changed, and not for the better. Objectors are not nearly as willing to settle for only their own children's exemption from whatever they object to. Increasingly, both conservative and liberal censors won't give up unless the book they object to is banned in general. This has resulted in increasing and more effective attacks on libraries. Fifty-one incidents involved library books in 1989, an increase from thirty-six in 1987–88.

The Most Censored Works of the 1980s

When writers of fiction for adolescents began their cautious attempts to move out of the long tradition of adhering to rigid taboos in the early and mid-sixties, as my own study reported in the *English Journal* in 1967 showed that they were doing, some censorship rumblings were expected and indeed came. But by the mid-seventies when writers were really treating life truthfully, an increase in censorship episodes was almost inevitable. Hazel Davis, in an article entitled "Sex and Fiction for Adolescents: Field Day for Censors and Anti-Censors," showed that this censorship was surely happening by 1979. My own article in *The ALAN Review* in that same year, "Coping with Censors and Comstocks," also demonstrated increasing censorship of young adult fiction. And the censorship grew by leaps and bounds during the 1980s. Following is a list of the most often challenged books during the 1980s according to the People for the American Way:

1. *The Chocolate War* (Cormier)—9 times
2. *The Catcher in the Rye* (Salinger)—8 times
3. *Of Mice and Men* (Steinbeck)—8 times
4. *The Adventures of Huckleberry Finn* (Twain)—7 times
5. *Deenie* (Blume)—7 times
6. *Go Ask Alice* (Anonymous)—7 times
7. *A Light in the Attic* (Silverstein)—7 times
8. *Forever* (Blume)—6 times

Other books read by young adults and frequently censored, challenged, restricted, or even burned during the past fifteen years include:

Blubber (Blume)
Brave New World (Huxley)
The Crucible (Miller)
The Diary of Anne Frank (Frank)
Flowers for Algernon (Keyes)
Harriet the Spy (Fitzhugh)
I Know Why the Caged Bird Sings (Angelou)
Iggie's House (Blume)
It's Okay If You Don't Love Me (Klein)
Lord of the Flies (Golding)
Love Is One of the Choices (Klein)
Nineteen Eighty-Four (Orwell)
Ordinary People (Guest)
Otherwise Known as Sheila the Great (Blume)
The Pigman (Zindel)

The Red Pony (Steinbeck)
A Separate Peace (Knowles)
Silas Marner (Eliot)
Superfudge (Blume)
That Was Then, This Is Now (Hinton)
Then Again Maybe I Won't (Klein)
To Kill a Mockingbird (Lee)

Most of these works have been challenged more frequently and with greater intensity within the last five years. And this list came from only one source, the American Library Association Office of Intellectual Freedom. It merely reveals the peak of the censorship iceberg.

Who Is Objecting and What Are They Objecting To?

And what were the objections? Here are some: espousing the state religion of secular humanism, discussion of the Renaissance, discussion of Leonardo da Vinci because his paintings glorify man instead of God, telepathy, the supernatural, discussion of religions, magic, witchcraft, people's power to change themselves, stories about dinosaurs because their existence indicates that the earth is older than the Bible tells us, one world government, feminism, homosexuality, sexuality, vulgarity, violence, pacifism, objectionable language, troublesome ideas about race relations, profanity, the "myth" of the Holocaust, four-letter words, unfavorable depiction of a former minister, behavior inappropriate to children, racist terms, bitterness and hatred, evolution, anti-Semitism, depressing content, lack of literary quality, boys cooking or girls playing baseball (called "improper roles").

Although this may seem a long list, it is a random one and leaves out much more than it includes. What is *not censorable*? Probably almost nothing. Certainly all of the plots, themes, characters, values, and words of which young adult literature is made are possibly objectionable to someone at some time for some reason. Lee Burress, writing in an issue of *Virginia English Bulletin*, summarized recent trends in censorship this way: "Among the characteristics of the books under attack are their contemporary nature, their generally American authorship, and their realistic treatment of their subjects" (76). What Burress describes here is the very essence of today's literature for young adults.

Often the censor is a single individual who makes one phone call, or simply drops a sentence or two in conversation with an administrator or school board member. It is not unusual for those solitary acts to cause a book to be removed from the library or the classroom. Or perhaps from the reading list. Many censorship watchers say that more censorship of the current holdings of school libraries results from a single complaint by a parent than from any other source. Many teachers, librarians, and administrators are so intimidated by a single call or the fear of a single complaint that materials are never ordered or are removed after any criticism, even in a nearby school. Since teachers have been fired for using challenged books, this is not surprising.

Of course, the censors always claim that they are not censors and that their only interest is quality education. Censorship groups always have names like Save Our Schools, Citizens for Quality Education, or Library Liberation Group. The epitome is Phyllis Schlafly's pro-censorship group of Eagle Forum called "Stop Textbook Censorship Committee." An interesting doublespeak name used by one censorship group is Educational Research Analysts in Texas. It is neither educational, nor research-oriented, and it is certainly not analytic, but actually a textbook censorship group headed by Mel and Norma Gabler. They intricately screen textbooks and have a strong impact on the Texas Textbook Commission and the publishing industry itself. Because the industry looks to populous states like Texas for textbook direction, the Gablers have had a significant impact on what does and doesn't get into books available to schools across the country.

Whatever the euphemism used to initiate censorship and to make it appear respectable, the effects are the same — limits to the diversity of ideas, opinions, and points of view to which young people should be exposed. Indeed, public schools and libraries in a free society have an obligation not only to provide, but also to encourage such diversity of opinions and points of view, thereby developing what tests show contemporary students lack so much — critical thinking ability. But how can schools do that in this present climate — a climate where nationally organized professional censors have been aiding and abetting challenges to school textbooks and library materials?

Results of Censorship:
A Sampling of Recent Incidents

Often restricted shelves are added to libraries where students may check out a book only with parental permission. Similarly, "opt out" procedures are sometimes provided for sex education and optional or substitute titles are added to reading lists. But compromising doesn't always work, and outright giving in to banning is all too frequent. In Kenosha, Wisconsin, for example, school officials worked for nearly three years on a sex education curriculum for K-12. Ninety-seven percent of the parents enrolled their children in it after the curriculum was adopted by the school board. But a small vocal minority called it "anti-parent, too explicit" and they also condemned the program for promoting "bad behavior." This minority got to the school board first and managed to get the board to drop the new textbooks. Next, they persuaded the board to scuttle the whole program just two weeks before it was to begin (PFAW 68).

In Caddo, Louisiana, a parent objected to *Huckleberry Finn* in a middle school because it, as the parent said, "looms with racism." The principal purged it from the required reading list. She would remove any book, she said, "if a single parent objected." She added, "It doesn't take but one thoughtful inquiry ... If a parent has a concern about language or image, for instance, we try to meet it ... We adapt our selections to social expectations" (People for the American Way 35). Another school in the district didn't need a single complaint to remove *Huckleberry Finn* from the library shelves. They said they did it "Just in case." That is the most unfortunate kind of censorship—done, not under pressure, but in fear that the pressure might come.

In Saint Paul, Oregon, high school students won't learn about the trials of black males in James Baldwin's *If Beale Street Could Talk* because, when a single parent complained, the board banned it rather than let students check it out with their parents' permission (PFAW 52). And in Vista, California, honors students won't learn about black life in segregated Arkansas in Maya Angelou's autobiographical *I Know Why the Caged Bird Sings* because it was banned by the school board despite the fact that it was on the state education department's approved reading list (PFAW 17).

In one recent case involving young adult literature in Panama City, Florida, a group of talented, dedicated English teachers at Mowat Middle School modified the traditional English curriculum to the point that in 1986 it was recognized by NCTE as one of 150 "Centers of Excellence." In addition to that, students were regularly winning writing contests, and ninth graders were rated on a twelfth grade level in reading comprehension, vocabulary, and grammar.

But not everyone was happy. Some parents lamented the loss of grammar workbooks, while others grumbled about books with violence, sex, and strong language. By the summer of 1986, the school was inundated by organized complainers, many mouthing identical charges. Teachers refused to alter the curriculum or to bowdlerize the library or textbooks, but they did much to placate angry parents. They encouraged any student who objected to a book to choose an alternative, and they required written permission from a parent before a student could attend a book fair or read novels that had been attacked. They held regular meetings with parents to explain their curriculum.

When some parents saw the classrooms, they were upset. One said, according to Peter Carlson, writing in the *Washington Post Magazine*, "It's like walking into a B. Dalton with desks ... There are books just lining the walls ... We don't turn our children loose in the theater and say, 'go see whatever movie you want to' ... why should we send them to school and have them exposed to books they shouldn't see yet?" (13).

Parents' major objections concerned two books—*I Am the Cheese* by Robert Cormier and *About David* by Susan Beth Pfeffer. Only four of ninety-two parents denied permission for their children to read the books. Nonetheless, one parent filed an official complaint saying that although her child would be allowed an alternate selection she would be "ostracized." The parent's complaint asked that the two books be withdrawn from all schools in the county until judged by the review committee.

In the fall of 1986, after a series of meetings of various committees, hearings and appeals before the school board, attempted arson, death threats to teachers and a local TV reporter, and much more, the superintendent not only removed the two offending books, but added that "any other material not specifically approved by the board may not be used in the future" (15). Before 1987 ended the teachers realized that nearly every book they taught would be judged by the same people who had rejected *I Am the Cheese* and *About David*. The teachers have now gone to court, and the case is working its way through the legal labyrinth.

Censorship surveys of recent years report that the goal of many censors has not changed—to use the public schools to impose their particular sectarian views. As stated earlier, some of the tactics have shifted from far-right scare words such as "secular humanism" or "globalism" to new vague categories, "offensive language," "the occult," and "new ageism." Tactics of Concerned Women for America (CWA), Eagle Forum, and Citizens for Excellence in Education (CEE) have become more mainstream. Instead of attempting to remove books only after they have been placed in classrooms or libraries, these and other groups have tried to get involved earlier in the policy process. They have taken an especially active role in school board elections and textbook selection committees.

"Offensive language" is a convenient charge becuse it is so vague that it can cover almost any language the objector wants it to. A few profanities such as "damn" or "hell" can be enough to justify the removal of both contemporary young adult novels and works which are considered almost modern classics such as Steinbeck's *The Grapes of Wrath* or Arthur Miller's *Death of a Salesman*. Charges are usually leveled without regard to context.

Censorship occurs on another level as well. Publishers frequently pressure writers to make changes in their works to avoid potential controversy. Jerry Weiss tells in *The ALAN Review* how T. Ernesto Bethancourt, a California Young Readers Medal Award winner, was treated by a paperback company that had bid successfully for several of his books in the Doris Fein mystery series. An editor of that paperback publisher suggested that Bethancourt change the color of Doris's hair to blond to make her less Jewish, since her religion might limit potential readership. Although Bethancourt refused, the publisher changed Ms. Fein's appearance on the paperback cover anyway (60).

It is also not unusual for editors to suggest that their authors choose less controversial subject matter, soften the language, or tone down the sex. Ann Rinaldi told Jerry Weiss that an editor wanted to use a selection from one of her works on the American Revolution in which she writes about George Washington's strategy of crossing the Delaware on Christmas Eve while the British troops were busy celebrating. But drinking and smoking and references to Christmas would have to be omitted. She protested, but finally gave in because, of course, it was to her advantage to make the changes so that students exposed to her work in this anthology might come to recognize her name and work and read more of her later. As Weiss says, "I have met several authors who have censored their own works to meet the requests of editors of texts: few young adult authors can afford the luxury of refusing since most do not receive huge advances or royalty checks. To be a writer one has to make sacrifices. If self-censorship leads to publication and additional revenue, how many will turn down such a request?" (59).

But writers don't always give in to such pressures, especially if they are among the more established authors. Recently Daniel Keyes, the much anthologized author of such works as *The Minds of Billy Milligan*, *The Fifth Sally*, and *Flowers for Algernon*, shared with me a letter he had received from a language arts editor of a major publisher. In that letter the editor requests using *Flowers for Algernon* in an eighth grade anthology but only if a few changes can be made to make it "acceptable to textbook adoption committees." Those changes would make their company's version the same as that published by two other major publishing houses. This was the first time Keyes had heard of any alterations to the text. They had been done by other publishers without his permission. The editor goes on to say how much they want his work represented in school books that aim to introduce youngsters across the country to the best in contemporary literature. Omitting Keyes would mean presenting an incomplete picture of American literature today and would impoverish young readers. That appeal was hard for him to resist, but he did.

How Censorship Can Be Dealt With: Authors Help

How can we begin to fight censors effectively now? A major step is to join with professional groups, both nationally and locally, to do such things as create self-help censorship packets for prevention and cure. We can create and disseminate intellectual freedom statements, sample selection policies, procedures for screening complaints, relevent articles and bibliographies, rationales, lists of words likely to trigger censors, and lists of people and groups who can help. Seminars, conferences, and consortia can help, too. And young adult writers are often willing to speak out in defense of intellectual freedom. Judy Blume, for example, says that she sees a tendency for adults who have lost control of their own lives to attempt to control their children's lives and thoughts. One way is through controlling what young adults read, but Blume points out that even if all of the books censors object to were removed you couldn't keep children from thinking about the same kind of things that are written about in those books. Fear of change is the motivation of many censors: the fear that children's values will change because they are exposed to other values isn't valid if there is communication between parent and child.

"Let children read whatever they want and then talk about it with them," suggests Blume. "If parents and kids can talk together, we won't have as much censorship because we won't have as much fear. Parents who believe that their children have the right to read, the right to information, the right to know, must become as vocal as the vocal minority" (Karlin).

Katherine Paterson tells us in *The New Advocate* that she has had readers object to the behavior of the title character in her Newbery Award winning book, *The Great Gilly Hopkins*. She says that the main point of the book is Gilly's inappropriate behavior. It includes her angry language — a defense against a world that has treated her as disposable. Paterson says, "A novel, as the French philosopher Jacques Maritain reminds us, is different from all other forms of art in that it concerns itself directly with the conduct of life itself. A novel cannot, therefore, set examples. It must reflect life as it is. And if the writer tells her story truly, then readers may find in her novel something of value for their lives" (6).

Paterson asks readers to think for awhile what the effects on schools would be if all the materials which might offend any group were removed. "What would remain? Certainly the Bible would be one of the first books to go, almost any novel, all of the dictionaries, encyclopedias, and don't count on those 'wholesome' teen romances making the cut. There are a lot of us mightily offended by that kind of literary toxic waste" (4).

Norma Klein wrote in the *Connecticut English Journal* a few years ago that she could write only about the people and the world she knows. She doesn't pretend they are the best people or even "normal" or typical people. The best fiction shows life as it is, and no two people see things exactly alike. She pleads, ". . . if any of you ever sit down to write a work of realistic fiction, I would hope, for my sake as a reader, that you would write of life exactly as it has appeared to you — all your truest thoughts and feelings and ideas — not just the cheerful surface most of us put on when we go about our daily routine, but the darker side as well: the terrors, the uncertainties, the confusion" (102).

Norma Klein also said in an interview in *Education Week* that if present censorship trends continue we will have no books which young adults will want to read. She concludes: "I believe children and adolescents are keenly aware of the hypocrisy around them. Juveniles search for honesty in literature ... If we censor our books and stop writing about the feelings that are so important to these children, we are betraying them" (9).

Establishing Effective Policies

Essential for dealing effectively with attempts at censorship and challenges to instruction are clear, established policies of material selection and procedures for complaints and complaint resolution. Problems tend to be resolved much more quickly and effectively when all involved — parents, students, teachers, administrators — are aware of district policies and procedures and can work within a complaint process which is already in place. Before challenges arrive, a materials selection policy should be developed which includes:

- a complaint form to be completed by anyone challenging instructional material
- a "broad-based" committee to examine challenges
- provisions to guarantee that challenged material remains available during review
- possibilities of alternate assignments
- defined procedures for dealing with complaints.

An in-place policy will help to guarantee a fair and effective study of the problem from all sides. Burress and Jenkinson in *The Students' Right to Know* and Bartlett in *Dealing with Censorship* provide excellent discussions on the topic and models for such a policy. Also, the American Library Association and the National Council of Teachers of English have developed forms which can be used in requests for reconsideration of works.

Remember that school systems that have developed and follow textbook complaint procedures are generally successful in fighting off censorship threats. Those that don't have such procedures are rarely successful. That was among the principal findings of the People for the American Way's 1988−89 *Attacks on the Freedom to Learn*.

Writing Rationales

In the initial selection of materials, a decision to use a work needs to be justified and supported. One way to do this is to develop rationales for the use of materials chosen. Writing an appropriate, thorough rationale can aid the teacher in making important decisions about which book truly fulfills the intended objectives. Taking the time and making the effort to prepare effective rationales allows teachers not only to preclude confrontation but also to become prepared to discuss and defend a book selection intelligently.

Diane P. Shugert, in *Dealing With Censorship*, puts forth eight questions which every rationale should answer:

1. For what classes is this book especially appropriate?
2. To what particular objective, literary or psychological or pedagogical, does this book lend itself?
3. In what ways will the book be used to meet those objectives?
4. What problems of style, tone, or theme or possible grounds of censorship exist in the book?
5. How does the teacher plan to meet those problems?
6. Assuming the objectives are met, how would the students be different because of their reading of this book?
7. What are some other appropriate books an individual student might read in place of this book?
8. What reputable sources have recommended this book? What have the critics said of it? (This answer cites reviews, if any are available.) (188)

A more thorough discussion of this topic, examples of rationales, and additional references, can be found in *Dealing With Censorship* (1979); *Rationales for Commonly Challenged Taught Books* (1983); and *Celebrating Censored Books* (1985).

Teaching About Censorship

Another way in which teachers can help to prevent censorship takes perhaps a more indirect, but arguably more effective form — that is, taking the time to teach about censorship. By exposing the issue to scrutiny, teachers can help students learn why books are censored, by whom, and how it affects them and their communities.

The ways to study censorship are numerous, limited only by a teacher's imagination. For example, celebrate National Banned Books Week. Designated annually (in the fall), this week provides a teacher with the perfect opportunity to begin a unit on censorship — studying the issues involved, reading *Huckleberry Finn*, examining community mores, and so on. Similarly, teaching books like *Huckleberry Finn* or *The Grapes of Wrath*, which have been censored (and continue to be), provides abundant opportunities to examine the issue of censorship and why the particular work would have been subject to challenges.

Other ideas could include studying the history of censorship. Looking at what has been censored over the years and how our society has or has not changed in regard to what gets censored can provide valuable insight into the issue. A good reference for such an activity is Hentoff's *The First Freedom: The Tumultuous History of Free Speech in America*.

Students can also participate in the writing of rationales for selected books. An activity such as this could give the students the opportunity to examine their own perceptions and impressions of a particular title as well as allowing them to study the issue of censorship prevention from the teacher's point of view.

For further suggestions of this nature, see the November, 1988, issue of the *English Journal*.

Procedures for Protecting Intellectual Freedom in Schools

Finally, some summary reminders on protecting against censorship:

1. Do the best professional job possible. Be well prepared. (See bibliography at the end of the chapter.)
2. Establish a materials selection policy before challenges arise.
3. Inform teachers, librarians, and administrators regularly of procedures so that they are aware of the current policies and procedures, and the necessity of complying with them.
4. Conduct community meetings on education goals, curriculum, and selection of instructional materials. Press attendance at these meetings and at all Board of Education meetings should be encouraged so that the community remains informed.
5. Give teachers strong support in the area of academic freedom to prevent closet censorship.
6. Include academic freedom in the bargaining contract.
7. Seek assistance from professional organizations.

8. Form coalitions with other professional and community groups.

9. Send letters of support to colleagues who are involved in censorship cases.

10. Write articles on censorship for submission to *The ALAN Review* or other publications.

11. Help an influential organization, such as your state NCTE affiliate, prepare a statement dealing with the right of students to read works of literature for adolescents.

12. Stay in contact with state and national organizations advocating intellectual freedom that might provide assistance in the event of censorship attacks.

The censors will always be with us. Author Harlan Ellison, according to Marian Lang, calls them monsters who are as prevalent as they are because "the two most common things in the universe are hydrogen and stupidity" (Lang 22). He says that the censors' real concern is power, not God or people, and that we will have to begin fighting them less politely. As we prepare for the fight, we need to remember that many of the books that appear on censors' lists affirm life. They are not immoral, and thus teachers and librarians must challenge anyone who interferes with our right to teach them or with readers' right to read them. We cannot afford to let American education become indoctrination. We must not let the censors make us all over into their image. What a drab, boring, sad society that would be!

Works Cited

Bartlett, L. 1979. "The Iowa Model Policy and Rules for Selection of Instructional Materials." In J. E. Davis (Ed.), *Dealing with Censorship* (202–214). Urbana, IL: National Council of Teachers of English.

Burress, Lee. 1986. "Are School Censorship Pressures Increasing?" *Virginia English Bulletin* 36.1 (Spring): 72–82.

Burress, Lee, and Edward B. Jenkinson. 1982. *The Student's Right to Know.* Urbana, IL: National Council of Teachers of English.

Carlson, Peter. 1987. "A Chilling Case of Censorship." *Washington Post Magazine* 4 January: 10–17, 40–41.

Davis, Hazel, and James E. Davis. 1979. "Sex in Recent Fiction for Adolescents: Field Day for Censors and Anti-Censors." *English Language Arts Bulletin* 20.2 (Fall): 29–34.

Davis, James E. 1979. "Coping with Censors and Comstocks." *The ALAN Review* 6.2 (Winter): 6.

———. 1979. *Dealing with Censorship.* Urbana, IL: NCTE.

———. 1967. Recent Trends in Fiction for Adolescents." *English Journal* 56.5 (May): 720–24.

Hentoff, Nat. 1980. *The First Freedom: The Tumultuous History of Free Speech in America*. New York: Delacorte. Reprinted in 1984 with new "Afterword" by Hentoff.

Karlin, Barbara. 1981. "Blume Speaks Out on Speaking Out." *Los Angeles Times* 18 October.

Karolides, Nicholas, and Lee Burress. 1985. *Celebrating Censored Books*. Urbana, IL: NCTE.

Klein, Norma. 1983. Interview in *Connecticut English Journal* 15.1 (Fall): 102.

———. 1984. Interview in *Education Week*. 9 September.

Lang, Marian. 1987. "The Real Fahrenheit 451." *OMNI* 9 (October): 22.

Paterson, Katherine. 1989. "The Tale of the Reluctant Dragon." *The New Advocate* 2.1 (Winter): 1–8.

People for the American Way. 1989. *Attacks On the Freedom to Learn: The 1988–89 Report*. Washington, D.C.: People for the American Way.

Shugert, Diane, Ed. 1983. "Rationales for Commonly Challenged Taught Books." *Connecticut English Journal* 15.1.

Weiss, M. Jerry. 1988. "A Dangerous Subject: Censorship!: *The ALAN Review* 15.3 (Spring): 59–61 + 64.

A Selected Bibliography on Censorship and Intellectual Freedom to Supplement the Works Cited

American Association of School Librarians. 1970. *Policies and Procedures for Selection of Instructional Materials*. Chicago: The Association.

American Association of School Librarians. 1969. *School Library Bill of Rights for School Library Media Programs*. Chicago: The Association.

American Library Association. 1989. *Intellectual Freedom Manual*, 3rd ed. Chicago: The Association.

Booth, Wayne. 1964. "Censorship and the Values of Fiction." *English Journal* 53 (March): 155–164.

Bosmajian, Haig A., Ed. 1987. *The Freedom to Read*. New York: Neal-Schuman Publishers.

Bradley, Julia T. 1987. "Censoring the School Library: Do Students Have the Right to Read?" *Connecticut Law Review* 10.3 (Spring): 747–71.

Burress, Lee. 1989. *Battle of the Books: Literary Censorship in the Public Schools 1950–1985*. Metuchen, NJ: Scarecrow Press.

Davis, James E. 1986. "Dare a Teacher Disturb the Universe? Or Even Eat a Peach? Closet Censorship: Its Prevention and Cure." *The ALAN Review* 14.1 (Fall): 66–69.

———. 1988. "Beyond Weather Reports: ALAN's Role in the Current Censorship Storm." *The ALAN Review* 15.3 (Spring): 62–64.

———. 1989. "Chained or Free? Which Will It Be? Censorship's New Wave and How to Confront It." *Michigan English Teacher* 39.7 (Spring): 2–5.

Donelson, Ken, and Alleen Pace Nilsen. 1990. "Censorship: Of Worrying and Wondering." Chapter 12 in *Literature for Today's Young Adults*, 3rd ed. Glenview, IL: Scott, Foresman and Company.

Donnerstein, Edward, Daniel Linz, and Steven Penrod. 1987. *The Question of Pornography: Research Findings and Policy Implications*. New York: Free Press.

Frangedis, Helen. 1988. "Dealing with the Controversial Elements in *The Catcher in the Rye*." *English Journal* 77.7 (November): 72–75.

Goode, Don J. 1984. *A Study of Values and Attitudes in a Textbook Controversy in Kanawha County, West Virginia: An Overt Act of Oppression in Schools*. Diss. Michigan State University.

Hansen, Eileen. 1987. "Censorship in Schools: Studies and Surveys." *School Library Journal* (September): 123–25.

Hoffman, F. 1989. *Intellectual Freedom and Censorship: An Annotated Bibliography*. Metuchen, NJ: Scarecrow Press.

Ingelhart, Louis E. 1986. *Press Law and Press Freedom for High School Publications*. New York: Greenwood Press.

Jenkinson, Edward B. 1979. *Censors in the Classroom: The Mind Benders*. Carbondale: Southern Illinois University Press.

Lewis, Felice Flannery. 1976. *Literature, Obscenity, and Law*. Carbondale: Southern Illinois University Press.

Last, Ellen. 1984. *Textbook Selection or Censorship: An Analysis of the Complaints Filed in Relation to Three Major Literature Series Prepared for Adoption in Texas in 1978*. Diss. University of Texas.

Limiting What Students Shall Read. Books and Other Learning Materials in Our Public Schools: How They Are Selected and How They Are Removed. Association of American Publishers, American Library Association, and Association for Supervision and Curriculum Development, July 31, 1981.

Little, Jean. 1989. "A Writer's Social Responsibility." *The New Advocate* 3.2 (Winter): 1–8.

Moffett, James. 1988. *Storm in the Mountains: A Case Study of Censorship, Conflict and Consciousness*. Carbondale: Southern Illinois University Press.

O'Neil, Robert M. 1981. *Classrooms in the Crossfire*. Bloomington: Indiana University Press.

Parker, Barbara, and Stephanie Weiss. 1983. *Protecting the Freedom to Learn*. Washington, D.C.: People for the American Way.

Paterson, Katherine. 1982. "Reading As a Revolutionary Activity." *The New Advocate* 1.3 (Spring): 137–42.

Reichman, H. 1988. *Censorship and Selection: Issues and Answers for Schools*. Chicago: American Library Association.

Reed, Arthea. 1989. "Are We Censoring Adolescence?" *The ALAN Review* 16.2 (Winter): 47–48.

Reiner, Constance, and Marcia Brock. 1988. "Books, Students, Censorship: Reality in the Classroom." *English Journal* 77.7 (November): 69–71.

Shannon, Patrick. 1989. "Overt and Covert Censorship of Children's Books." *The New Advocate* 2.2 (Spring): 97–104.

Shugert, Diane, Ed. 1983. "Rationales for Commonly Challenged Taught Books." *Connecticut English Journal* 15.1 (Fall). (Available from NCTE)

Simmons, John S. 1989. "On Stemming the Tide." *The ALAN Review* 16.3 (Spring): 14–17.

Thompson, Edgar H. 1986. "Being Prepared: Writing Rationales for Frequently Challenged Books." *Virginia English Bulletin* 36.1 (Spring): 104–107. (Available from NCTE)

West, Mark I. 1988. *Trust Your Children: Voices Against Censorship in Children's Literature*. New York: Neal-Schuman Publishers.

Williams, Carole A. 1988. "Studying Challenged Novels: Or, How I Beat Senioritis." *English Journal* 77.7 (November): 66–68.

Contributors

Sandy Asher is the author of sixteen books, including six novels for young adults and two nonfiction books for young writers. Her award-winning plays for juvenile and adult audiences have been produced nationwide. She is writer-in-residence at Drury College in Springfield, Missouri.

Sue Ellen Bridgers' books include *Home Before Dark*, *All Together Now*, *Notes for Another Life*, *Sara Will*, and *Permanent Connections*. She lives in the Great Smoky Mountains of North Carolina.

James E. Davis, professor of English at Ohio University in Athens, is a past president of the National Council of Teachers of English. A former high school teacher, he reviews regularly for *The ALAN Review* and is a member of its editorial board. In addition to chapters in several books, he has contributed over one hundred articles to journals of NCTE and its affiliates. He has edited the *Ohio English Bulletin*, *FOCUS*, the book *Dealing with Censorship*, and co-edited the 1988 edition of *Your Reading*, the junior high/middle school booklist for NCTE.

Donald R. Gallo is professor of English at Central Connecticut State University and a former president of ALAN. He is the author of *Presenting Richard Peck*, compiler and editor of NCTE's *Speaking for Ourselves*, and editor of several anthologies of short stories and plays written for teenagers by young adult novelists, including *Connections* and *Center Stage*.

Jeanne M. Gerlach is assistant professor of English education and curriculum and instruction at West Virginia University. She has taught English/language arts at all levels (K–C) and has worked as an educational consultant to businesses and corporations. Additionally, she has served as consultant to several National Writing Project sites and co-directs the West Virginia Advanced Writing Project. Past chair of the NCTE Committee on Women in the Profession, she has published articles in various professional journals. She is co-editor of *Missing Chapters: Ten Pioneering Women in NCTE and English Education*.

Ted Hipple is professor of English education at the University of Tennessee, where formerly he chaired the Department of Curriculum and Instruction. Active in NCTE, he also chaired the Conference on English Education and the Secondary Section of the Council. He was one of the founders of ALAN, the Assembly on Literature for Adolescents of NCTE, served that organization as its president, and has been its Executive Secretary for the last several years. He has written widely in English education and adolescent literature, with numerous pieces in journals such as *The ALAN Review* and *English Journal*.

Patricia P. Kelly, a former English teacher and department head, is associate professor of English education at Virginia Tech, where she is director of the Southwest Virginia Writing Project. The 1989–90 president of the Assembly on Literature for Adolescents, NCTE, she is also co-editor of *Virginia English Bulletin* and editor of *SIGNAL*, the publication of IRA on adolescent literature.

Virginia R. Monseau is associate professor of English at Youngstown State University, Ohio, where she serves as Coordinator of English Graduate Studies. She teaches courses in adolescent literature, children's literature, and composition, and frequently works on outreach projects with area schools. A former high school English teacher, she has published articles and reviews in *English Journal*, *The ALAN Review*, *Children's Literature Association Quarterly*, *CEA Forum*, and other journals. She is co-editor of *Missing Chapters: Ten Pioneering Women in NCTE And English Education.*

Richard Peck has written twenty novels for readers of all ages, but his favorite readers remain those two groups of the young: adolescents and the puberty people. After twelve years of army service, teaching, and textbook editing, he entered the young adult field in 1972 with *Don't Look and It Won't Hurt*. His *Are You in the House Alone?* and *Dreamland Lake* were Edgar Allan Poe award winners, and three of his novels, *The Ghost Belonged to Me*, *Are You in the House Alone?*, and *Father Figure*, reappeared as feature-length films. In 1990 he received the School Library Journal/Young Adult Services Division Author Achievement Award from the American Library Association.

Gary M. Salvner, a former elementary and secondary teacher, is professor of English and secondary education at Youngstown State University, Ohio. He teaches courses in English methods, children's literature, and adolescent literature, and co-directs a collaborative school-college program on writing assessment and instruction in the Youngstown area. He is the author of *Literature Festival*, a book of writing games designed to evoke student response to literature and is editor of the *Ohio Journal of the English Language Arts*.

Barbara G. Samuels, a lover of reading since childhood, now teaches children's literature and adolescent literature at the University of Houston-Clear Lake in the hope that she will be able to influence others to find pleasure in reading. A former president of the Assembly on Literature for Adolescents of NCTE, she has written about adolescent literature in *English Journal*, *Journal of Reading*, and *The ALAN Review*. She is a reviewer for *The ALAN Review* and *SIGNAL*. As co-director of the Greater Houston Area Writing Project, she frequently demonstrates reading-writing connections using books for children and young adults.

Linda K. Shadiow became addicted to reading when her grandmother gave her a copy of a Bobbsey Twins book in the 1950s. An avid under-the-covers flashlight reader from that point on, she decided to become a teacher of English and then to become a teacher of English teachers. She has taught English in several states and is now an English and education professor at Northern Arizona University. She has been director of the Commission on

Curriculum for the National Council of Teachers of English and Associate Executive Director of the Center for Excellence in Education at NAU, where she is currently a special project associate for the executive vice president. And now, in addition to reading books by flashlight, she occasionally also drafts book chapters.

Lois T. Stover is assistant professor of secondary education at Towson State University, where she teaches undergraduate and graduate courses in curriculum development, methods of teaching, writing as thinking, and young adult literature. She has published in *Journal of Teacher Education*, *The ALAN Review*, *Action in Teacher Education*, *Art Education*, *Music Educator's Journal*, *Language Arts*, and *English Journal*. Her current research interest is young adult literature from other countries and the cross-cultural similarities and differences in the developmental tasks of adolescents reflected in the literature.

Eileen Tway was professor of teacher education at Miami University, Ohio. A teacher of language arts and children's literature, she wrote numerous books, book chapters, and articles in addition to editing "The Resource Center" column for *Language Arts*. A past president of the Ohio Council of Teachers of English Language Arts, she also served as a trustee of the NCTE Research Foundation. She was the recipient of the 1990 Arbuthnot Award, given by the International Reading Association to the nation's outstanding teacher of children's and young adult literature.